GETTYSBURG REBELS

Gettysburg REBELS

**FIVE NATIVE SONS
WHO CAME HOME
TO FIGHT AS
CONFEDERATE
SOLDIERS**

Tom McMillan

REGNERY
HISTORY

Regnery History™ is a trademark of Salem Communications Holding Corporation; Regnery® is a registered trademark of Salem Communications Holding Corporation

Cataloging-in-Publication data on file with the Library of Congress

ISBN 978-1-62157-592-4

Published in the United States by
Regnery History, an imprint of
Regnery Publishing
A Division of Salem Media Group
300 New Jersey Ave NW
Washington, DC 20001
www.RegneryHistory.com

Manufactured in the United States of America

10 9 8 7 6 5 4 3 2 1

Books are available in quantity for promotional or premium use. For information on discounts and terms, please visit our website: www.Regnery.com.

Distributed to the trade by
Perseus Distribution
www.perseusdistribution.com

Contents

To At,
who encouraged me to dream

And to Colleen,
who made sure that I did

AUTHOR'S NOTE

I was different from other Gettysburg battlefield trampers. I was often drawn to obscurity.

I would whisk past Devil's Den and Little Round Top and the field of Pickett's Charge to find myself at an often-ignored corner of the Emmitsburg and Wheatfield Roads, where a plain iron tablet next to an old stone foundation reads simply, "Wentz House." How poetic.

It was here that an elderly Adams County resident, John Wentz, crouched in his cellar during the battle of Gettysburg on July 2, 1863, unaware, at least at first, that his son, Henry, who had grown up in that house, was posted six hundred yards away as an artillery sergeant in the Confederate army.

Henry Wentz's homecoming as an enemy soldier has intrigued me since the day I first read about it in Harry Pfanz's *Gettysburg: The Second Day*. I wanted to learn more about him—to read and study more, to advance the story in my own mind—but, alas, very little was available in books. Like many other soldiers in the Civil War, Henry did not write about his experiences, or if he did, nothing has survived. No one has seen his photo or any of his possessions. He was, and is, a mystery—and perhaps he preferred it that way.

But I decided to explore. I came up with an idea to write a book about two young men from Gettysburg who had fought as Confederates in the battle of Gettysburg—Henry Wentz and Wesley Culp, whose name is better known because of his family's hometown roots. In the process, however, I learned that three brothers named Hoffman had also grown up in Gettysburg and become Rebel soldiers, and that all three had direct connections to Culp.

Thus, *Gettysburg Rebels* was born.

The research was a challenge because Culp was killed in the battle, and none of the others wrote about his actions during this cataclysmic period in the nation's history. Aside from Culp's, no portraits of the men exist (though perhaps an unknowing descendant will dig into a box and come forward with one after this is published). But I decided that a lack of such traditional evidence should not deter me. These men's stories still deserved to be told.

Uncovering those stories took me on an amazing journey to places I'd never been (Shepherdstown and Martinsburg) and some I'd never heard of (Linden and Warrenton), in addition to Harpers Ferry and Gettysburg. I scanned countless pages of oversized county deed books that probably had not been opened for a hundred years and sifted through wills, tax records, church records, newspaper advertisements, family files, obituaries—and, of course, military service records and pension applications at the National Archives. I met and was helped by many wonderful people along the way.

The story in these pages is certainly not the complete account of Henry Wentz, Wesley Culp, and the three Hoffman brothers, but I'm convinced it is the closest anyone has come. Perhaps it will spark more dogged research and the uncovering of more clues (maybe even a photo).

In the meantime, I hope that you enjoy the narrative presented here—the story of five young men who grew up in the North, fought for the South, and marched on their old hometown with an invading army in July 1863.

However you judge them, they will no longer be obscure.

Tom McMillan
Pittsburgh, Pennsylvania
December 2016

INTRODUCTION

Fifty miles from the Gettysburg battlefield, on a gently sloping hill behind the Green Hill Cemetery mausoleum in Martinsburg, West Virginia, a weather-beaten and barely legible tombstone marks the final resting place of one of the fascinating figures of the American Civil War.

Henry Wentz
Died December 10, 1875
Aged 48 Years

The stark memorial offers no tribute to his four years of artillery service for the Confederate States of America, makes no mention of his deeds on fields of honor at Manassas, Sharpsburg, Mechanicsville—or, hauntingly, Gettysburg. It is as though the friends and family of Henry Wentz did not comprehend the extraordinary role in

America's great cataclysm of a man who invaded his old hometown with a foreign army and fired on the house where he grew up.[1]

Born in nearby York County, Pennsylvania, in 1827, Wentz was just turning nine years old when his family moved to the Gettysburg area.[2] His father, John, bought a one-and-a-half-story log and weatherboard house along the Emmitsburg Road in Cumberland Township, barely a mile from the Gettysburg town line and adjacent to a peach orchard that would one day merit its own place in American history. Henry spent his formative years there, maturing into adulthood and becoming a local land owner himself before moving to northwestern Virginia in 1852. He settled in Martinsburg (in what became West Virginia), found work as a plasterer, joined a local militia unit called the Martinsburg Blues, and enlisted in the Confederate army when war broke out in 1861.[3]

If Orderly Sergeant Wentz felt a strange queasiness two years later as the Army of Northern Virginia thundered into south-central Pennsylvania, he would not have been alone. Four other men in Robert E. Lee's invading force had grown up in Gettysburg. John Wesley Culp, from one of the borough's most prominent families and a private in Company B of the Second Virginia Infantry, was immortalized when he fell in battle near his cousin's farm.[4] The three remaining Gettysburg Rebels, however, were unknown even to Civil War historians for well over 130 years.

These were the Hoffman brothers—Robert, Frank, and Wesley. Their father, C. W. Hoffman, had been one of Gettysburg's leading citizens, but in 1856 he suddenly, and somewhat mysteriously, pulled up stakes and moved to northwestern Virginia, with profound consequences for the lives of four future Civil War soldiers. Wesley Culp, a sixteen-year-old apprentice in Hoffman's Gettysburg carriage-making business, went with his boss, helping him open a new shop in Shepherdstown, in what became West Virginia. Culp joined the local militia known as the Hamtramck Guards and eventually entered the Confederate service when the unit became Company B of the Second Virginia Infantry in 1861. And yet most historians have overlooked the story of Hoffman's own sons, who also moved south with their father.[5]

Robert Newton Hoffman, the eldest of C. W. Hoffman's surviving sons, worked alongside Wes Culp at his father's carriage shop in Gettysburg. Like Culp, Robert joined the Hamtramck Guards after arriving in Shepherdstown and enlisted in Company B of the Second Virginia when their adopted state seceded in April 1861. He was with Culp at the battle of First Manassas and other major engagements with the famous Stonewall Brigade. Though no longer in a combat role by the time of the Gettysburg campaign, Robert came north with Lee's army and served throughout the campaign.

Francis William "Frank" Hoffman, the middle brother, enlisted in the Confederate army as an infantryman at the start of the war but soon transferred to artillery service. He served in Company A of the Thirty-Eighth Battalion Virginia Artillery for four years until being wounded at Petersburg, Virginia, in March 1865. Frank's company arrived on the field at Gettysburg on the morning of July 3 and played a key role in the great cannonade that preceded Pickett's Charge.

Wesley Atwood Hoffman followed his older brothers into the Confederate service in March 1862, enlisting in Company A of the Seventh Virginia Cavalry, the "Fauquier Mountain Rangers." Though his Gettysburg service is more difficult to document than his brothers', there is strong circumstantial evidence that he was with the Seventh Virginia throughout 1863 and during the Gettysburg campaign, when it took part in the battle of Brandy Station in early June, guarded the mountain passes under General William "Grumble" Jones on the move north, and fought in the cavalry action at Fairfield on July 3.

The first mention in print of the Hoffman brothers' connection to the battle came only in 1995, when the great Gettysburg researcher William Frassanito identified Robert in his book *Early Photography at Gettysburg*. Frank's presence as an invading soldier on his native soil was overlooked until 2015, when James A. Hessler and Wayne E. Motts briefly mentioned him and Robert in a sidebar in *Pickett's Charge at Gettysburg*. The third brother, meanwhile, has been a cipher to Civil War historians for more than a century and a half; Wesley Hoffman's service in the Confederate cavalry is detailed here for the first time.[6]

I have scoured the military, legal, and family records to reconstruct the stories of all five Confederate soldiers who returned to Pennsylvania as invaders in 1863. Though the names of Wesley Culp and Henry Wentz have been known to serious students of the Gettysburg campaign, the two are barely mentioned in the classic single-volume histories of the battle, and their stories are almost never told together. Culp is familiar largely because of his connection to the Gettysburg heroine Jennie Wade and because he fell in battle on "his uncle's farm," but I have uncovered convincing evidence that puts the previously accepted date, site, and family relationship in dispute. Wentz merits a mere eight sentences in Harry W. Pfanz's 438-page epic, *Gettysburg: The Second Day*, and even Pfanz can only conclude that his role "must remain as one of the tantalizing mysteries of Gettysburg." My goal has been to conduct a more thorough examination of the Culp and Wentz stories and to place them in context with the heretofore anonymous Hoffman brothers.[7]

The book will also probe the fascinating and complex background of C. W. Hoffman, whose prominence as a Gettysburg business owner and civic leader is understated by historians who identify him only as a "carriage-maker." Hoffman had direct connections to four of the soldiers—his three sons and Wes Culp—exerting a strong influence over the Gettysburg Rebels. It is also possible that he knew Henry Wentz, for modern-day Hoffman descendants say C. W.'s sister lived as a tenant on the Wentz property in the late 1840s (when Henry was still at home). Gettysburg in the mid-nineteenth century was a *very* small town.[8]

Beyond those personal details, *Gettysburg Rebels* will highlight the astoundingly inefficient communication within the Confederate army during the campaign, a weakness that prevented Lee and his senior staff from realizing they had five men from Gettysburg in their ranks. Brigadier General James Walker of the Stonewall Brigade was aware that Wes Culp had Gettysburg ties, allowing him to visit his sisters in town on the night of July 1, but there is no evidence that Walker conveyed this important information to his division commander, Edward Johnson, or to his corps commander, Richard Ewell. None of the other colonels or generals overseeing Culp, Wentz, or the Hoffmans made any mention of the hometown connections in their battle reports or postwar memoirs. We are left to conclude that no one in authority other than Walker was aware of the potentially rich sources of local intelligence among the Confederates' own ranks.[9]

By contrast, some of the foot soldiers in Company B of the Second Virginia were well aware that both Culp and Robert Hoffman were from Gettysburg—Private Benjamin S. Pendleton requested that pass from General Walker for his friend Culp on July 1—and one member of Henry Wentz's artillery battalion knew that a fellow soldier had family living on the Gettysburg battlefield. But apart from Pendleton's request for Culp's pass, it appears that none of these men in the ranks thought to pass the information up the chain of command.[10]

Thus was Robert E. Lee deprived of rare intelligence assets that could have provided crucial information during his bold and historic invasion. It was not uncommon for Civil War commanders to identify soldiers in their units with local ties and temporarily assign them as scouts or guides. General Thomas "Stonewall" Jackson tapped Private David Kyle of the Ninth Virginia Cavalry for such a role at the battle of Chancellorsville because Kyle had once lived and hunted nearby; Kyle, it was said, knew "every hog-path." The need for local knowledge was especially acute at Gettysburg because General J. E. B. Stuart's Confederate cavalry did not reach the field until the afternoon of the second day of the three-day battle. "Lee was entirely in the dark as to the terrain and any features of any likely battlegrounds," writes Stephen W. Sears in *Gettysburg*, his history of the campaign. Had Stuart been on hand earlier, as expected, Sears believes, he would have been "in position to reconnoiter most of the ground between the converging armies." But he was not. Certainly, any of the five Gettysburg rebels could have helped in that regard.[11]

One of the famous missteps in Confederate strategy took place early on the morning of July 2, when Lee sent his topographical engineer, Captain Samuel Johnston, to scout the Union left flank. A Virginian with no previous knowledge of the Adams County landscape, Johnston informed Lee that from the summit of the hill known to history as Little Round Top he saw no enemy troops in the vicinity—a compelling report for the commander of an invading army and one that had a powerful influence on Lee's battlefield assessment that morning. But as Harry Pfanz writes, "Captain Johnston made an incorrect report to his commanding general." Historians have concluded that Union troops were indeed present in the area of the Peach Orchard and Little Round Top that morning. Lee's July 2 battle plan was therefore based on a hopelessly flawed scouting report.[12]

How did Johnston make such a mistake? The eminent Civil War historian Allen C. Guelzo offers one possible explanation: "Federal troop movements made Johnston's claim to have ridden straight up to the summit of Little Round Top unopposed and with nothing to observe simply incredible—unless, of course, Johnston had not been anywhere near the Round Tops in the first place." The captain apparently did not have an Adams County map in his possession, and it is possible that he mistook one of the many other hills in the region for Little Round Top. We can never know for sure, but under any circumstances and regardless of where he went or what he saw, he could have used a local man to guide him.[13]

Unfamiliarity with the terrain took another toll later on July 2, when Confederate troops under General James Longstreet were marching into position to attack the flank that Johnston had already misidentified. Hoping to surprise the Federals, Longstreet instructed his division commanders to avoid being spotted by troops from a Union signal corps posted on Little Round Top. The unfortunate Johnston accompanied them to show the way. Alas, when they crossed a bald hill near the Fairfield Road about three miles from their destination, they came within long-range view of the flag-waving signal men. The 14,500 Confederates were compelled to turn around and counter-march several miles to reach the assigned position, costing them valuable time and delaying the start of the fateful attack.[14]

By way of contrast, a rebel artillery battalion of twenty-six guns under Colonel Edward Porter Alexander had faced the same challenge earlier—on the same hill, with the same perspective of Little Round Top—and had made it into position undetected. Turning off the road and cutting across fields, they zig-zagged down the slope into a narrow valley and onto the edge of Warfield Ridge, then waited idly while the counter-marching infantry found its way. Was it mere coincidence that Alexander's battalion included Captain Osmond B. Taylor's Virginia Battery, and that the battery's orderly sergeant was the onetime local Henry Wentz? Neither Alexander nor Taylor mentioned Wentz in his battle report, so perhaps their seamless arrival at the assigned position was simply good luck. We can never know for sure.[15]

But this was Wentz's back yard. When the rebel gunners crossed the rise beyond the Fairfield Road and began their descent to the valley, the site of his boyhood home was visible in the distance. His parents and youngest sister still lived in the house where he was raised. Colonel Alexander, trained as an engineer, had been assigned by Longstreet earlier that morning to reconnoiter the ground and find an acceptable route for his unit, but it strains credulity to think that Wentz would not have mentioned his intimate knowledge of the landscape to his fellow soldiers if not to any of his commanders. Wouldn't someone have passed it on?[16]

Sadly, neither Wentz nor any of the Hoffman brothers wrote about their experiences in the Civil War, and Culp was killed in action during the battle, so we are left to speculate about the thoughts, emotions, and actions of these soldiers as they approached their hometown. Few men have found themselves in such remarkable circumstances. Of the 75,000 rebel soldiers who came north with Robert E. Lee that summer, five had spent their childhoods playing in the streets and fields of the town that would become the bloodiest battlefield of North America. The mystery and poignancy of the story of the Gettysburg Rebels make it one of the most intriguing episodes of the Civil War.

One

INVADERS

Private John Wesley Culp trudged dutifully down Carlisle Street and veered left into the town square. How many times had he made the turn before? Hundreds? *Thousands*? Even in the falling darkness of July 1, 1863, the familiar sights of his hometown greeted him. The carriage shop where he'd worked as an apprentice in the mid-1850s was nearby on Chambersburg Street, and his oldest sister's home was a block away on West Middle Street. One of his many cousins lived on York Street, just a few doors from the square. For a foreign invader from Company B of the Second Virginia Infantry, it all must have seemed so surreal.[1]

The bustling crossroads town of Gettysburg had been home to the Culp family for four generations. Wesley's great-grandfather, Christophel Culp, bought a sprawling 233-acre farm on the southeast side of town in 1787, and by 1860 more than seventy Culps were listed in the Gettysburg census. They included Wes's father, Esaias Jesse Culp, who operated a tailor shop on Baltimore Street before passing

1

away in 1861, and Esaias's first cousin Henry Culp, who inherited the original family farm. Henry's property featured a rocky, tree-covered protuberance that towered over the rolling landscape. It would soon be known to American history as Culp's Hill.[2]

Just that morning, lead elements of General Robert E. Lee's Army of Northern Virginia had clashed with Federal forces on the town's western ridges, and now the rest of Lee's vaunted army was finally catching up. General Edward Johnson's division of the II Corps had taken a circuitous route, weaving its way from Carlisle, Pennsylvania, through Scotland and Green Village before traipsing down the Chambersburg Pike toward Gettysburg. Wes Culp, whose regiment belonged to the famed Stonewall Brigade in Johnson's division, may have sensed his destiny as he approached the borough. He was one of five men from Gettysburg who had come north with Lee's army, but his was the family with the deepest local roots.[3]

Great-grandfather Christophel Culp was seventeen years old in 1744 when he sailed into Philadelphia from Germany on the *Friendship*, one of the ships "importing foreigners." The original spelling of his surname was Kolb or Kalb, and he would be variously identified over the years as Christophel Kolb, Stophel Kolp, Christopher Kolb, Christopher Culp—even Staphael Kolp—before "Christophel Culp" became the settled American version of his name.[4]

Christophel married Maria Catherina Leise in about 1760 in Berks County, and the couple had six children—including two sons whose descendants would figure in Gettysburg's Civil War history. Christophel was a rebel himself, enlisting in the Pennsylvania militia from Lancaster County in 1777, though the fifty-year-old private's service in the Revolutionary War was probably limited to the symbolic home guard in Lancaster.

In 1787 Culp uprooted his family again, purchasing a farm in Cumberland Township in modern-day Adams County that had been

owned briefly in the 1770s by Samuel Gettys, the father of Gettysburg's founder, James Gettys.[5] Culp's son Peter bought the farm in
1798,[6] and his son Henry in turn became the owner in 1841. Wesley
Culp has sometimes been misidentified as the nephew of Henry Culp
(and thus said to have been killed on or near "his uncle's farm"), but
Wesley's father was Henry's first cousin. Wesley and Henry were first
cousins once removed.[7]

Wesley was a descendant of another of Christophel's sons,
Christian, a wheelwright who contributed to Gettysburg's burgeoning carriage industry and lived with his wife, Barbara Rummel, less
than two blocks from the town square. Among their five children
was Esaias Jesse Culp,[8] born in Gettysburg in 1807, a devout Methodist Sunday school teacher, a doting father, and a skilled tailor. In
the early 1830s he moved his young family and tailoring business
fourteen miles to Petersburg, in northeast Adams County, where
Margaret Ann Sutherland Culp gave birth to the couple's third child
and second son in July 1839. Christened John Wesley, after the
founder of Methodism, he would come to be known by his middle
name.[9]

County tax and church records for Esaias Culp show that Wesley
likely spent the first seven years of his life in Petersburg (now York
Springs). By the spring of 1847, however, Esaias had returned to Gettysburg, as this advertisement in the town's *Republican Compiler*
newspaper indicates:

NEW TAILORING ESTABLISHMENT

The subscriber respectfully informs the citizens of Gettysburg and vicinity, and the public generally, that he has
opened a Tailoring Establishment in South Baltimore
Street, in the room occupied by Daniel Culp as a Chair
Ware-room, a few doors south of the Post Office, where

he will at all times be happy to accommodate those who may patronize him, assuring them that he feels himself able to make a first-rate FIT. His charges will be reasonable as at any other establishment in the county. Country produce taken in exchange for work. He has made arrangements to receive the New York and Philadelphia fashions, quarterly, and will therefore be prepared to make garments in the most approved styles.

Esaias J. Culp
Gettysburg, April 5, 1847

Esaias's son William, having learned the tailoring trade from his father, worked as a "coach trimmer" for the local carriage maker Charles William Hoffman, preparing the lace, lining, and other trimmings on coaches destined for lucrative markets in Maryland and Virginia.[10] In the mid-1850s, at the age of fifteen or so, Wesley was apprenticed in the same establishment. Eager and talented, he was probably the smallest man in the shop, barely more than five feet tall. One brief account of his childhood says he was "much smaller than the other boys" and "most likely endured a great deal of teasing and bullying." But Wes, too, had learned the tailoring trade from his father and refined that skill to become one of Hoffman's most valuable employees.[11]

In the spring of 1856, when Hoffman moved his business fifty miles south to Shepherdstown, Virginia, he asked Wesley, his older brother William Culp, and some of the other workers to come along. It must have been a tempting opportunity for young men who had rarely set foot outside of Adams County. William, twenty-five, married, and just starting a family, declined the offer, but Wesley, still only a teenager—unsettled, single, and adventurous—decided to follow Hoffman.[12]

Wesley Culp. *Gettysburg National Military Park*

Shortly after arriving in Virginia, Wesley joined a militia unit known as the Shepherdstown Light Infantry, commanded by a local veteran of the Mexican War, Colonel John F. Hamtramck. The militias of the nineteenth century appealed to a young man's sense of civic responsibility and offered a social life. For the transplanted northerner, the Shepherdstown Light Infantry was a source of new friends. Colonel Hamtramck commanded the respect of his volunteers. The son of a daring Indian fighter and a graduate of West Point, he had briefly served in the War of 1812 while still a teenager and led a Virginia state regiment in the Mexican War. His second-in-command in Mexico had been Major Jubal Early, who would lead a Confederate division at Gettysburg.[13]

One of Shepherdstown's most distinguished citizens after returning from Mexico, Hamtramck was elected to five consecutive one-year

terms as mayor from 1851 to 1854. Is it any wonder that the Shepherdstown Light Infantry so readily attracted young men of the region to
serve as the town guard? Wes and the others drilled on weekends and,
dressed in fancy uniforms with horizontal white chest piping, appeared
at parades and other patriotic events. Shortly after Hamtramck's death
in 1858, the unit was reorganized under new officers and officially
renamed the Hamtramck Guards.[14]

Three years later, almost to the day, the Guards marched twelve
miles to Harpers Ferry to enlist in the Civil War. Wesley Culp was
among those answering the call of his new country, signing his enlistment papers on April 20, 1861 (the same day that his brother William
committed to the Union army). The Guards were formally mustered
into the Confederate service on May 11 as Company B of the Second
Virginia Infantry and assigned to a brigade under the soon-to-be-
famous commander Thomas Jonathan Jackson. They would bear the
name Hamtramck Guards throughout the war.[15]

Wesley and his unit had their first taste of battle on July 21, 1861,
near Manassas, Virginia, along the banks of a meandering creek
called Bull Run. It was here, in the war's first major engagement, that
General Jackson earned his legendary nickname ("There is Jackson
standing like a stone wall!" a fellow officer shouted.) The Confederates wavered early but hurled back federal forces with a vicious counterattack that had the bluecoats fleeing in terror, sending shock waves
rippling to the front lawn of the White House, thirty miles away.
Many had hoped for—predicted, even—a quick and seamless victory
for the Union. The rebel forces under Stonewall Jackson, including
the Hamtramck Guards, let it be known that they would not be sub-
dued so easily—and that there would be more battlefield horrors to
come.[16]

There were. Wesley endured long marches, picket duty, and
relentless drilling through the fall and winter of 1861–1862. He

was captured by Federal troops while on furlough in March 1862, shortly after the battle of Kernstown, but defiantly rejoined his unit after being released from a Union prison later that year. He'd become a hardened veteran by the age of twenty-three. During the march north in mid-June 1863 he even encountered his brother's regiment, the Eighty-Seventh Pennsylvania Volunteers, at Carter's Woods during the second battle of Winchester. A few days later, on June 18, Wes and the men of Company B splashed right past their old homes when they crossed the Potomac at Shepherdstown onto nominally Union soil in Maryland. By this point it was apparent that Robert E. Lee had designs on Pennsylvania, and a handful of his men faced the peculiar prospect of invading their native state.[17]

Johnson's division marched through Hagerstown, Maryland, on June 22 and churned toward the Pennsylvania border. We know the men were in or around Chambersburg, Pennsylvania, until June 26 because Wesley addressed a short letter at that time to his sister, Ann E. Culp Myers, in Gettysburg. After advancing as far north as Carlisle and setting up camp, they were abruptly ordered to countermarch to the Gettysburg area on June 29. "In obedience to orders," Johnson wrote in his official report, "I countermarched my division to [Green Village], then eastwardly, via Scotland to Gettysburg." They arrived on the evening of July 1, a few hours after major fighting had ended for the day.[18]

Darkness now cloaked the battlefield. Turning off the Chambersburg Pike, Johnson's foot-weary men "moved along the Gettysburg and York Railroad to the northeast of town." They took a position near Hanover Road, on the extreme left of the Confederate line, and threw out a thin line of skirmishers.[19] Other units, including the Second Virginia marched boldly through the center of Gettysburg rather than following the railroad.

Benjamin S. Pendleton, Wesley's friend from Shepherdstown and a member of Company B, who became an orderly on General Walker's staff during the Gettysburg campaign, recalled the route with striking clarity years later. "We came in on the Carlisle Road and the head of the column turned left at the square. There were few citizens of the town to be seen for there had been fighting in the streets of the town before we arrived."[20] Aware that one of his comrades had grown up there, he noted, "The townspeople had made themselves scarce, so that no one welcomed or recognized Wes Culp on his homecoming."[21]

———

A few hours before midnight on July 1, campfires crackled along the Chambersburg Pike in Greenwood, Pennsylvania, about fifteen miles from Gettysburg. The anxious gunners of Colonel E. P. Alexander's reserve artillery battalion knew they would be moving shortly to the site of the first day's action, where, as Alexander put it, "we heard enough to assure us that the little dispute was not entirely settled." Many of the men tried to steal a few minutes of sleep before the order to start the fateful march, but one of them, Sergeant Henry Wentz of Taylor's Virginia Battery, likely peered out from his post and pondered the eerily familiar territory up ahead.[22]

His parents, John and Mary Wentz, and his youngest sister, Susan, still resided in the house in Cumberland Township where he had grown up. It had been eleven years since Henry left home at the age of twenty-five to start a new life fifty miles to the south in Martinsburg, Virginia. He had boarded with a family there, found steady work as a plasterer, immersed himself in the local culture, and like so many rambunctious young men of his generation, enlisted in a militia unit. But he never could have imagined that he would one day be an officer in Robert E. Lee's vaunted Army of Northern Virginia, returning home to make war.[23]

Henry's great-grandfather, Frederick Wentz, was thirteen in 1743 when, like Christophel Culp, he arrived in Philadelphia from Germany. The next two generations of the family drifted west to York County, until Henry's father, John, bought two acres at the intersection of the Emmitsburg Road and Millerstown Road in Adams County in 1836.[24] A weaver by trade (but often simply a "laborer"), John was fifty and had fathered nine children by two wives by the time he settled in the Gettysburg area. Henry, the third of the four children born to the second wife, Mary, was born in York County in 1827 and was nine years old when the family moved to the site now marked by the "Wentz House" sign along modern-day Business Route 15 in the Gettysburg National Military Park.[25]

There is little record of Henry's life before the Civil War, but there seems to have been nothing remarkable about his upbringing or

The modern-day Wentz House sign at the corner of the Emmitsburg and Wheatfield Roads. *Author photo*

appearance. He was listed in Confederate military records as standing five feet eight inches, with black hair, hazel eyes and a dark complexion. The carriage business was prospering in Gettysburg in the mid-nineteenth century, and Henry took a job in town working for David Ziegler, a partner in the Danner and Ziegler Carriage-Making Establishment on East Middle Street. Ziegler and his partner, J. B. Danner, had purchased the business in 1846, promising in a newspaper advertisement to conduct their business "on an extensive scale" with "a large number of the best workmen engaged." Carriage-making promised a prosperous livelihood for a young man turning twenty years old.[26]

In 1850, another career possibility opened up for Henry when his father, perhaps hoping to quell the young man's wanderlust, gave him nine acres of prime Adams County farm land along the Emmitsburg Road, diagonally across the intersection from the Wentz family home and directly across from Joseph Sherfy's peach orchard. (By the time of the Civil War, this land abutted farms owned by George Rose and James Warfield.)[27]

John Wentz's attempt to anchor his son to Gettysburg didn't work. Henry moved to Martinsburg in 1852, ostensibly to continue his work in the lucrative carriage industry, possibly with the ambition of opening a carriage shop of his own. But while he may he have dabbled in carriage-making and other jobs for a few years after settling in Virginia, his occupation in the 1860 Martinsburg census (and all existing records thereafter) is given as "plasterer." He boarded with a family headed by another plasterer, George Toup—apparently his boss *and* landlord.[28]

Henry's interest in military affairs was piqued early on when he came across a Martinsburg militia unit known as the Blues, led by Ephraim G. Alburtis, the editor of the influential *Berkeley County Republican*. Alburtis and the original roster of Martinsburg Blues had volunteered for duty in Mexico in 1846, serving in the Virginia regiment commanded by Colonel John F. Hamtramck of Shepherdstown. Alburtis managed to keep his small unit intact as a home guard following the war, no doubt using his newspaper connections and prominent position as two-term county clerk of courts to attract a new wave of recruits.[29]

The Virginia Convention voted to secede from the Union on April 17, 1861, stoking tempers and fracturing loyalties in the northwestern part of the state near the Pennsylvania border. Some citizens in the Martinsburg area were staunchly pro-Union, while others favored secession. Men from the same towns and neighborhoods scrambled to enlist in armies representing different sides. The nineteenth-century *Aler's History of Martinsburg and Berkeley County* describes the complex mix of sentiments in the area:

> The minds of the grandsons of Berkeley were pervaded in 1861 by the same spirit which animated the heroes of 1776 and 1812, and emulating their noble example, a full representation volunteered who were willing to take up arms; and, if need be, sacrifice their lives in defense of the principles which they had adopted. These heroic men enlisted on both sides. Men equal in intelligence and courage, honesty of purpose and stubborn determination, whose forefathers had fought side by side for the independence of their country during the Revolutionary War; only differing, perhaps, in the circumstances and influences which had educated them into a decided opinion upon the great questions then at issue.[30]

Alburtis and his men chose the Confederacy. Henry Wentz enlisted on April 19 in Martinsburg, originally for one year but soon afterward committing to a term of "three years or the war." The unit was mustered into the rebel army as Company B of the First Virginia Light Artillery, known less formally as the Wise Artillery (after Henry A. Wise, the revered "War Governor" of Virginia). Their transition from home-guard militia to a wartime artillery company was clumsy and time-consuming, in large part because Alburtis's men, though eager, "knew nothing whatsoever about cannons." Complicating matters, the few guns they possessed were outdated smoothbore six-pounders. One early observer judged the battery to be "little more than symbolic." But with the assistance of a sharp young lieutenant from West Point named John Pelham, the Wise Artillery began to round into form by the early summer of 1861.[31]

Wentz was introduced to the war at the battle of First Manassas on July 21. The green gunners of the Wise Artillery were hustled into action on the key terrain of Henry House Hill, where they supported the troops of General Thomas Jackson (including Wesley Culp and the Second Virginia). Inexperienced and nervous as the Wise men were, Pelham thought they deserved "the highest praise" for their first performance under fire. Over the summer and early fall of 1862, they would develop into seasoned warriors in the Seven Days' campaign on the Virginia peninsula and at Antietam.[32]

Wentz served under an ever-changing list of commanders (Alburtis and Pelham were followed by James S. Brown and John L. Eubank in the first two years alone), but he was always well regarded by the officer in charge. Entering the Confederate service as a corporal on Alburtis's staff, he was promoted to first sergeant (also called orderly sergeant) shortly after Brown took command in February 1862, a rank he retained through the remainder of the war.[33]

When the Confederate high command reorganized its artillery in the fall of 1862, the Wise Artillery was disbanded and its men reassigned to compatible units. Wentz was one of sixty-eight who were transferred on October 8 to a company led by John Eubank, the secretary of the last Virginia convention on secession before the war, whose career as a commander would be short lived. Eubank battled through illness to lead his newly-strengthened unit at the battle of Fredericksburg in December, a resounding Confederate victory, but a medical examination in March declared him unfit for further service. He was promptly replaced by one of his lieutenants, Osmond B. Taylor.[34]

By the time the Gettysburg campaign got underway in June 1863, Taylor's four-gun battery was part of a larger artillery battalion under E. P. Alexander and attached as a reserve unit to General James Longstreet's corps of the Army of Northern Virginia. When marching orders from Longstreet arrived at his headquarters in Milford, Virginia, on June 3, Alexander knew instantly "that it meant another great battle with the enemy's army." After finally crossing the Pennsylvania border on June 26, however, his gunners spent four mostly idle days in camp at Chambersburg and had advanced only nine miles to a small village near the Cashtown Gap by July 1. "Back at our camp at Greenwood, we knew nothing of the fighting until later in the afternoon," Alexander remembered years later. Then, almost hauntingly, "rumors began to arrive."[35]

Shortly after dark on July 1, Longstreet sent word to move the guns forward to the newly-designated battlefield. The "little dispute" had not, in fact, been settled. "We had a little breakfast and corn coffee before starting," Alexander said, "and then a lovely march over a fairly good pike by a bright moon." Historians continue to debate the implications of Longstreet's order for the course of Civil War, but for Henry Wentz they were personally momentous. At long last, he was headed home.[36]

Late in the evening of July 1, a few hours before Wentz's unit had broken camp out along the Chambersburg Pike, a dust-covered soldier in the butternut uniform of the Confederate army made his way down East Middle Street toward the intersection with Baltimore Street. He was cautious, pensive, purposeful. The rebels held the town after overrunning two Union corps on Gettysburg's western ridges that afternoon, but this was no time to draw attention to oneself as an invader. The citizens were jittery and frightened—some downright angry—and many had loaded muskets in their parlors for protection.

Wesley Culp crossed Baltimore Street in the darkness and found a familiar address along West Middle Street. After hesitating for a moment, he raised his hand and rapped on the door.

There was shuffling inside, and he heard nervous whispered voices. The gunfire had stopped for now, but the eerie silence wouldn't last for long. "It's me!" he wanted to say, but he didn't dare raise his voice, lest a neighbor recognize the sound of a traitor. He waited until he heard soft footsteps approaching and saw the latch being lifted.

The door opened ever so slightly, and their eyes met for the first time in years.

"Why, Wes!" exclaimed his older sister, Ann E. Culp Myers, "You're here!"[37]

Two

A MAN CALLED
C. W.

arch 1856. Dust billowed as the caravan of carriages clat-
tered away from the two-story home in the second block
of Chambersburg Street in Gettysburg. Curious onlook-
ers gathered to gawk at the spectacle.[1]

For almost seventeen years, an enterprising German named
Charles William Hoffman had raised his eight children and operated
his multifaceted business here on the north side of the street, a block
from the town square. What began as a modest carriage factory in
1839 had expanded to include a thriving blacksmith operation, a
buggy repair shop, a steam mill, and, by 1854, an enterprise that sold
"clothing of all kinds made to order by experienced workmen." Hoffman had become one of the town's most prominent citizens: a three-
term borough councilman, a trustee of the Methodist Episcopal
Church, and a member of Gettysburg's delegation to the 1854 state
temperance convention in Harrisburg. In the mid-1850s he also served
on a committee that established the Evergreen Cemetery on a hill

south of town, where, a decade later, Abraham Lincoln would deliver the Gettysburg Address. But now C. W. Hoffman was heading south.[2]

––––––––

Upheaval had been part of his life almost from the start. Born on August 5, 1815, in Cologne, Germany, Charles William Hoffman immigrated with his parents to Baltimore in early 1817. His father, Francis William Hoffman, was a music teacher from a distinguished background whose elopement with his pupil Anna Barbara Esser in 1814 probably prompted the parental disapproval that precipitated the move to the United States.[3]

Francis "played the organ in a cathedral in Baltimore after coming to America," but a second child was born shortly after his arrival, and the strain of providing for a growing family in a foreign land began to overwhelm him. "He was a musician," one descendant wrote, "and knew not how to make a living for his wife and family." Over the next thirteen years, the Hoffmans embarked on a series of moves around the region that took them as far west as Greencastle, in Franklin County, Pennsylvania, where three of their nine children were born, before returning to Baltimore by 1830. On November 22 of that year, the *Baltimore Patriot and Mercantile Advertiser* reported that "Francis W. Hoffman" was an applicant "for the benefit of the insolvent laws of Maryland." Francis was broke.[4]

The family relocated one more time—to Gettysburg, possibly as early as 1831 and certainly by 1833, where Francis decided to try his hand at the town's burgeoning carriage business in a futile attempt to make ends meet. Soon after the birth of his ninth child, in 1833, he disappeared. The *Ancestral Record of Francis William Hoffman and Anna Barbara Esser* reports that he "went to Baltimore to sell some carriages and was never heard from again. The supposition is that he either was waylaid and killed for his money from the sale of the carriages, or that he returned to Germany."[5]

It is impossible to gauge the full impact of Francis's sudden disappearance on his oldest son, Charles, who was seventeen at the time. He had been put to work at a young age to help his father provide for the family, but from the struggles of his teenage years he learned basic business principles and the difference between success and failure, developing a relentless work ethic that would serve him well as he grew to adulthood. Charles was driven to succeed. "[He] was a self-made man," one of his granddaughters wrote with pride decades later. "He had no opportunity to go to school as he had to help his father make a living. He had only three months schooling but was a good businessman.... [He] was alert as to business and investments."[6]

Charles was twenty-one years old when he married Sarah Ann Taylor in Gettysburg on September 6, 1836. A year later, he purchased a carriage shop on West Street, a few blocks from the square, and Sarah gave birth to their first child, Charles Wesley, on April 2, 1838. Four more boys and three girls followed, all born in Gettysburg between 1838 and 1855.[7]

An advertisement in the *Adams Sentinel and General Advertiser* on April 8, 1839, read:

COME AGAIN!

The Subscriber returns his sincere acknowledgements
to the public for the liberal patronage heretofore extended
to him, and begs leave to inform, that he has

REMOVED HIS SHOP

to the one formerly occupied by George Richter, in
Chambersburg Street, a few doors west of Mr. Thompson's Hotel, where he is prepared to execute all work

entrusted to his care with neatness and dispatch. He hopes, by strict attention to business, to merit and receive a share of public patronage.

C. W. Hoffman

The man who from now on would be known as "C. W." had become a major player in Gettysburg's dominant industry. The town was a national leader in the production of carriages from 1800 to 1860, and at one point fifteen percent of its workers earned their wages from carriage-related businesses. C. W. Hoffman, at age twenty-four, now had his own stake in that legacy.[8]

The old Richter property, on the northwest corner of Chambersburg and Washington Streets, would be Hoffman's home and workplace for the next decade and a half.[9] The plant included "a blacksmith shop for iron work and tires, a cabinet-making shop for construction of carriage bodies, a trimming shop which provided canvas covers and other trim, a paint shop for painting the carriages and a silversmith shop for plating silver and other exterior metals." Contemporary descriptions of his holdings include two brick "dwelling houses," two brick stables, a "large Coach Maker Shop," a blacksmith shop, a frame coal house, a wood shed, several back buildings, and three other substantial lots fronting Chambersburg Street. The two-story brick family residence anchored the complex.[10] For a small Pennsylvania town in the 1840s, C. W. had quite a spread.

Personal tragedy struck in 1843 when little Charles Wesley Hoffman died at the age of five. By then, however, there were two other children—Robert Newton, born in 1840, and Francis William, born in 1842—and more were on the way. Another son, Wesley Atwood, came along in 1844, and a daughter, Sarah Elizabeth, was born two years later. With Mrs. Hoffman now caring for four little ones under the age of seven in the main house and C. W. tending to his expanding carriage and blacksmithing businesses next door, the north side of the second block of Chambersburg Street was a decidedly bustling place.[11]

Having established himself as one of Gettysburg's most prominent businessmen, C. W. entered the political arena in 1846 and was elected to a one-year term on the borough council. Consecutive terms were not permitted, but he regained his seat at the next opportunity, in 1848. In February of that year, he joined a number of local dignitaries—including Professor Michael Jacobs, the Reverend S. S. Schmucker, attorneys David McConaughy and D. A. Buehler, and businessmen Henry Fahnestock and Edman W. Stahle—in the Adams County Temperance Convention, which declared that "the evil against which we have enlisted demands the same kind of legislation which has been pursued in regard to horse-racing, gambling, profanity and other immoralities."[12]

Hoffman's business continued to grow, and soon he was offering shovel cultivators, second-hand buggies, "all kinds of blacksmithing" services, and even fruit trees—all in addition to the carriage shop. The arrival of another son in 1849 brought the number of children to five (along with three other relatives and five boarders) at the residence on Chambersburg Street.[13]

Religion, especially Methodism, was an essential part of life for C. W. and his family. As early as 1833, not long after they'd arrived in Gettysburg, C. W. and two of his sisters, Mary and Henrietta, were listed on the membership rolls of the Methodist Episcopal Church on East Middle Street. Having served the church in various capacities throughout the 1840s, C. W. joined the board of trustees in 1851.[14]

His growing stature at the church led to his appointment three years later to the influential committee raising funds for a new public cemetery, called "Ever Green," where "the dead shall repose together without distinction of sect, rank or class." The Gettysburg *Star and Banner* reported in January 1854 that the committee had already approved a site, "the first hill on the Baltimore turnpike, west side, embracing lands of George Shyrock and Conrad Snyder," a spot that would become famous nine years later as "Cemetery Hill."[15]

Expanding his business empire, Hoffman had teamed with Thomas and David Warren two years earlier to open a factory on Middle Creek "on the road from Gettysburg to Emmitsburg" for the manufacture of "cloths, cassinets, carpets, stocking-yarn, and carpet-chains…in the best style and at reasonable rates." At the start of 1854, he embarked on perhaps his most ambitious business enterprise—a steam mill for sawing timber and chopping grain, located around the corner from his carriage shop on Franklin Street, the most expensive and valuable of his business holdings.[16]

Having been out of elected office for six years, Hoffman was determined to solidify his leadership stake in the community and exert even more influence by resuming his political career. Gettysburg borough councilmen were now able to serve more than one-year terms, and C. W. was voted in for three years. With broad political support, multiple business interests, and religious and social prestige, Hoffman was part of the town's elite.[17]

Until, that is, an incident in the summer of 1854, little known today even among Gettysburg historians but vividly described in local church records:

On Monday, the 26 day of last June, said C. W. Hoffman imprudently and unnecessarily engaged with one John Barrett in a cruel fight by striking with a stick or club, throwing stones, and striking with iron—Hoffman using the stick and stones and Barrett using the iron with the intention of doing severe bodily harm; and in which both were badly injured. All of which showed highly improper and immoral conduct and sinful tempers and actions on the part of said C. W. Hoffman and shamefully outraged the cause of God.[18]

Hoffman and two other men, who seem to have been the aggressors, were charged by an Adams County grand jury with assault, battery, and inciting a riot.[19] A committee of Hoffman's church, conducting their own investigation, "unanimously refused to recommend him to mercy" and expelled him from the congregation "for the good of souls and reputation of the church."[20]

Despite his newfound infamy, Hoffman tended to his businesses, which straddled Chambersburg and Franklin Streets, as though no assault had ever taken place. An August advertisement in the Gettysburg *Star* announced, "The subscriber has completed his new Steam Mill and is now prepared to SAW TIMBER and CHOP GRAIN at usual rates and short notice. Hannover prices in Cash will be paid for Rye, Corn and Oats delivered at the Steam Mill, west of Warren's Foundry, Gettysburg." Nevertheless, the damage to his reputation in the community had been done.

Hoffman and his two accomplices—his brother John and another Gettysburg carriage-maker, William Graham—appeared in court on August 24. The record of the proceedings is sparse, but the jury found the three defendants "guilty of an assault and battery" and "not guilty of a riot." C. W. was fined forty dollars plus court costs and

ordered to remain "in custody until the sentence is complied with."
John Hoffman was fined twenty dollars and William Graham ten for
their presumably less culpable roles in the attack.[21]

On August 28, the day before the church committee was to hear
his appeal, C. W. attended his first borough council meeting since the
incident with Barrett, offering a well-timed proposal to permit
improvements to the Methodist Episcopal Church. The following day
the committee members again found him guilty of "immoral conduct" but offered to reinstate his membership if he confessed his
wrongdoing and promised "to do better in the future."[22]

The reason for the assault that changed Hoffmans' life remains a
mystery. Perhaps it was a difference of opinion over temperance. C.
W. was a teetotaler, while Barrett was known to deal in "spirituous
liquors." The most plausible theory, however, rests on the previously
undisclosed involvement of William Graham, who in the early 1850s
had been John Barrett's partner in a carriage-making business just
around the corner from C. W.'s workplace on Chambersburg Street.
Is it possible that Barrett was attacked by the three men because of a
simmering business feud?[23]

Barrett and Graham had formed their partnership as far back as
April 21, 1851. A newspaper advertisement from two years later
indicates that Graham was now the man in charge:

> If you want a vehicle that can't be beat! The partnership
> between Barrett & Graham having been dissolved by
> mutual consent, the undersigned respectfully informs the
> public that he continues the carriage-making business at
> the old stand in Washington Street.... [H]e flatters himself

that his work is a little ahead of any turned out by any other establishment in the place.

But Graham's sole ownership didn't last. By March 13, 1854—barely three months before the attack—Barrett was back in charge. What caused the original breakup is uncertain, but the two men had clearly gone their separate ways by this time—perhaps not by "mutual consent."

Barrett trumpeted the change in a new ad using eerily similar language to the one previously placed by Graham:

> If you want a vehicle that can't be beat! The undersigned, having purchased the carriage-making establishment of Wm. Graham, respectfully informs the public that he will continue the said business at the old stand in Washington Street.... [H]e flatters himself that his work is a little ahead of any turned out by any other establishment in the place.

The evidence of a connection between Graham's and Barrett's business dealings and the attack is purely circumstantial. Did C. W. have his own beef with Barrett? Did he and his brother enter the fray on Graham's behalf? Were other factors involved? Something caused C. W. Hoffman to risk his health, his good name, and his future in Gettysburg in a vicious armed assault on a fellow citizen. More than 160 years later, however, we simply can't be sure what it was.

———

C. W. did not leave town immediately. For a brief period, there were even signs that his life in Gettysburg might return to normal.

On November 6, he attended a borough council meeting, only his second appearance in that official capacity since the attack on Barrett in June. The next day, local officials held opening ceremonies for the new "Ever Green" Cemetery with musicians, vocalists, orators, and "exercises appropriate to the occasion." The first burial plots went up for sale that afternoon, Hoffman's name was listed prominently in a newspaper advertisement with other members of the cemetery's board of managers.[24]

But the respite didn't last, and by early 1855 there were already hints that Hoffman was plotting a move away from Gettysburg and Adams County. Borough records show that he never attended another council meeting, even though he had two years remaining on his term. Then, on February 26, he made a very public show of his intentions with the following ad in the *Republican Compiler*:

For Sale or Rent
   The subscriber offers for Sale or Rent the GETTYSBURG STEAM MILL. He will run the mill only until the 15th of March next.
                                                    C. W. Hoffman

Even with the turmoil and embarrassment that followed the assault and conviction, C. W.'s customers and business associates must have been stunned. He had spent countless hours and resources to fund and build the steam mill, the crowning achievement of his Gettysburg business development. When the mill opened in August, the *Compiler* expressed the town's excitement in a breathless report: "The machinery works well, and the Mill no doubt proves a great convenience. The song of steam always sounds like enterprise, and it delights us to hear it." Now, after only six months, C. W. was putting it up for sale.[25]

The remainder of 1855 was devoted to wrapping up his business in Gettysburg. Hoffman's name was included on a borough balance sheet published in early April in the *Star*, but his career in politics came to a sudden end a month later when the council appointed S. S. McCreary to fill his seat. It is not known whether Hoffman had resigned or had been forced out.[26]

During the spring or summer, he started to make plans to move his family and carriage business across the Mason-Dixon Line to Shepherdstown, Virginia, on the banks of the Potomac River about fifty miles to the southwest. Virginia and Maryland were fertile markets for a Gettysburg carriage maker in the mid-nineteenth century, and C. W. had been intrigued by Shepherdstown as a potential place of business since the early 1850s. He had purchased property there as early as 1852, perhaps with an eye to expanding his operation,[27] but he soon turned his attention back to Gettysburg, where all his other activities from 1852 through the summer of 1854 were consistent with an intention to set down even deeper roots. But the incident with Barrett and the accompanying disciplinary action—and humiliation—must have convinced him that it was time for a change as soon as he could get his affairs in order.

Hoffman was already familiar with Shepherdstown, so it was a natural and convenient destination. In March 1856, he satisfied his self-imposed deadline by acquiring several buildings on Princess Street for a new carriage shop, which he would oversee with his brother John. He was unable to sell the Gettysburg steam mill at this time, and he would not put his other Gettysburg properties up for sale until 1858, but he had made enough arrangements regarding his other businesses that he was able to move his family and carriage operation by the end of the month. His oldest son, Robert, now almost sixteen, would play an active role in the family's transition to Shepherdstown.[28]

Robert, who "was taught the carriage trade and would drive a string of carriages when he was just a boy," had been helping out in the carriage shop for years. He would have been familiar with another young man from Gettysburg, Wesley Culp, a sixteen-year-old apprentice who accepted C. W.'s offer to join the new enterprise in Shepherdstown. With Robert's younger brothers Frank and Wesley, the caravan leaving Gettysburg in March 1856 included four future soldiers in the Confederate army.

Three

TO VIRGINIA

J ust west of a natural ford in the river that allowed Indians and wildlife to cross the "Pawtomack" for centuries, Thomas Shepherd had laid out fifty acres of his wide-ranging tract of land in a neat pattern of lots and streets. The small settlement, incorporated as the town of Mecklenberg by the Virginia General Assembly in 1762, came to be known as "Shepherd's Town" following Shepherd's death in 1776. By that time, it had already established itself as a bastion of American patriotism.[1]

In 1775, when the Second Continental Congress put out an emergency call for two companies of "Virginia Volunteer Riflemen" to help General George Washington in his stand against the British at Boston, a commander recruited a hundred men from Mecklenberg, drilled them in military basics behind the old Entler Tavern, and led them on the grueling "Beeline March" to Cambridge, Massachusetts—six hundred miles across five states in twenty-four days—for which they are recognized as the first organized troops in the history of the U.S. Army.[2]

The little river town began to flourish after the Revolution. The Potomac supported bustling waterfront commerce along the Virginia-Maryland border, and one of its local branches, Town Run, powered the workplaces of tanners, potters, millers, smiths, and other industrious craftsmen. James Rumsey conducted a successful trial of a steamboat on the Potomac in 1787, and the first post office and first newspaper in western Virginia was established there in the early 1790s, as brick homes and shops replaced the original wooden structures along German Street. Shepherd's Town—later contracted to Shepherdstown—was well positioned to welcome a fresh wave of businessmen and industrialists heading into the nineteenth century.[3]

The town's location by the river and its ford linking Northern states with the Shenandoah Valley had ensured its future as a vital migration and trade route. The placement of the federal arsenal at nearby Harpers Ferry in 1799 and the arrival of the Chesapeake and Ohio canal along the opposite bank of the Potomac in the 1830s increased the opportunities for commerce. When the Baltimore and Ohio Railroad steamed into Jefferson County, arriving at the river junction of Harpers Ferry in December 1834, travel and the shipping of goods became easier and cheaper than ever.[4]

But as industry and commerce expanded and agriculture continued to thrive, a related institution—slavery—became a growing and commonly accepted presence in the region. The 1810 federal census counted 3,488 slaves among Jefferson County's population of 11,694, almost 30 percent of the total, "more than enough to do the work of the whites," as an unrepentant local history puts it. In January 1835, a group of the county's slave owners petitioned the General Assembly to assist them in recovering runaway slaves, arguing that their "position along the frontier near Pennsylvania rendered slave property insecure." Retrieving runaways in a neighboring state where slavery did not exist was "attended with much difficulty," they said. Pennsylvania's laws "prohibited the capture of a fugitive and…its citizens were hostile to such action." Later that year, the General Assembly responded by incorporating the Virginia Slave Insurance Company to protect owners against losses from the "absconding of slaves."[5]

By 1850, not long before C. W. Hoffman of Gettysburg cast his eye toward Virginia, the county population had grown to 15,357 and included 4,341 slaves.[6]

———

In the spring of 1856, Lot 119 in Shepherdstown was a prime location for a carriage factory. Existing buildings at the corner of Princess and New Streets, already fitted for carriage work, were easily adapted for C. W. Hoffman's new business, and he took possession of the property, just a block from the town's main thoroughfare on German Street, within sight of the Entler Hotel and other local landmarks and near a spot where slaves were bought and sold, on March 24.[7]

Charles Edwin "Ed" Skelly joined Wesley Culp in the move from the Gettysburg shop to Shepherdstown. Hoffman's brother John, a blacksmith by trade, added another layer of leadership and support to the enterprise. The new complex comprised a "two-story brick house, two-story shop, carriage shed, corn house, stable, two-story brick carriage house and a frame paint shop with [a] smoke and ice house attached."[8]

Wes Culp lived a few doors around the corner on New Street. The tradeoff for the independence he felt in leaving Gettysburg, however, was that he now had few friends in town other than Skelly, Robert Hoffman, and another carriage worker with vague Gettysburg ties named Jeremiah B. Sheffler.[9] Joining the Shepherdstown Light Infantry, which he did with Robert Hoffman and Sheffler shortly after arriving in Virginia, was a way to prove his loyalty to his new home and perhaps more easily fit in.[10]

———

Whether C. W. Hoffman ever intended to make Shepherdstown his long-term home can never be known. He left no written record of his plans. But he had clearly grown restless by the start of his second winter in Virginia and was already envisioning his next life-changing move. In January 1858, he announced in a newspaper advertisement that he was finally selling his extensive Gettysburg properties, identifying ten lots that would have been well known to his friends and associates back in Pennsylvania. But the last item in the advertisement was perhaps unexpected: "No. 11 Coach Establishment in Shepherdstown, Va.... The location is an admirable one for business, and improvements in good order. If not sold by the 1st of March, the above properties will be for RENT."

He was leaving. Again.

It is unclear why C. W. felt the urge to move from Shepherdstown so quickly, but he seems never to have settled into society there as he had in Gettysburg. He took no leadership positions, served on no committees, bought no additional property, placed no advertisements in the local newspapers. His carriage shop had quickly become known for its consistently excellent craftsmanship, but now, at age forty-three, and after almost twenty years as a carriage-maker, he may have been seeking a new and more enticing opportunity. "I imagine he wanted to try his business in some other location," wrote his granddaughter Ruth Hoffman Frost. What's more, there was legal trouble back in Gettysburg, where he was the subject of multiple legal judgments for not paying his bills.[11]

Like his move from Gettysburg, Hoffman's departure from Shepherdstown was gradual, probably because he needed time to sell his Adams County property, resolve debts, and untangle other business matters. But a little more than a year later, in the summer of 1859, he purchased a massive 585-acre farm on the border of Fauquier and Warren Counties in northeastern Virginia, about fifty miles south of Shepherdstown. The farm, known as "Linden" (apparently for its preponderance of linden trees), was an unconventional acquisition, one that promised stark changes in his way of life, accustomed as he was to working in business districts near town squares. Ruth Hoffman Frost, who visited often in later years, remembered it as an idyllic setting with lush fields and spectacular views.[12]

The line dividing Fauquier and Warren counties [ran] through the farm. The farm was really on the top of the mountain, for the water in branches ran either way. They raised grain, wheat, and buckwheat, and had all kinds of fruit, apples and grapes from the vineyard, and dried all kinds of fruit.

The house stood on the top of a hill, the railroad a way off down in front in a deep cut. The view was grand, looking over on the hills beyond. We would come up a drive from the front gate, along each side being large linden trees, and immense cherry trees in the yard. Here, grandmother had flowers around the house and a little down the slope to the left stood rows of white bee [h]ives. Around the right of the parlor in the yard was a large tree where we had a wooden swing. A path led on through the side yard and over a stile across a wheat field.[13]

Hoffman now had "eleven horses, 15 cows, 2 oxen, 60 head of other cattle, one hundred and thirty five sheep, fifty hogs, four farm waggons, one cart, one wheat fan and trashing machine, cutting box, corn shelter, six ploughs, six shovel ploughs [and] two grindstones"— far more animals and implements than he had ever owned before. The deed for the property at the county courthouse also lists saddles, shovels, pitchforks, one set of blacksmith's tools, three mule colts, various household items, and—the last items mentioned—"one negro woman, Lucy, and her future increase; one boy, Tom; one boy, William, and all other property.... "[14]

It still leaps off the page more than 150 years later.

Having lived among slave owners for four years, Hoffman was becoming a slave owner himself. His granddaughter mentioned that C. W. "had his negroes" at Linden, and her narrative also refers to a "negro wench," to "darkies," and to "a good old negro cook." The 1860 U.S. Census for "Slave Schedules" identifies him as the owner of seven slaves.[15] C. W. had become thoroughly implicated in the institution that would soon provoke the American Civil War.

Robert, Frank, and Wesley Hoffman, all in their teens, made the move to Linden with their parents in 1859, but Robert and Wesley had, with their father's encouragement, occasionally attended classes at Dickinson Academy (later Dickinson College) in Carlisle, Pennsylvania.[16] Robert had entered with the class of 1861 and Wesley with the class of 1862, though neither received a degree. Prevented by his father's business failures from pursuing an education himself but determined that his sons would receive every opportunity to advance themselves through academic achievement, C. W. "had a room furnished for them [at Dickinson] to occupy as their turn would come to use it." Frank apparently had no interest in educational pursuits, but

Robert and Wesley dutifully traveled to Carlisle and became part-time residents and scholars before the family left Shepherdstown.[17]

Though Robert gave up on his studies after the family moved to Linden, he never turned his back on Shepherdstown. He returned often between 1859 and 1861, maintaining his connections with the Hamtramck Guards and with a young lady who had caught his fancy, Ellen Louisa Humrickhouse. Conveniently enough, two of Ellen's brothers were active members of the Hamtramck Guards. After a two-year courtship, Robert and Ellen were married in Shepherdstown in May 1861.[18]

Wesley Culp also was forced to make adjustments in his living and work arrangements when the Hoffman family left Shepherdstown. He found a job in Martinsburg, ten miles away, in a carriage factory run by John C. Allen, who also became his landlord and something of an older brother. But Wes likewise kept his membership in the Hamtramck Guards, frequently returning to Shepherdstown on weekends to drill and socialize with his militia friends and former co-workers. In June 1860, he wrote to his sister in Gettysburg that he planned to visit Shepherdstown in early July to "see my friends" and go "on a spree." He didn't mention his participation in the annual Fourth of July parade that year, but it is known that the Hamtramck Guards played a central role in the celebration—the last to be held on the streets of Shepherdstown before they all marched off together to secede from the Union and fight in the Civil War.[19]

Four

DRUMBEATS
OF WAR

For years, John Brown had dreamed of an armed insurgency of slaves that would end the scourge of slavery in America. As far back as 1833 he had talked of wanting to "do something in a practical way for my fellow men who are in bondage," and by 1837 he had determined to "consecrate [his] life to the destruction of slavery." Two decades later, he was ready to strike. On the night of Sunday, October 16, 1859, Brown gathered twenty-one men from his self-styled Provisional Army of the United States at a farmhouse in the Maryland hills overlooking the strategic river town of Harpers Ferry, Virginia, where a hundred thousand guns lay virtually unguarded in the U.S. Armory and Arsenal. "Men," Brown said, "get to your arms. We will proceed to the Ferry."[1]

Twelve miles south of Shepherdstown and forty miles from the free-state soil of Pennsylvania, Harpers Ferry seemed to Brown to be the perfect place to incite a slave rebellion. The "peculiar institution" he so despised had been a way of life for decades in Jefferson County, and the federal armory and arsenal there offered an enticing symbolic target. Brown envisioned a midnight raid to overrun the arsenal and commandeer its weapons, striking terror into the hearts of nearby plantation owners (some of whom would be captured and forced to free their slaves). Fortified with fresh recruits from among the newly-emancipated bondsmen, Brown and his Provisional Army would then use their mountain hideout to shield thousands of others escaping to freedom in the North.[2]

It all went well for the first few hours. Brown and his raiders slipped into town at half past ten and by midnight had seized control of the armory, the arsenal, a nearby rifle factory on Lower Hall Island, and the bridge over the Potomac River. A short time later, Brown dispatched several men to nearby Halltown to abduct Colonel Lewis Washington, a prominent local slave owner and the great-grandnephew of George Washington. They confiscated some of his most valuable possessions, including a sword that once belonged to Frederick the Great and a pistol presented to President Washington by Lafayette, but the biggest strategic prize they bagged was Colonel Washington himself. "I wanted you particularly for the moral effect it would give our cause, having one of your name our prisoner," Brown told him. He promptly granted freedom to at least three of Washington's slaves.[3]

Startled residents of the Ferry awoke the next morning to find the place under occupation. Calls for immediate assistance went out to militia units in nearby towns, including Shepherdstown and Martinsburg, and to a small detachment of U.S. Marines sixty miles away in Washington, DC. The conductor of a B&O passenger train that Brown allowed to pass through on its way to Baltimore sent a frantic telegraph to the outside world: "They say they have come to free the slaves and intend to do it at all hazards."[4]

Brown had once told the ex-slave and abolitionist Frederick Douglass that "something startling" would be needed to focus the country's attention on the future of slavery.[5] By the morning of October 17, he had indeed startled the country.

The next two days brought sporadic armed clashes that would reverberate far beyond Harpers Ferry. The Martinsburg militia trapped Brown in the armory's engine house on Monday, and the marines took him prisoner on Tuesday, but news of his ill-fated incursion to free the slaves did indeed spark a new national debate on the propriety of human bondage. The *Richmond Enquirer* declared, "The Harpers Ferry invasion has advanced the cause of disunion more than any other event that has happened since the formation of the government," and John Brown's raid came to be seen as the unofficial first battle of the Civil War.[6]

The young men who flocked to the Ferry with militia units—tailors and farmers, students and blacksmiths—were ill-equipped citizens with little formal military training, but they came away on October 18 as battle-tested soldiers. Many veterans of the brief but deadly conflict would enlist in the Confederate army eighteen months later, among them two Gettysburg rebels, Henry Wentz and Robert Hoffman.

Though he would later insist to interrogators that his overriding objective was freeing the slaves *without* bloodshed, Brown made his true intentions known early on the first night of the raid. "I have possession now of the United States armory," he told two terrified prisoners shortly before midnight on October 16, "and if the citizens interfere with me, I must only burn the town and have blood."[7]

As if to underscore the point, more prisoners were seized that night and marched to the armory complex. Early the next morning, a defiant citizen, the grocer Thomas Boerly, opened fire on Brown's command post and was promptly gunned down, suffering a "ghastly" mortal wound. As panic spread quickly through the river valleys, militia units in nearby Shepherdstown, Martinsburg, and Charles Town were summoned to the aid of their brethren. A prominent resident of Shepherdstown, Alexander Boteler, a U.S. congressman and future member of Stonewall Jackson's staff, heard that morning that "a number of armed abolitionists from the North—supposed to be some hundreds—had stolen into the Ferry during the previous night, and having taken possession of the national armories and arsenal, were issuing guns to the Negroes and shooting down unarmed citizens in the streets." He was stunned.[8]

Boteler rode at once to Harpers Ferry, but before leaving, he noticed militiamen mustering in Shepherdstown from their farms and shops. Some twenty years later he recalled, "The only military organization of the precinct—a rifle company called 'The Hamtramck Guards'—had been ordered out, and as I rode through town the command was nearly ready to take up its line of march for the Ferry, while a goodly number of volunteers, with every sort of fire-arm, from old Tower muskets which had done service in colonial days to modern bird-guns, were joining them." He added, "I observed, in passing the farms along my route that the Negroes were at work as usual."[9]

The scene was repeated in towns throughout the region. The first militia units to reach Harpers Ferry came from Charles Town, just seven miles away. Arriving at 11:30 a.m., they immediately seized the railroad bridge over the Potomac, cutting off the Provisional Army's escape route into Maryland, and occupied a strategically-located building overlooking the entrance to the armory. Brown sent out emissaries under a flag of truce to seek a cease-fire, but they were answered with bullets.[10] Around three o'clock, Henry Wentz and the rest of Ephraim Alburtis's newly renamed Wise Artillery arrived from Martinsburg, about the same time as the Hamtramck Guards from Shepherdstown.[11]

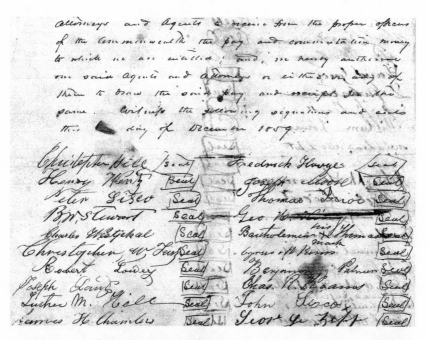

Henry Wentz's signature (left column, second from the top) appears on a list of Wise Artillery members in the "John Brown's Raid Unit Records" at the Library of Virginia in Richmond. *Author photo*

Wentz's presence is confirmed by unit records for the John Brown Raid located at the Library of Virginia; by contrast, there is no direct evidence that Robert Hoffman or Wesley Culp was with the Hamtramck Guards at Harpers Ferry. It is possible that they were away from Shepherdstown in mid-October 1859 and therefore unavailable for duty on such short notice. But militia records from the pre-Civil War era are notoriously informal and incomplete, and Robert's daughter maintained that he took part in suppressing the raid.[12]

Wentz's Martinsburg militia and Hoffman's Hamtramck Guards approached the town in mid-afternoon and met on the road from Bolivar about a mile from Harpers Ferry. The Martinsburg men were marching behind the Guards when Alburtis received orders "that the company from Shepherdstown should take the street coming into Harpers Ferry, entering the armory at the east gate, and my command should enter [the armory at] the upper end." The Hamtramck Guards at this point angled toward the railroad bridge, while Alburtis's troops aimed directly down Potomac Street toward the fire engine house, into the thick of the fighting.[13]

A small group of Brown's insurgents posted just outside the engine house sensed the mounting pressure and opened fire. Alburtis's unit, which he estimated at more than fifty men, recoiled briefly but returned the fire, forcing the raiders back inside the small brick building. It was

The restored Engine House at Harpers Ferry where John Brown was captured—now identified as "John Brown's Fort" at the Harpers Ferry National Historic Park. *Author photo*

a fortress-like structure of "dead brick walls on three sides, and on the fourth, large doors, with window sashes above, some eight feet from the ground." Brown's men were trapped inside with ten of their high-profile prisoners as the militiamen kept surging, "dashing on, firing and cheering, and led by the gallant Captain Alburtis." Colonel Lewis Washington was still a captive in the engine house, but Henry Wentz and the Martinsburg troops helped to free about thirty other citizens who had been left behind as unguarded prisoners in the adjacent guard house.[14]

As Alburtis himself remembered it,

> We were fired on by the men in the engine house and the pay office. The fire was returned and they retreated into the engine house, from which they kept up a continual fire through the door, which was kept four or five inches ajar. This fire was very briskly returned by our men.... We had a small piece of cannon, which we proposed to bring to bear on the engine house, but were directed not to do so on account of endangering the prisoners.[15]

Alburtis always believed that his men could have ended the stand-off that afternoon: "Had the other companies come up, we could have taken the engine house then." Recollections of combat, however, can be shaped by starkly differing perspectives. A correspondent for a Virginia newspaper wrote that the Martinsburg men were "poorly armed, some with pistols and others with shot-guns, and when they came within range of the engine house, where the *elite* of the insurgents were gathered and were exposed to their rapid and dexterous use of the Sharps rifles, they were forced to fall back, suffering pretty severely." One of Brown's raiders later remembered, "We shot from under cover, and took deadly aim...one and another of the enemy were constantly dropping to the earth."[16]

As evening fell on Harpers Ferry, neither side could gain a decisive advantage, and a tense stalemate developed. Brown's core group hunkered down in the engine house, perhaps preparing for a final stand. Outside, Alburtis's unit joined the Hamtramck Guards and numerous other militia companies in what amounted to an overnight siege. It had been a stressful day for the Guards as well. According to the *Shepherdstown Register*, they had killed three of the "rioters" in a firefight near the bridge. Some of the militia eased the tension with refreshments from local taverns and became intoxicated, leading one observer to believe the town was in a state of "drunken mayhem," with men firing their guns wildly into the air.[17]

The hope for a breakthrough came just before midnight on October 17, when a company of ninety U.S. Marines on assignment from President James Buchanan arrived from Washington, DC. Their temporary commander was a fifty-two-year-old U.S. Army colonel named Robert E. Lee, an accomplished military engineer and Mexican War veteran, who had been home visiting his family in Arlington, Virginia. Buchanan appointed Lee to lead the inexperienced marines to Harpers Ferry and selected another army man, Lieutenant J. E. B. "Jeb" Stuart, to serve as his assistant. Together, the two future Confederate commanders would oversee the U.S. effort to capture Brown and end the raid.[18]

Lee briefly considered a midnight assault on the engine house but decided against it "for the fear of sacrificing the lives of some of the gentlemen held by them as prisoners." Instead, he wrote an official demand for surrender that Lieutenant Stuart would present to Brown under a flag of truce at daylight. Lee's letter was a reasonable and generous effort to put an end to three days of hostilities at Harpers Ferry, but in hindsight it drips with historical irony:

Colonel Lee, United States army, commanding the troops
sent by the President of the United States to suppress the

insurrection at this place, demands the surrender of the persons in the armory buildings. If they will peaceably surrender themselves and restore the pillaged property, they shall be kept in safety to await the orders of the President. Colonel Lee represents to them, in all frankness, that it is impossible for them to escape; that the armory is surrounded on all sides by troops; and that if he is compelled to take them by force he cannot answer for their safety.[19]

Wentz and Hoffman would have been among those watching when Jeb Stuart approached the engine house at seven o'clock in the morning and spoke with Brown through a slight opening in the door. The now-ragged abolitionist held a cocked rifle in one hand and adamantly refused to surrender, a decision that came as no surprise to Lee. "Knowing the character of the leader of the insurgents," he wrote in his official report, "I did not expect it would be accepted." Stuart was under orders that he should not negotiate, so he stepped away and gave a pre-determined signal by waving his hat in the air. At that point, twelve marines charged the engine house, battering the door with sledgehammers and a heavy ladder.[20]

Lieutenant Israel Green was the first U.S. soldier inside, and he claimed the honor of subduing and capturing the fifty-nine-year-old Brown. The marines quickly overran the tired and hungry raiders, killing or wounding some and taking others prisoner. "The insurgents who resisted were bayoneted," Lee said. "Their leader, John Brown, was cut down by the sword of Lieutenant Green, and our citizens were protected by both officers and men." The final line of Lee's report underscored the speed and efficiency of the attack that ended one of the most famous raids in American history: "The whole was over in a few minutes."[21]

Shortly after noon, an injured and exhausted Brown was carried to the paymaster's office on the armory grounds, where he was interrogated by a group that included Lee, Stuart, Lewis Washington, and Governor Henry A. Wise of Virginia. Reporters and anti-slavery politicians also peppered him with questions. The tone of Brown's rambling comments alternated between "courtesy and defiance" as he readily admitted his intention to free the slaves and forever abolish "this great wrong against God and humanity." In conclusion, however, he issued a warning to the slave-holding states that was equally haunting and prophetic.[22]

> I wish to say furthermore that you had better—all you people at the South—prepare yourselves for a settlement of the question that must come up...sooner than you are prepared for it. You may dispose of me very easily. I am nearly disposed of now; but this question is still to be settled—this Negro question I mean—the end of that is not yet.

Brown received a perfunctory trial in nearby Charles Town, the county seat. One of his original defense attorneys was Lawson Botts, who had led part of the local militia opposing Brown at Harpers Ferry (and who would later command a company alongside the Hamtramck Guards in the Second Virginia Infantry). After four days of testimony, the jury deliberated for just forty-five minutes on November 2 before finding Brown guilty of murder, treason against Virginia, and conspiring with slaves to rebel. He was sentenced to "hang by the neck until you are dead," with the execution set for December 2.[23]

Amid rumors of an abolitionist plot to storm the jail and free Brown, a "considerable portion of the Virginia militia was mobilized" in and around Charles Town. Martinsburg's Wise Artillery and

Shepherdstown's Hamtramck Guards were among a force of 1,500 militiamen stationed there in late November and early December. Henry Wentz was certainly there, and Robert Hoffman and Wesley Culp might have been as well.[24] All of them were affected by the news and civic upheaval. The young men from Gettysburg who had come to Virginia in the 1850s would not be the same after Brown's historic raid. They had experienced the roots of national rebellion before it officially began.

Brown was forced to ride to the gallows on the lid of his own coffin. Four other raiders would be executed within the month at Charles Town, but it was the spectacle of Brown's death in the public square that became an abolitionist legend. A Virginia militia captain felt he was representing millions of Southerners when he shouted, at the moment the trap released under Brown, "So perish all such enemies of Virginia! All such enemies of the Union! All such foes of the human race!" But to abolitionists everywhere, to free blacks, and to millions of progressive thinkers in the industrialized North, the old man was now the martyred symbol of the anti-slavery crusade.[25]

Years later, Frederick Douglass put Brown's uprising in perspective. Speaking in 1881 at Storer College, a school for blacks at Harpers Ferry, he told the students,

> If John Brown did not end the war that ended slavery, he did at least begin the war that ended slavery.... Until this blow was struck, the prospect for freedom was dim and shadowy and uncertain. The irrepressible conflict was one of words, votes and compromises. When John Brown stretched forth his arm the sky was cleared. The time for compromises was gone—the armed hosts of freedom stood face to face over the chasm of a broken Union—and the clash of arms was at hand. The South staked all upon

getting possession of the Federal Government, and failing to do that, drew the sword of rebellion and thus made her own, and not Brown's, the lost cause of the century.[26]

––––––

Sectional strife continued to fester as the calendar turned to 1860, especially in the small towns of northwestern Virginia, where memories of Brown's incursion were still fresh. Brown himself had predicted on the day of his death that "the crimes of this guilty land will never be purged away but with blood." New York Senator William Seward had issued a stern warning about "irrepressible conflict" between the geographical regions, and many Southern states, including Virginia, responded by holding their own military conventions to reorganize the militia system and recruit new units.[27]

That is not to say that drumbeats of a coming civil war dominated every facet of daily life for Southern citizens—not even for the militiamen who were future Confederate volunteers. Writing from Martinsburg in June 1860 to his sister in Gettysburg, Wesley Culp never even raised the subject. One of the few surviving documents in Wesley's own hand, the letter reads:

My Dear Sister

i reseaved your kind and welcom letter and was verey glad to hear from you you nead not look for me at the fourth of July for i cant com and i doant no when i cin be thair mebey not for a year or too for if i git dun work hear in the fall i will go to the west and hunt my fortune and if i cant find it i cin starve but i doant think the peopil of the west will leave a good lookin boy like me starve sis i am a goin to send you a nother doler this weak and then you cin go and get yir bonit and i will send you the other won next weak or weak after for sure i want to go to Shepherdstown in the Sunday befoar the fourth and se my friends and git on a spree for i will be twenty won a bout that time and you said i should git on a spree when I was twenty won i would like to se a birth day gift comin from that place about that time i woush you would go and se our brother and ast him wether he got a letter that I roat to him about three weeks a go a bout our bugey tell him if he got it i would like if he would answer it tell him grist was to start out with it this weak to sell

i will cloas my letter by given my love to all my friends good by rite sune i remain your borother J Wesley Culp[28]

He wrote again on August 21, 1860, expressing concern about the recent illness of their father, Esaias, who had turned fifty-three years old that year:

My Dear Sister

I reseaved your and fathers letter on Saturday and i was verey glad to hear from you but sorey to hear that father is sick i will send him five dolers in this letter and when i rite to him i will tri and send him some more for i think to help him along.... [29]

It is not known how often Wes returned to Gettysburg to visit his family and friends after moving to Shepherdstown in 1856. He most likely went home in the fall of 1856 when his mother passed away, and he may have been there when his father remarried in July 1859. His sisters Ann and Julia paid him frequent visits in both Shepherdstown and Martinsburg, and the tone of his June letter indicates

Published here for the first time is the original copy of Wesley Culp's June 1860 letter from Martinsburg to his sister in Gettysburg. This is the second page, which includes his signature. *Courtesy of Culp descendant Michael Fahnestock*

that he at least considered Julia's invitation to return home for the Fourth of July celebration in 1860. But he decided against it, opting for a "spree" with his friends in Shepherdstown.[30]

Indeed, Wes and his militia unit would be among those leading the Shepherdstown celebrations. The *Shepherdstown Register* reported that the Hamtramck Guards, "accompanied by a number of citizens, at the spirited notes of the fife and the soul-inspiring music of the drum, assembled at their Armory at 12 o'clock and took up their line of march toward the Big Spring." A hearty holiday dinner was served upon their arrival, followed by speeches and celebratory toasts, some of which underscored the coming national divide.[31] Albert Humrickhouse, the uncle of Robert Hoffman's fiancée, toasted the Union, declaring, "Our fathers fought for it, and their sons must protect it." The Declaration of Independence was read by a future Confederate general named Edward Gray Lee, and the keynote speech was delivered by Henry Kyd Douglas, a future member of Stonewall Jackson's staff. The diversity of opinion from a Union supporter and two soon-to-be rebel officers must have unsettled Culp, Hoffman, and the other young men in the audience.[32]

Given the chance to offer toasts of their own once the formal program was completed, Shepherdstown citizens expressed starkly different viewpoints. C. W. Yontz proudly toasted Virginia: "So long as she contains the graves of Washington, Jefferson, and Madison, she must be faithful to her glorious title of Old Dominion—for she is first in war, first in peace, and first in the hearts of her citizens." R. P. McGinley countered with a salute to the Union: "May the Ship of State ride safely to port over the troubled waters of Sectionalism and the enemies that cast her against the breakers of fanaticism."[33]

The *Register*'s generally patriotic report could not ignore the sense of unrest that hung over the festivities. "Another anniversary of American Independence dawned upon us Wednesday last, and with its coming we found the spark of National pride, enlivened as in days gone by, in the breast of every American, notwithstanding inroads calculated to quench or partially extinguish it." The somewhat awkward merry-making continued until four o'clock, when the Hamtramck Guards led the match back to town, randomly "firing several salutes through the streets."[34] In a little more than nine months, Wes Culp, Robert Hoffman, and their friends in the Guards would be aiming those same guns at United States soldiers.

The 1860 presidential election threatened to further weaken the bond between North and South. With four major candidates, including the controversial Republican, Abraham Lincoln, who opposed the expansion of slavery, the election promised "to be the warmest ever known in the political annals of our country," the *Register* reported. Jefferson County voters were especially perplexed by the choices confronting them on Election Day. Many supported slavery but had no interest in seceding from the Union.[35]

They could agree only on their disdain for Lincoln and the so-called "Black Republicans." A county history records that "support of Lincoln's candidacy was out of the question" because "his views in opposition to slavery extension were too well-known and there were too many slave-owners in the county to expect them to vote for a man with such opinions." But warring factions of the Democratic Party had nominated two competing candidates, Stephen Douglas and John Breckenridge, both of whom supported the states' right to permit slavery but who held differing views on the expansion of slavery and secession. A fourth group, known as the Constitutional Union Party, offered an alternative in John Bell, who sidestepped the slavery issue and ran on a platform committed "to the maintenance of the Union and the Constitution."[36]

On Election Day, November 6, Bell, the compromise candidate, carried Jefferson County with 959 votes. Breckenridge and Douglas neutralized each other, Breckenridge drawing 458 votes to Douglas's 440. Lincoln did not receive a single vote. The results underscored that citizens here supported the "peculiar institution" but opposed seceding from the Union.[37]

Lincoln, not even on the ballot in most of the slave-holding states, took less than 40 percent of the national popular vote, a fractured and chaotic result that sent the country hurtling toward civil war. South Carolina was the first state to break with the Union as a result of Lincoln's victory, passing its secession ordinance on December 20, two and a half months before the new president even took office.[38]

Throughout 1860, with debate over the election raging and the odor of disunion in the air, transplanted Northerners in Southern states faced a decision about their immediate future. Would they stay to prepare for the war, or would they return home? Edwin Skelly, one of the young men from Gettysburg who had come south in 1856 to work in C. W. Hoffman's carriage shop, was among the most decisive. He headed back north in time to appear in the 1860 Gettysburg census and would eventually enlist with other townsmen, including William Culp, in the Eighty-Seventh Pennsylvania Infantry. Others did more soul-searching but reached similar conclusions.[39]

At one point, a group with distinct pro-Union sympathies approached Wesley Culp with travel plans, telling him they were heading north and expecting him to join the exodus. "No," Wes replied with equal parts bravado and defiance. "I am going to stay here, come what may."[40]

Five

CONFEDERATE
RECRUITS

The ink had barely dried on South Carolina's secession ordinance in early January 1861 when attention turned once again to the federal armory and arsenal at Harpers Ferry. Fifteen months after John Brown's insurrection, another U.S. Army officer was ordered to "assume the military command of the armory." The concern this time, however, was a raid by local militia and others sympathetic to the secessionist cause.[1]

Lieutenant Roger Jones and his hand-picked company of sixty-eight troops were given the task of preventing "the success of an attack on the United States property there, should one be attempted"—a tricky assignment, and not only because Jones was warned not to agitate the residents by "making a display of your force." Secessionist fervor was not yet strong in Virginia, which would be among the last of the Southern states to follow South Carolina's lead. Pro-Union sentiments ran deep in the Old Dominion, the home of seven of the first eleven U.S. presidents.[2]

Seven states had already seceded and the Confederate States of America had been formed before Virginia opened its convention on the subject on February 13, 1861. The 85-to-45 vote against secession on April 4 must have been a relief to Jones and his men at Harpers Ferry. They could relax, conduct meaningless daily drills, and bide their time without fear of reprisal.[3]

But the situation changed dramatically two weeks later, when the newly-formed Confederate army attacked U.S. forces at Fort Sumter, South Carolina. On April 15, President Abraham Lincoln called for seventy-five thousand volunteers to suppress the rebellion and maintain the "existence of our National Union." The secretary of war, Simon Cameron, informed Governor John Letcher that Virginia's quota would be three regiments of 2,340 men, all of whom would be expected to take up arms against their Southern neighbors. The reaction, whether Lincoln or Cameron expected it or not, was furious.[4] "I have only to say that the militia of Virginia will not be furnished to the powers at Washington for any such use or purposes as they have in view," was Letcher's seething response. "Your object is to subjugate the southern states, and a requisition made upon me for such an object...will not be complied with. You have chosen to inaugurate civil war."[5]

The Virginia convention secretly voted to secede from the Union on April 17, but by that time local militia units were already massing for an ad hoc insurrection of their own. Even before the vote was taken and well before the results were made public, the former governor and future Confederate soldier Henry Wise had organized a plan to seize the federal property at Harpers Ferry for the state. On April 18, Lieutenant Jones frantically informed U.S. Army headquarters that Southern troops pouring into the region appeared to be planning such an assault. "There is decided evidence that the subject is in contemplation," he wrote, "and has been all day." Jones soon learned that several companies of militia had gathered at the small village of Halltown, "about three or four miles from here on the road to Charles Town, with the intention of seizing the government property, and the last report is that the attack will be made tonight."[6]

Indeed, a force of at least three hundred militiamen had assembled at Halltown to await reinforcements and further instruction, the Hamtramck Guards of Shepherdstown among them. Two Gettysburg Rebels were about to enter the Civil War.[7]

Robert N. Hoffman enlisted in the Confederate war effort on April 18 at Halltown under his old militia commander from Shepherdstown, Captain Vincent M. Butler. Although Hoffman had moved with his family fifty miles south to Fauquier County in 1859, he made frequent and extended trips to Shepherdstown to visit his fiancée, Ellen Louisa Humrickhouse. On his enlistment form, he gave his occupation as "coach maker," an indication that he was spending much of his time in Shepherdstown working at the carriage shop on Princess Street now operated by his uncle, John Hoffman.[8] He was almost certainly there when war broke out in mid-April 1861.[9]

According to his daughter's family history, Robert had tried to leverage the threat of civil war to hasten their wedding date. "She did not like the idea of marrying and he going off to war," Ruth Hoffman Frost wrote. "She tried to persuade him to wait to see if there really would be war, but he refused to take no for an answer." The Harpers Ferry adventure intervened, however, and they would not be married until May 16, when Robert sneaked home for the ceremony.

The Harpers Ferry region was in a state of agitation and excitement as Hoffman reported for duty with the Hamtramck Guards. Lieutenant Jones had just received a stark warning from General

Winfield Scott that three trains of additional rebel troops were reportedly on the way from Manassas with the intention of seizing the federal armory, and he sent scouts on horseback to confirm the presence of the "three to four hundred men" already at Halltown. "[H] aving become satisfied that an attempt would be made to seize the arsenal and workshops during the night," he later recalled, "I made preparations for the destruction of the place." Two years earlier, the Hamtramck Guards and other militia had rushed patriotically to Harpers Ferry to save federal property from insurgents. Now the presence of the same Guards four miles away was enough to cause the U.S. Army to consider burning the arsenal down.[10]

The Southern volunteers left Halltown for the Ferry at about eight o'clock on the night of April 18. "The men, flattered with the idea of being foremost in the enterprise, sprung to arms and formed their column with alacrity," records the regimental history of the Second Virginia Infantry. There had been questions for a time about the legality of seizing a U.S. military installation while Virginia was still a part of the Union, but those concerns quickly faded as more units gathered and secession fever spread through the ranks. "The men were Virginians first, United States citizens second." They reached Bolivar Heights, about a mile from the Ferry, and stopped to await the arrival of additional troops before making a final push.[11]

At ten o'clock, however, all such plans were pre-empted when "a sudden flash illuminated the gorge." Lieutenant Jones had decided that his position was untenable, even though his highly professional troops were facing lightly-organized militia units that could hardly be mistaken for a functioning army. The news that the Halltown troops were en route to the Ferry so unnerved Jones's men, he recalled, that "one of my parties had determined to retire and go home under the belief that it was utter folly to attempt to resist." Determined to prevent the thousands of federal arms from falling into enemy hands,

Jones gave orders to set fire to the armory buildings and blow up the munitions. "Having taken this step, there was but one course left to me to save my command from the exasperation of a disappointed mob," he said. "I immediately commenced a retreat to Hagerstown on the way to Carlisle, Pennsylvania."[12]

Explosions at the arsenal thundered through the valley. Searing heat from the burning buildings temporarily delayed access to the armory complex, but the militia units that were now the vanguard of the new Confederate army—the Hamtramck Guards, Botts Greys, Jefferson Guards, and Nelson Rifles—swept into Harpers Ferry and seized the armory without firing a shot. By morning they would learn that the fires had destroyed fifteen thousand arms, but many structures had been saved by the quick actions of local citizens wielding water buckets, and the arsenal's cherished weapons-producing machinery remained intact. When the Star-Spangled Banner was replaced by the flag of Virginia over the armory, everyone knew that secession was on.[13]

The soldier who identified himself in military service records as "John W. Culp" formally enlisted in the Confederate cause on April 20 at Harpers Ferry. It probably had taken Wesley Culp a few days to react to news of action at the Ferry and make the twenty-mile trek from Martinsburg to reconnect with the Hamtramck Guards.[14]

Culp's original muster document offers little additional information other than incorrectly listing his age as twenty-two (he was still only twenty-one at the time) and identifying his occupation as "tailor" (because he likely handled much of the sewing work for John Allen's carriage operation in Martinsburg, as he had for C. W. Hoffman back in Gettysburg and Shepherdstown). It is known that a sympathetic officer from Shepherdstown named Henry Kyd Douglas furnished him with a specially-made musket because he was one of the smallest men in the unit—"very little, if any, over five feet" tall.[15]

Culp arrived in Harpers Ferry on April 20 to find that all hell had broken loose. Local militia companies had theoretically taken over the town from Jones's retreating U.S. troops, but these were ragged, poorly-trained, and undisciplined units, and no one appeared to be in overall command. As had happened during a lull in the John Brown Raid two years earlier, whiskey from local taverns flowed freely and an atmosphere of drunken mayhem prevailed. "Few took the war seriously," wrote the author of the Second Virginia regimental history. "Most discovered they were enjoying this 'heyday of amateur soldiering.'" Even Henry Kyd Douglas talked of the "lightheartedness with which all duty was done" and admitted that "nothing was serious yet; everything [was] much like a joke."[16]

The merriment and general disorder came to an abrupt halt on April 29 when a resolute colonel from the Virginia Military Institute arrived and took command. Thomas Jonathan Jackson had not yet earned the nickname "Stonewall," but he brought with him a reputation for sternness, eccentricity, and an unwavering adherence to military protocol that set him apart from others in the fledgling Southern army. Jackson did away with whiskey and other distractions, reassigned the unqualified militia commanders, and began to mold his undisciplined and joyriding mob into regular companies and regiments. Reveille sounded at five a.m. The men drilled endlessly and marched at least seven hours a day.[17]

Within a month, a more formal Confederate military organization had developed, and Jackson was given command of the First Brigade, Virginia Volunteers—made up of the Second, Fourth, Fifth, Twenty-Seventh, and eventually the Thirty-Third Virginia regiments. Under his rigid leadership, they would become the most famous unit in the Confederate army, known to history as the

"Stonewall Brigade." The Hamtramck Guards were officially mustered into the army on May 11 as Company B of the Second Virginia Infantry, and its members—including Hoffman and Culp—took their place among the South's most improved and best disciplined foot soldiers. Decades later, Ruth Hoffman Frost boasted that her father served "in Stonewall Jackson's Brigade." A close friend and comrade of Culp's once told a reporter, "We of the Stonewall Brigade thought we were good soldiers, and history says so, too."[18]

Jackson realized early on that he had to hammer the independence out of individual militia companies if he wanted to form a cohesive unit. Company B, for instance, could not simply be "Shepherdstown in martial display." Amidst all the seemingly mindless marching and drilling, the men learned the complex military maneuvers that were needed to function efficiently on the battlefield. They did not always look the part of an army, the gray and yellow uniforms of the Hamtramck Guards contrasting with the blues and greens of other units, men carrying their own weapons from home, but in time and after relentless practice, Jackson had drilled into them to a degree of military competence. Companies and regiments were now fully aligned into a productive and systematic brigade.[19]

In mid-June, Jackson's men were pulled out of Harpers Ferry and directed toward Shepherdstown and Williamsport in response to a rumored threat from federal troops under General Robert Patterson. Believing that Patterson might try to enter Virginia through Shepherdstown, Jackson ordered the Second Virginia to guard the ford there and burn the bridge across the Potomac River, an act of destruction that made for a bitter homecoming for the boys of Company B. Henry Kyd Douglas, a native of Shepherdstown who once lived in a house overlooking the town from the Maryland side, never forgot the rage he felt as the assignment was carried out. It was the moment he appreciated the calamity that civil war would visit on the country.[20]

I was with the company that set fire to [the bridge], and when, in the glare of burning timbers, I saw the glowing windows in my home on the hill beyond the river and knew my father was a stockholder in the property I was helping to destroy, I realized that war had begun. I knew that I was severing all connection between me and my family and understood the sensation of one, who, sitting aloft on the limb of a tree, cuts it off between himself and the trunk, and awaits results. Not long after, when I saw the heavens lighted up over in Maryland one dark night and knew that the gorgeous bonfire was made from the material and contents of my father's barn, I saw that I was advancing rapidly in a knowledge of the meaning of war; and my soul was filled with revengeful bitterness.[21]

Most of the men who had lived in Shepherdstown and were now committed to fighting for the Confederacy, including Culp and Hoffman, shared those feelings. Shots had not been fired, but troops from both sides were on the move, and the scent of war was in the air. Jackson kept his brigade in almost constant motion during the second half of June, changing camp seven times in seventeen days, ricocheting between Martinsburg and Winchester and keeping an eye out for signs of Patterson's prowling federal force. If something happened—and it was expected soon—his men would be ready. Barely two months after the mad dash of raw, untrained militiamen to seize the arsenal at Harpers Ferry, these transformed troops "were in perfect trim and knew each other well and felt like soldiers."[22]

———

The same scenes played out that spring in towns and hamlets across Virginia, though nowhere else under the command of a figure as domineering as T. J. Jackson. Recruits poured in, and entire militia units pledged themselves to the Southern cause. On April 19 at Martinsburg, Henry Wentz followed the lead of his seemingly omnipresent militia commander, E. G. Alburtis, and enlisted with others from the Wise Artillery in Company B, First Regiment, Virginia Light Artillery. He entered with a low-level leadership role, serving as a first corporal on Alburtis's staff.[23]

The peculiar challenge for Alburtis, Wentz, and the others, however, was that "Wise Artillery" was a misnomer. The men were an artillery unit in name only. Responding to John Brown's raid two years earlier, they had stormed the Harpers Ferry armor with shotguns and pistols, and neither Alburtis nor the soldiers in the ranks had any practical knowledge of how to handle cannons on a battlefield. This quickly came to the attention of Confederate General Joseph E. Johnston, who designated a promising twenty-two-year-old, John Pelham, as "drill master" for Company B, a young man so eager to join the rebel cause that he had quit the U.S. Military Academy that spring before graduating.[24]

Pelham's arrival in mid-June might have opened a rift in the command structure, especially given the loyalty of the Martinsburg men to their long-time militia captain. Alburtis, a month shy of his forty-fourth birthday, was "surprised to find that his new aide was a soldierly-looking beardless boy." But Pelham handled the situation deftly, showing respect for Alburtis's authority, deferring to him at times, and tactfully asking for permission to assist with artillery instruction. It was not long before he was essentially running the battery.[25]

One of Pelham's first achievements was improving the unit's equipment and ordnance. As recently as April 30, Alburtis had notified a fellow Confederate officer that his company still possessed only "two iron 6-pound guns...and the old Roman pattern sabre," and there was little improvement in the six weeks before Pelham's arrival.

The Wise Artillery, writes one historian, was "armed with four smoothbore six-pounder bronze guns, was without horses and had received no training at all in field artillery use." Worse, writes another, Pelham's sixty-two recruits were "undisciplined and knew nothing whatsoever about cannons."[26]

But Pelham went to work, drilling his raw recruits every day for the next month in fields between Winchester and their home in Martinsburg. The young lieutenant leaned on J. E. B. Stuart to acquire several teams of horses, and he and his men ingeniously fashioned caissons and limbers from discarded crates and ammunition boxes. Improvisation was part of the Confederate modus operandi. Through dogged repetition, and under Pelham's watchful eye, Wentz and the others learned to load, ram, aim, and fire their cannons. Hassler credited Pelham with transforming Alburtis's battery "from an awkward squad into the most polished gunnery unit in General Johnston's army." Even if that is the overstated opinion of a fawning biographer, it is clear that Pelham had molded the disparate Martinsburg militiamen into an artillery company capable of operating with military precision on the field of battle.[27]

———

Roughly fifty miles to the north, against this backdrop of unrest and rampant rebellion, patriotic citizens of Gettysburg had gathered in the town square to answer President Lincoln's call for volunteers. On April 20, the same day that Wes Culp enlisted in the Confederate army, his brother William and a company of eager recruits from Gettysburg and Adams County were mustered into service for the Union. The ranks included the prominent local businessmen C. H. Buehler and Edward G. Fahnestock and one of Wes's boyhood friends, a nineteen-year-old granite cutter named Johnston H. "Jack" Skelly Jr.[28]

Each man signed up for a term of three months, all anyone in the North thought it would take to suppress the annoying insurrection. Perhaps no one had taken the time to consider that Union forces would be as green and unfamiliar with military protocol as their Southern counterparts. The president invoked patriotism in his April 15 proclamation, asking that "all loyal citizens favor, facilitate and aid this effort to maintain the honor, the integrity and the existence of our national Union, and the perpetuity of popular government, and to redress wrongs already long enough endured." In Gettysburg and other small towns from Maine to Pennsylvania, the response was swift and overwhelming.[29]

Buehler, who had been captain of a local militia company known as the Independent Blues (and who had served on a temperance committee years earlier with C. W. Hoffman), called for an emergency meeting two nights later "in view of the demand for the services of the patriots of the country." Although the Blues had ceased to be an active unit in recent years, the belief was that they could be quickly reassembled and fortified with new members, and "the call was quite handsomely responded to." The Adams *Sentinel* reported that the meeting was held "at early candle-light" on Wednesday, April 17, and volunteers poured into Sheads' and Bachlers' Hall to cast their lots with the Union. Buehler was elected captain and Fahnestock became first lieutenant. William Culp was named second corporal. The Gettysburg war effort was on.[30]

Patriotic fervor gripped the borough and the county. By Friday evening, April 19, citizens had erected a massive 120-foot flag pole, dubbed the "Liberty Pole," in the town square. A local attorney and future Union soldier, J. J. Herron, made a patriotic speech during the flag-raising ceremony, noting that the flag still had thirty-four stars— including one for each of the seceded states. The next day brought much pomp and circumstance, as more than a hundred men of the reconstituted Independent Blues (who would soon become Company E of the Second Pennsylvania Infantry) were officially registered with the Union army. William Culp, Jack Skelly, and the others marched through the streets in "citizens' dress" for the final time before heading off to the battlefields of northern Virginia.[31]

"A most impressive scene was witnessed in the Square on Saturday evening," the *Sentinel* reported.

> The Blues paraded, and marched around the beautiful pole just erected, from which the Stars and Stripes had just commenced to stream, and there with uplifted head and bare heads, took the solemn obligation of fealty to the United States and the State of Pennsylvania. For the time, there was a solemn stillness, and all felt deeply the thrilling interest of the scene. They left for the war on Monday morning, 150 strong, and a finer-looking set of young hearty soldiers can rarely be found. Not one of them, we venture to say, will disgrace the flag of this country.[32]

The nation's newest soldiers boarded a train on Monday, April 22, believing they were headed for the state capital in Harrisburg. Orders changed quickly, however, and they set up camp for the next five weeks on a fairground at nearby York, where they received uniforms and equipment befitting an actual army and were drilled incessantly in the fundamentals of war. Skelly wrote to his mother that they drilled three times a day, from "daylight" until "breakfast," from ten a.m. to twelve noon, and then again from three p.m. to six p.m., after which "we are clear till 9 o'clock." Spirits were high, and the men proudly deemed themselves "ready for any emergency."[33]

In early June they moved their temporary quarters to Chambersburg, about twenty-five miles west of Gettysburg. Up to that point, the adventures of war had barely taken them beyond the borders of Adams County. But Company E and the other Pennsylvania troops were now under the overall command of the elderly General Patterson, whose newly-formed "Department of Washington" had been assigned to operate "against the Rebel army in the Shenandoah Valley, which was now threatening the contiguous parts of Maryland and Pennsylvania." William Culp, Skelly, and the other Gettysburg foot soldiers could not have known it at the time, but Patterson's battle plan would soon bring them close to the two Gettysburg Rebels in the Second Virginia.[34]

Patterson moved his troops into Maryland in mid-June, pitching tents and setting up headquarters near the Virginia border, within striking range of the Confederacy. "We are camped about seven miles from Shepherdstown, Virginia, where [brother] Ed worked," Jack Skelly wrote to his mother on June 16. "I don't know whether we will get there or not. We never know where we are to go when we leave." Responding to the Union threat, Confederate General Joseph Johnston sent Jackson's Virginia brigade to Martinsburg to support a regiment of cavalry that had already been placed there under J. E. B. Stuart. The two sides kept a wary eye on one another from a safe distance, probing and feinting, until Patterson's much larger force crossed the Potomac River near Williamsport, Maryland, on July 2. The invasion of Virginia had begun.[35]

Woefully outnumbered, Jackson's only hope was to fight a delaying action on the road to Martinsburg, and so he encountered the blue-coated foe for the first time near a sharp bend in the Potomac called Falling Waters. Coming over a rise, the naive and untested Confederate troops gulped hard as they got their first glimpse of the Union army—"flags flying and bayonets glistening in the morning sun...drawn up in battle lines a half-mile down the road." The Fifth Virginia Infantry took the lead, with the Second Virginia (and Wes

Culp and Robert Hoffman) serving as part of the reserve. But Jackson's 380 men could only hope to impede and annoy a Union force of more than three thousand before eventually giving way. It was not much of a battle at all.[36]

Johnston, for his part, was delighted with Jackson's first performance under fire. "In retiring, he gave [Patterson] a severe lesson in the affair at Falling Waters," the general bragged in his official report. "Skillfully taking a position where the smallness of his force was concealed, he engaged them for a considerable time, inflicted a heavy loss and retired when about to be outflanked, scarcely losing a man, but bringing off forty-five prisoners."[37]

Not surprisingly (and as often happened in the Civil War), the enemy perspective differed substantially from Johnston's report. In the eyes of the Union, the opposing Confederates had been overwhelmed and forced to retreat in panic. Writing with the bravado of a first-time soldier, Jack Skelly told his mother that "we expected a hard battle here, but they would not stand [and] fight. They left as soon as they heard we were coming." In reality, the Second Pennsylvania had arrived as a follow-up unit shortly after the brief exchange of gunfire, running about three miles to reach the field, Skelly wrote. "But we were too late. If we had been fifteen minutes sooner, we might [have] had a chance at them."[38]

In the wake of the Confederate retreat, the Gettysburg soldiers found discarded knapsacks, blankets, haversacks, canteens, and tents. "They left everything they could get off," Skelly wrote. One additional piece of intelligence was unexpected, however, and it was especially compelling to the folks back home. "Wes Culp was along with them," Skelly reported in a letter to his mother on July 5. "He was seen by some of the citizens of Martinsburg when they went through."[39]

It was stunning, almost repulsive, news. With the possible exception of Culp's sisters, it was the first time that anyone in Gettysburg knew that one of their own was now fighting with the Confederate army—and had just come within minutes of staring down a musket barrel at his friend and older brother.

This would indeed be a different kind of war.

Six

"LIKE A STONE WALL"

The second-oldest of C. W. Hoffman's surviving sons was Francis William, born in Gettysburg in 1842 and named for his pioneering grandfather.[1]

Early in the summer of 1861, as enthusiasm for independence grew in Virginia and rumors of skirmishes with the Union army caused a stir, nineteen-year-old Frank Hoffman and other young Virginians began to weigh their options for military adventure.

Frank's opportunity came in late June with a call for volunteers in Fauquier County. Recruitment started on the twenty-second in Markham, "a tiny station along the Manassas Gap Railroad," the ranks filling so quickly that the newly-dubbed "Markham Guards" were mustered into the Confederate army on July 1. The enlisting officer was a major from nearby Alexandria, George W. Brent, who had been sent to Fauquier by General P. G. T. Beauregard to rally support for the Southern cause. Frank promptly signed up for one year of service, a commitment he would later extend for the duration of the war.[2]

The Guards elected a local medical doctor, Robert Stribling, as their first commander and captain. Two of the company's junior officers had impressive bloodlines—Lieutenant William C. Marshall was the grandson of Chief Justice John Marshall, and Sergeant D. M. Mason was the grandson of the Revolutionary patriot George Mason—but most of the other recruits, including Frank, were common farmers from western Fauquier County, most of them lacking even rudimentary militia experience.[3]

Stribling quickly herded the men into barracks at the Goose Creek Baptist Church (known locally as the Old Stone Church), equipped them with "Mississippi rifles," and implemented a program of "recruiting, uniforming and drilling." By mid-July the roster had grown to a full complement of one hundred men and four officers, and the Guards had started to behave like a formal military unit. The men were especially proud of their new uniforms, "stitched together" by the "ladies of Markham" from cloth donated by the government of Fauquier County. It was an all-encompassing hometown war effort.[4]

Frank Hoffman and the Markham Guards sensed that they would see their first combat when a Federal force of thirty-five thousand men left Washington, DC, on July 16 and marched menacingly toward Manassas Junction. But despite their proximity to the eventual battlefield, and even though General Beauregard was aware of their presence, they never got the call. One historian speculates that the Guards may have been held out of action because Dr. Stribling's wife had fallen ill and he would not leave home until she recovered. Whatever the reason, the Fauquier County men were relegated to reserve status on July 21 as the Union and Confederate armies clashed in the battle of First Manassas, the first major conflict of the Civil War.[5]

The Guards *did* make it to Manassas less than two weeks later, on August 1, when they were officially designated Company G of the Forty-Ninth Virginia Infantry under Colonel William "Extra Billy" Smith, a former governor of Virginia. But these connections with Extra Billy and the infantry were short lived. Having captured thirty cannons in its victory at Manassas, the Confederate army suddenly needed additional artillery battalions, and in October Company G was re-designated the "Fauquier Artillery"—known officially in Confederate military records as Company A, Thirty-Eighth Battalion, Virginia Light Artillery.[6]

Like Henry Wentz and the Wise Artillery before them, the men of the Fauquier Artillery "knew nothing whatsoever about cannons." Assigned to a brigade in James Longstreet's division, they went into camp near Centreville, Virginia, where "Stribling had plenty of time to school them in the tools and tasks of the artilleryman." Frank Hoffman and his unit spent a relatively quiet winter and saw no action during the first calendar year of the war. Battlefield experience continued to elude them.[7]

The same could not be said for three other Confederates from Gettysburg.

Thomas Jackson's Virginia brigade buzzed with anticipation as the foot soldiers struck their tents at Winchester on the afternoon of July 18, 1861. Just that morning, a small Confederate force had briefly engaged Union troops at Blackburn's Ford near Manassas Junction, about fifty miles to the southeast. The war, it seemed, had finally arrived.[8]

Jackson's men, including Wes Culp's and Robert Hoffman's Second Virginia Infantry, gathered their belongings and fell into line.

Their overall commander, General Joseph E. Johnston, had been ordered to move his small army to Manassas with all possible speed, and Johnston had picked Jackson to lead the way. "Every moment is precious," one of Johnston's aides had scribbled furiously in a note to regimental officers about an hour into the march. "The General hopes that his soldiers will step out and keep closed, for this march is a forced march to save the country."[9]

Hyperbole aside, it is no wonder that the scene at Manassas spooked the Confederates. A Union army of thirty-five thousand men under General Irvin McDowell had left Washington two days earlier in pursuit of the twenty-two-thousand-man Confederate force under General Beauregard. The rebels' numbers weren't their only disadvantage—they were ill-equipped and largely ignorant of battlefield doctrine. As Beauregard was quick to note in his official after-action report, "very few" of the men "had ever belonged to a military organization." But an indecisive McDowell hesitated to press the early advantage after locating his prey along the banks of Bull Run (perhaps, at least in part, because Confederates under a rising star named James Longstreet had bloodied two Union brigades at Blackburn's Ford in the surprise preliminary encounter on the eighteenth). By the time the battle was fought in earnest on July 21, Johnston's ten thousand men had arrived from Winchester to even the odds.[10]

The journey to Manassas was not without its challenges, especially for the Second Virginia. Starting on the afternoon of July 18, the men "footed it fast and furious" on a rugged forced march through Frederick and Clarke Counties, splashing across the Shenandoah before piling into railroad cars at Piedmont "like so many pins and needles" on the morning of July 19. Grousing that the cars were intended for freight and cattle, a number of the men commandeered a more comfortable coach outfitted for gentlemen passengers. By evening, they had arrived at Mitchell's Ford near Bull Run and caught their first sobering glimpse of the field of battle.[11]

The two sides eyed each other nervously until 5:30 on the morning of July 21, when the thunder of Union artillery announced the beginning of the battle. Jackson had his men up and on the move by then, but they spent the first five hours shuttling back and forth in defensive positions along the banks of Bull Run. It was not until eleven o'clock that they were deployed into a line of battle along the crest of Henry House Hill. The Second Virginia was near the center of the line, posted just to the left of an artillery battery, "southeast of the Henry house and slightly in front of a pine thicket." The Thirty-Third Virginia was on its left.[12]

Until that point, the battle had been a predominantly Union affair. Having pushed the rebels off Matthews Hill, Federal troops pursued the scattered remnants of General Bernard Bee's Georgia brigade as they scrambled toward the Henry house. Beauregard remembered that they "had come around the base of the hill and the Stone Bridge into a shallow ravine which ran to a point on the crest where Jackson had already formed his brigade along the edge of the woods." From a purely military perspective, this was a defining juncture of the battle. But Jackson's soldiers, including Culp and Hoffman, were about to witness one of the most celebrated episodes in the brief history of the Confederate States of America.[13]

As a dirt-encrusted and battle-weary Bee drew back with his men, he saw the resolute Jackson calmly surveying the field, determined to fight back and preserve the rebel cause. Stirred by the sight, Bee gathered his wits and waved toward the hill, shouting, "Look! There is Jackson *standing like a stone wall*! Rally behind the Virginians!"[14] Bee's men rallied—and a Confederate legend was born.

"Stonewall" Jackson's rock-hard brigade was joined by others at the center of the battle. Henry Wentz joined Culp and Hoffman on the field when the Wise Artillery from Martinsburg and other artillery units rumbled in. Generals Beauregard and Johnston also arrived on the scene. "Steady men, steady," Jackson told the troops. "All's well. All's well."[15]

But all was not well, and Jackson knew it. Smoke hung thick over the battlefield as the momentum went back and forth. The Thirty-Third Virginia, on the far left of Jackson's brigade, charged and temporarily captured a Union battery, only to be driven back. Again, the Federals countered. The Second Virginia fell back amid the confusion, but a hundred men rallied with another of Jackson's regiments, the Fourth Virginia, to eventually secure the Confederate left. "Although exhausted and partially disorganized," reads the regimental history, "the Second Virginia stood firmly with the newly proclaimed 'Stonewall' Jackson until victory was won."[16]

"General Jackson said the Second and Fourth Regiments pierced the enemy's center," wrote Henry Kyd Douglas of Shepherdstown's Company B. "My part of the line was driven back at first; then we went in again and fought it through, and found, when the smoke cleared and the roar of artillery died away and the rattle of musketry decreased into scattering shots, that we had won the field and were pursuing the enemy."[17]

The final, desperate Union attack of the day came at four in the afternoon, just beyond Henry House Hill at a place called Chinn Ridge. But fresh brigades from Joseph Johnston's army (one of them under a cantankerous former West Pointer named Jubal Early) overwhelmed the blue troops and sent them reeling. As S. C. Gwynne describes it in his biography of Stonewall Jackson, "the retreat soon became a rout, and the rout a full-scale panic. Soldiers by the thousands now merged into an unruly, terrified, disorganized mob several hundred yards wide and several miles long whose single thought was to flee to the safety of Washington, D.C."[18]

For the wide-eyed men of the newly-christened Stonewall Brigade and the rest of the rebel army, the sight of United States troops scurrying across the Stone Bridge after the first major battle of the war was astounding and thrilling. But victory at Manassas had also been purchased at a steep cost. Four hundred Confederate soldiers had been killed and 1,600 were wounded. The Second Virginia alone suffered what would be its greatest losses of the Civil War in its first combat action, with fifteen killed and fifty-three wounded. (Although Company B, it should be noted, recorded no casualties.) Any illusions these new soldiers had about the "romance" of war had quickly dissipated on the crest of Henry House Hill.[19]

The Wise Artillery likewise took no casualties, but Henry Wentz and the others had been in the thick of the action. Young John Pelham was in temporary command of the unit that day because Alburtis was deemed "too ill to take the field." Originally stationed near McLean's Ford, Pelham and the Martinsburg men were summoned to the front at eleven a.m., following Colonel William N. Pendleton's artillery toward Henry House Hill. According to a history of the battery written by Robert H. Moore II, "Pendleton and the batteries were greeted by General Thomas J. Jackson, who directed the batteries to the crest of the ridge opposite the Henry house." General Beauregard later mentioned their role in his official report.[20]

Manning four smoothbore guns, the green Wise artillerists performed well in their debut. They had been wheeled into position on the right of the Stonewall Brigade to face the advancing wave of blue. "My men were cool and brave and made terrible havoc on the enemy," Pelham said. "The highest praise is due them. We shot down three U.S. flags and dislodged the enemy from several positions. I was complimented several times on the field of battle by general officers and a great many times after the battle was over by other officers."[21]

Pelham's elation was typical of the rebels' reaction. The president of the new Confederate States, Jefferson Davis, reached the field from Richmond that afternoon and, according to Beauregard, "had the happiness to arrive in time to witness the last of the Federals disappearing beyond Bull Run." Stonewall Jackson wrote glowingly to a friend that "the First Brigade was to our army what the Imperial Guard was to the First Napoleon." There was little doubt among any of them that July 21, 1861, would go down as one of the greatest days in the history of the young Confederacy. And three of the Gettysburg Rebels—Culp, Wentz, and Robert Hoffman—were there.[22]

William Culp of the Second Pennsylvania never made it to Manassas for a potential confrontation with his younger brother.

He and his Gettysburg comrades had expected to return home during the third week of July because their ninety-day enlistments, signed on April 20, were about to expire. But as happened so often in the war, their travel plans were changed. "We expected to leave for home yesterday," Jack Skelly wrote to his mother on July 16, "but we were all fooled." Indeed, General Robert Patterson's Union force of eighteen thousand men was sent to shadow Joseph Johnston's Confederate troops, including the Second Virginia, and to keep them from reinforcing Beauregard near Manassas. It was an assignment that could have altered the outcome of the battle and, with it, perhaps, the war.[23]

The foot soldiers were oblivious to the specifics, but they all knew there was trouble ahead. "We are seven miles from the main body of the rebels," Skelly wrote. "They are camped about Winchester.... We intend to take Winchester, if it can be taken.

"I don't know when we'll get home. Now we did expect to get home the last of this week or the beginning of next. I suppose some of us will never return alive if we get into battle.... "[24]

Skelly need not have worried. Patterson, a sixty-nine-year-old veteran of the War of 1812 and the Mexican War, never displayed the verve needed to confront and pin down Johnston in northwestern Virginia. On July 17, he essentially retreated to a camp near Harpers Ferry. Johnston and the rebels departed Winchester the next day, stealing a march on their vacillating foe to reach Manassas and provide a lifeline to Beauregard's outnumbered force. The newly-arrived troops, including the Second Virginia, helped to balance the odds and turn the battle in the Confederates' favor.[25]

Members of the Second Pennsylvania were mustered out of the army on July 24, having yet to experience any substantial combat. But although the men from Company E returned to their homes in Gettysburg by the end of July, their respite from the war lasted only two short months. On September 25, 1861, answering yet another call from President Lincoln, William Culp and Skelly re-enlisted in the Union army, this time in Company F of the Eighty-Seventh Pennsylvania Infantry. They were joined by Jack's older brother, Ed Skelly, who had gone to Shepherdstown with C. W. Hoffman and Wes Culp in 1856 but had returned to Gettysburg in 1860, and by one of the Culp brothers' many cousins, David Culp.[26]

For much of the next year and a half, the Eighty-Seventh guarded railroad lines, became adept at repetitive drilling, and took part in "tiresome" marches "over rugged mountains and swollen streams." On occasion they were assigned to "look after straggling bands of the enemy," but most of their activities during this time were conducted far from the chaos of the front lines. It was not until June 1863 that the men of Company F met their destiny on a field of battle, against a rebel force that included the Second Virginia and Private

John Wesley Culp—their friend, cousin, brother, and now mortal enemy.[27]

———

Robert Hoffman's commitment to the Confederate cause was never questioned. He was among the first wave of Virginians to take up arms near Harpers Ferry in April 1861, and he would serve with the Second Virginia until May 1864, when he was captured by Union troops near Spotsylvania Court House and confined to a federal prison camp. He grudgingly signed his oath of allegiance to the Union in late May 1865 after more than a year in custody. But Robert's personality and priorities at the start of the war were markedly different from those of other soldiers in his unit, and they were reflected by a decision he made five days after the battle of First Manassas.[28] He went AWOL.

"Absent without leave, not mustered, since July 26" is the notation for Robert N. Hoffman in the two-month muster roll conducted at the end of August 1861, and military service records show that he did not return to the unit until October 16. He would go absent again from November 13 until the end of December and also for the entire "month of July 1862." Even with the spotty attendance record, however, Robert was present as an infantryman with Company B for the battles of Falling Waters, First Manassas, Kernstown, Winchester, Port Republic, and Gaines's Mill in the first fifteen months of the war, and it is likely that he was with the regiment on July 1, 1862, at Malvern Hill before departing on his month-long sojourn. According to the records, he was back in time for both the battle of Cedar Mountain (August 9) and Second Manassas (August 29–30).[29]

The circumstantial evidence is that Robert went home to the family farm in Linden during these periods, defying military protocol out of obligation to his father and the family's business holdings. Because

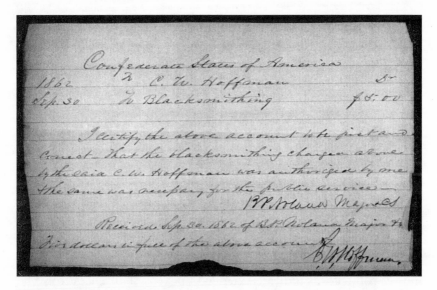

The Confederate army regularly purchased goods and services from C. W. Hoffman, as indicated by this 1862 receipt. *www.fold3.com, Confederate Citizens File, Chas. W. Hoffman*

of its proximity to Washington, DC, and the Mason-Dixon Line, Fauquier County saw vast troop movements during this period by both the Union and Confederate armies. Union soldiers in particular camped regularly near Linden, where they learned that C. W. Hoffman ran a blacksmith shop, a cooperage shop (to make barrels, buckets, drums, etc.), and a general merchandise store in addition to his massive farm. It was not long before they became aware that he was providing supplies and services to Confederate troops. Robert's unauthorized trips to Linden may have begun out of concern for the safety of his parents, his wife (who had moved there from Shepherdstown at the start of the war), and his younger siblings, but he almost certainly tried to assist his father with the growing daily challenge of operating business ventures in a war zone.[30]

There is no record that he was punished for his lengthy absence following the battle of First Manassas, however, and he was allowed to return without penalty to the "tedious and monotonous" routine of Confederate camp life. Nor was there any known discipline meted out after his second departure from the army on November 13. Robert managed to rejoin his unit at its camp near Winchester in early January 1862, when he was greeted by nature's own form of retribution—a near-constant torrent of "rain, snow, sleet and slush" that dogged the regiment for more than three weeks. He and his fellow soldiers then settled into winter quarters at another site near Winchester, where the men, according to the regimental history, "managed to exist most miserably."[31]

While other first-time soldiers longed for the comforts of home under these extreme conditions, Robert was one of the few who were bold enough to act upon such impulses. Four separate entries in his muster roll records indicate extended unexcused absences from the army, and it is likely that he slipped home on other occasions during lulls in the action. All three Hoffman brothers exhibited the same tendency during the war. (Wesley, the youngest, enlisted in the Confederate cavalry in March 1862.) The lure of home was strong. "Both armies were passing Linden," Ruth Hoffman Frost wrote in her family history, "and when the men dropped out of the ranks and would come to the house they would be constantly on the watch for the enemy—they would hide them in the attic or in the cellar under grandma's room."[32]

Encountering such a challenge regularly, the Hoffman women devised their own ingenuous system for duping the enemy and frustrating their efforts to gather intelligence. "Mother said when they would have any of the men concealed about the place and the northern army came through they would try to see how nice they could treat them and would cook and fix them the best meals possible to keep them from searching the house," Ruth wrote.[33]

Despite the precautions and subterfuge, however, Robert had a potentially perilous encounter with Union troops near Linden—most likely in 1862, although his daughter never specified the date or accompanying battle.

> My father came in at one time when they were shearing sheep. He was up with the men, but came down to the house [to look] around. He noticed some men off in the distance and thought he had better investigate. He always kept his horse nearby ready to ride.... Some distance in front of the house was a foot bridge, across the cut, in which the railroad ran. He told mother he would ride over and look around. When he rode across the bridge he could see the infantry coming up in this cut—the enemy. He was away in a hurry, off to Front Royal where his command was stationed. [He] gave the alarm and the Confederates won the battle which followed. After my father had gone, these two men he had seen came on over to the house and asked mother if she knew who the man was that had ridden off across the hill. She was very nervous and frightened, but she told him she did not know who it was.[34]

Even though he was assisting with efforts to supply the army and providing occasional intelligence, Robert's repeated absences began to wear on his regimental and brigade commanders. In September 1862, after Second Manassas, he was pulled out of the infantry and reassigned to a staff position in the regiment's commissary department.[35] His days as a front-line fighter were over. There would be another transition in mid-June 1863, when he was assigned to "drive cattle" to feed the troops as the Confederate army invaded the North during the Gettysburg campaign. It was in this role that he signed a receipt for twenty-five head of beef cattle "for the use of the Stonewall Brigade" at a camp near Carlisle, Pennsylvania, on the morning of June 30,

1863—one day before the start of the battle of Gettysburg. Later that year he would be reassigned again, this time as a member of the regimental band.[36]

But that was all off in the future.

In the fall of 1861, when Robert slinked back to the army following his first lengthy unauthorized absence, the Confederate war effort was still in its infancy. Individual soldiers were naïvely unaware of military protocol, and regimental commanders were learning on the job. Victory at Manassas had emboldened the revolutionary spirit of the men in the ranks, especially in the Stonewall Brigade, but they had no understanding of the challenges of extended warfare and were utterly ignorant of what lay ahead. All they could do was hope for a more decisive battle to gain their independence as the calendar turned to 1862.

Seven

1862: YEAR OF TURMOIL

Stonewall Jackson's direct command of the Stonewall Brigade was short-lived. In October 1861, less than three months after the battle of First Manassas—and largely because of his fierce resolve on the blood-stained fields near Bull Run—he was promoted to major general. One month later, on November 4, he was given command of a newly-designated Rebel military district in the Shenandoah Valley.[1]

The news of his departure hit the brigade like a thunderbolt. "We all had the blues," one of them wrote, "for we did not want to part with him as our commander. Besides, we all wanted to go with him." Representatives of each regiment were invited to meet individually with Jackson before he departed for the Valley, and it did not take long for the men to see that he shared their sorrow. "I want to take the brigade with me, but cannot," Jackson confided to Henry Kyd Douglas of Shepherdstown's Company B. "I shall never forget them.

In battle I shall always want them. I will not be satisfied until I get them."[2]

The soldiers in the ranks, "restless and eager," begged Jackson for one final address as their brigadier, and "Old Jack" agreed to meet with them all in a field near the tents of the Second Virginia regiment. Privates such as Wesley Culp and Robert Hoffman (back from one of his unexcused leaves of absence) had to wander only a short distance from their campground to observe the spectacle. Jackson spoke for two minutes in a "sharp earnest" voice, wrote Douglas, who recorded the remarks within a quarter of an hour of their delivery.[3]

"Officers and men of the First Brigade, I am not here to make a speech, but simply to say farewell," Jackson began.

> I first met you at Harpers Ferry, in the commencement of the war, and I cannot take leave of you without giving expression to my admiration of your conduct from that day to this, whether on the march, in the bivouac, the tented field, or on the bloody plains of Manassas, where you gained the well-deserved reputation of having decided the fate of the battle.... [4]

Tears streamed down faces of the same soldiers who had fearlessly charged Union cannons near the banks of Bull Run. At the climax of his speech, the general "rose on his stirrups, threw the reins upon the neck of his horse, and stretching out his gauntleted right hand...concluded in a voice that sent a thrill through all that [were present]":

> In the army of the Shenandoah you were the First Brigade; in the army of the Potomac you were the First Brigade; in the second corps of this army you are the First Brigade; you

are the First Brigade in the affections of your general; and I hope by your future deeds and bearing you will be handed down to posterity as the First Brigade in our second War of Independence. Farewell![5]

For all the emotion of Jackson's valedictory, his separation from the Stonewall Brigade was remarkably brief. "Appalled" by the quality and experience of the troops at his new camp in the Valley, he immediately demanded reinforcements. His appeal to army headquarters included a specific request for the men of his former command. Over the protest of Joseph Johnston, the Stonewall Brigade was transferred to the Valley District "with the least practicable delay."[6] The date on the order was November 7. Jackson and his men had been apart for all of three days.[7]

Having already survived longer than Northern skeptics imagined possible, the Confederate States of America continued on its aggressive war footing early in 1862. That suited the new commander of the Valley District just fine.

Stonewall Jackson's promotion put him in command of a division with three brigades of infantry, including the Stonewall Brigade. Ordered to pin down invading Union troops in the Shenandoah Valley, he rushed to the crossroads town of Winchester in mid-March when it was reported that the Federals were withdrawing from the Valley, leaving behind only a small rear-guard force to stand in his way. The Stonewall Brigade setting the pace, Jackson led his 3,400 men on a maniacal forced march of thirty-seven miles in less than thirty hours, arriving at Kernstown, four miles south of Winchester, on the afternoon of March 23.[8]

But the intelligence was wrong. The Union force he faced was not a "rear guard" but a full division that outnumbered him more than two to one. The disparity became apparent shortly after the rebels opened the battle. Jackson's aide, Sandie Pendleton, scrambled up a hill and spotted a mass of blue-clad troops—perhaps as many as ten thousand—ready to defend Winchester. But Jackson considered it too late for a withdrawal, stubbornly telling Pendleton, "Say nothing about it. We are in for it!"[9]

His men fought gallantly, especially the Second Virginia. The regiment lost seven color-bearers that day, and its tattered battle flag—torn by fourteen bullets, the staff shot in two—bore witness to the ferocity of the action. Late in the afternoon, Colonel James Allen led the men of the Second on a desperate charge to the cover of a stone wall, where they held out for more than an hour with the rest of the Stonewall Brigade until running low on ammunition. At about six, outnumbered and about to be overwhelmed, they began to fall back under orders from their new brigade commander, Richard B. Garnett.[10]

Quickly assessing the situation and deeming it futile, Garnett opted to save his brigade to fight another day. Everyone, including the other regimental commanders, agreed it was a prudent and logical decision—everyone, that is, but Jackson. Dashing around for reinforcements at the height of the chaos, trying to stem the rebel retreat, he had been stunned to see a full brigade—*his* brigade, the *Stonewall Brigade*—running away from the enemy. He was apoplectic.[11]

Jackson never forgave Garnett for the battle of Kernstown. When rebel troops regrouped a few days later at Mount Jackson, Virginia, he stripped the brigadier of command and placed him under arrest. Proceedings for a court martial were suspended because of the progress of the war, and Garnett was eventually transferred to command of a different Virginia brigade (in place of the wounded George Pickett), but the damage to his reputation lingered. Historians have theorized that his reckless bravery in Pickett's Charge at Gettysburg—in which he was killed leading his men on horseback—was an effort to remove the stain of Jackson's rebuke.[12]

But March 23, 1862, had been a destructive day all around for the Confederates. The Stonewall Brigade alone lost forty dead, 151 wounded, and 152 captured or missing—343 casualties out of 1,148 engaged, or thirty percent. Among its five regiments, the Second Virginia suffered the most damage with ninety casualties, including fifty-one captured—most of whom were detained "during the withdrawal and the ensuing confusion in the early evening darkness."[13]

At least eight of the captured men were from Company B of the Second Virginia. One of them had been away on a long furlough since early February—probably in Martinsburg or Shepherdstown—and was apparently seized by Union troops as he tried to reunite with his unit near Winchester.[14] Wesley Culp, expatriate, was now a prisoner of war.

The details of Wes Culp's capture and time in captivity remain murky. Military service records provide only the most basic information—that he was "taken prisoner whilst on furlough" in March 1862 and released in a prisoner exchange five months later. But it appears that his experience as a POW was substantially more complex than the official story line. Letters and local newspaper accounts reveal a mysterious itinerary: captured, released, and captured again within a two-month span; a stint in a Union jail at Baltimore, where he was visited by his brother, an enemy soldier; and a summer languishing in a Federal prison camp at Fort Delaware until the two sides agreed to exchange captives on August 5.[15]

Muster roll record for Wesley Culp ("Jno. W. Culp") from later in 1862, indicating that he was taken prisoner "whilst on furlough" before being exchanged. *www.fold3.com, Military Service Records for John W. Culp*

Culp's odyssey started innocently enough on February 11, 1862. Jackson was encouraging the "liberal granting of furloughs," and Culp received a furlough from the Second Virginia after ten months of active duty. He was listed as "absent" on his company muster roll at the end of February and remained on furlough for at least thirty-one days, eventually being reimbursed by the army for "rations" from February 11 through March 13. The most likely scenario is that, trying to rejoin his unit in late March, he ran afoul of Union troops just as Jackson was assailing Kernstown. One historian surmises that Culp and others had "wandered into Federal hands" immediately following the battle on March 23.[16]

Most captives from the Second Virginia were sent directly to Fort Delaware and held there "until exchanged in August," but Wes, willing to sign an oath of allegiance, was detained only briefly. He wrote about it in a letter to his sister Ann back in Gettysburg, and she in turn broke the news to relatives and neighbors, including Elizabeth Skelly, Jack's mother, who lived across the street.[17]

"Did you know Wes Culp was taken prisoner at Winchester [Kernstown] but is released on parole," Elizabeth wrote to Jack in a letter dated April 16. "He wrote to Ann. God only knew what he suffered while he was a prisoner. Do you all pity him? Ann tries to excite sympathy."[18]

Beyond confirming Culp's capture and release, Mrs. Skelly's suggestion that his older sister was trying to "excite sympathy" is perhaps the earliest indication that Gettysburg citizens were not altogether pleased that one of their former residents had taken up arms for the South.

Despite his oath of allegiance to the United States, Culp returned to the Confederate army shortly after his release and was reunited with the Stonewall Brigade for the next phase of its spring campaign in the Shenandoah Valley. In early May, the men embarked on a series of forced marches "up and down, over and across" the Valley, once pounding out thirty-six miles in a single day. Under the oppressive pace, many fell ill or straggled behind the main body. During one such marathon it was reported that "Federal scouts nabbed at least 18 of the stragglers."[19]

Confederate service records offer no specifics, but it was probably on one of these marches that Culp was taken prisoner by Union troops for the second time. Back in Gettysburg, the June 3 edition of the *Sentinel* reported with a mix of glee and indignation that "our young townsman, Wesley Culp, was taken prisoner at the battle of Winchester [Kernstown]—took the oath of allegiance to the U. States—was released—then joined a band of guerillas, and has been captured again. He is good and ripe for summary process, or at least ought to be."[20]

The next stop for Wes was a federal prison in Baltimore, where he was detained under guard through the middle of June. By coincidence, his brother William was stationed near Baltimore with the Eighty-Seventh Pennsylvania Infantry, at a place they called Camp McKim, and obtained a pass to visit Wes in prison on June 11. He described the strange meeting the next day in a letter to his sister Ann:[21]

Dear Sister:

I recieved [sic] your letter while at the point of rocks and couldn't answer it sooner We got back day before yesterday and I got a permit from the provost marshal yesterday to see Wesley I was with him a bout two hours and a half he is well and is getting along as well as can be expected under the sercimstances he says that he is treated first rate he thinks he will get out in a few days I want to go and see him this afternoon or tomorrow morning Juley has gone to Shepherdstown she went last Saturday I haven't herd from her since neather has Wesley he tolde me to tell you not to be uneasy about him for he is well and will soon get out the provost marshal tolde me they couldn't do any thing with him Well I must close as they are calling me for to go and drill I will write to you as soon as I see him again I will (try) to see him as oftin as I can but it is hard to get a permit to see eny person in the jail no more but remain your affectionate Brother

W. E. Culp[22]

Wesley didn't "get out" of prison as soon as he had hoped, however, and William never had the chance to visit him again. Transferred to the federal prison camp at Fort Delaware, Wes was released in a massive prisoner exchange on August 5. It is possible that he returned to his unit in time for the battle of Second Manassas, August 28–30, (the service records are unclear) but he certainly had made it back to the ranks by October 14, when he signed a receipt for reimbursement as "J. W. Culp."[23]

The men of the Second Virginia sat out the battle of Antietam in September but contributed to the substantial victory at Fredericksburg on December 13–14, at one point conducting a "sharp fight" on the Confederate right. The Stonewall Brigade then went into winter quarters southeast of Fredericksburg, as, apart from some shivering picket duty, a year of tumult for Wes Culp and his battle-hardened comrades came to a quiet close.[24]

C. W. Hoffman was having his own problems in the spring and summer of 1862. The Union troops who often passed through

Fauquier County and camped near his farm in Linden were increasingly aware that C. W. and his family were aggressively supporting the Southern cause. It was only a matter of time before they swooped in to take *him* prisoner.

C. W. had shown himself to be shrewd and enterprising since the early days of his carriage operation back in Gettysburg, and the prospect of doing business with the Confederate army had intrigued him from the start of the war. Receipts for his dealings with the "Confederate States" date back to July 25, 1861, just four days after the battle of First Manassas. Although the vast majority of C. W.'s records have been lost, a handful of items remain, including receipts from the fall and early winter of 1861 (53½ bushels of corn and eighteen sacks of grain, one wagon and two horses with harnesses, 161¾ bushels of corn). Two receipts survive from the first quarter of 1862—a purchase of three thousand shingles and various unidentified "articles."[25]

Hoffman's support for the rebels went beyond foodstuffs and farm animals. His two oldest sons, Robert and Frank, had volunteered for the Rebel army at the start of the rebellion in 1861, and a third son, Wesley, enlisted with Company A of the Seventh Virginia Cavalry in March 1862. C. W.'s wife also did her rebellious best to aid the South. Sarah Ann Hoffman acquired "several large Howe sewing machines...and made clothes for the soldiers" and teamed with other ladies to "plait straw and shucks to make their hats."[26]

By 1862, the enemy had become a more regular and oppressive presence in Fauquier County, especially near Linden. "When the Federal troops came through they would leave their worn-out horses and take the good ones," Ruth Hoffman Frost wrote in her family history. "[They] would come to the house and take away anything they could find to eat, carry honey in the comb from the cellar in the hands, the kitchen floor being strewn with the honey as they came through, also taking off chickens and meat out of the smoke house."

Difficult as it was, however, "things were even worse after grandpa was taken prisoner."[27]

C. W. Hoffman never took up arms against the United States, but his support for the rebellion became so well-known (and perhaps so disruptive) that Union troops took him captive near his farm in the spring of 1862. He was promptly transported to a Federal prison camp in Washington, DC. No date for the arrest is given, but it most likely took place in mid-to-late May, when Union General John Geary's troops were patrolling in the region. Word of C. W.'s detention appeared in the Gettysburg *Compiler* on June 2:

> C. W. Hoffman, formerly of this place, was recently captured near Linden, Va. by Gen. Geary's command, and sent to Washington. It is said he has been connected with the rebel army, and has three sons in that army.[28]

The next day, the *Sentinel* reported this version of the news:

> We learn that C. W. HOFFMAN (coach-maker), formerly of this place, has been in the Rebel army for some time, with his three sons. He was captured a few days ago, near Linden, Va., by General Geary's command, and is now in prison in Washington. How much better to have joined his fortunes with the Union-men, than send down his name to his posterity as a traitor.

Coincidentally, the *Sentinel* carried the news of Wes Culp's capture in the same June 3 edition, but the paper never reported (and perhaps did not know of) the direct connection between the two men—that Wes had worked at C. W.'s carriage shop on Chambersburg Street and had followed him south to Shepherdstown in 1856.

Neither newspaper mentioned that the three Hoffman sons had all been born and raised in Gettysburg.

C. W. was detained only briefly following his arrest, possibly for as little as one month, but his unexpected absence meant hardships on the home front at Linden. "Things were much worse for the women," Ruth Hoffman Frost wrote, "there being none of the men left at home—only Charlie, who was just a young boy [of twelve]." The Hoffman women persevered and fought back against Union occupation in any way they could. Family legend has it that C. W.'s wife once kicked a stool from beneath a Union soldier who was trying to reach for supplies. "She would also cut the cords which held the chickens after they had been tied on the soldiers' saddles."[29]

Fortunately for the family, C. W. was back at his farm by July 16, when he sold a bay horse and two saddles to Company A of the Seventh Virginia Cavalry. His captivity clearly had not deterred him from supporting the Confederate cause. But the relentless entrepreneurial spirit that was behind so much of his business success got the best of him once again in September, when he traveled seventy-five miles south to Charlottesville, Virginia, to sell his wares in a different market. This time he even ran afoul of his own government officials in Richmond.[30] The Richmond *Dispatch* reported on September 12, 1862:

> A citizen of Fauquier, named C. W. Hoffman, was arrested yesterday at Charlottesville, Va. and sent to Richmond for refusing to take Confederate money. Hoffman is a German, and formerly lived in the North. He came over from Fauquier with a load of something to sell, and first attracted notice by his announcement that he would take nothing but Virginia Bank notes, and going to the town Treasurer of Charlottesville and demanding that description of

currency in exchange for incorporation which he held. The Provost Marshal here will dispose of the case as justice may seem to require.[31]

C. W. was taken to Richmond's Castle Thunder prison, established just one month earlier for "political prisoners, Unionists and deserters." Standing on the site of a former tobacco factory and warehouse, Castle Thunder became notorious for its brutal treatment of inmates and at one point was investigated by the Confederate House of Representatives. C. W., however, was detained there for only one day. He did not hesitate to boast to authorities that he had "three sons in the Confederate army" and somehow convinced them that he "had sold all goods for Confederate money, except a lot of cloth, which he could not replace with Virginia funds." He returned to Fauquier County by September 30, when he signed a receipt for five dollars (presumably in Confederate money) for his blacksmithing work.[32]

C. W. managed to stay out of the news—and prison—for the remainder of 1862, but he had earned the distinction of having been arrested by both the Union army and the Confederate government during the second year of the Civil War.

Henry Wentz's year was calm by comparison. He was promoted to first sergeant of the Wise Artillery early in 1862, saw his battery reorganized and then disbanded, was assigned to a new unit, and took part in fighting in the Peninsula Campaign and at the battles of Antietam and Fredericksburg. He barely had time to ponder his fate.[33]

The upheaval began early in the year with the resignation on January 25 of his long-time militia captain, Ephraim G. Alburtis, who had become too ill to lead the unit, which he had commanded in some form since the end of the Mexican War in 1848. Wentz had joined the original Martinsburg Blues after arriving from Gettysburg in the early 1850s, followed Alburtis to Harpers Ferry in 1859 in response to the John Brown Raid, and was one of his first recruits when the Civil War broke out in 1861. Alburtis thought enough of the thirty-four-year-old to name him first corporal at the start of the war and promote him to sergeant shortly after First Manassas.[34]

Fortunately for Wentz, Alburtis wasn't the only one to recognize his value. James S. Brown, named captain of the Wise Artillery on February 1, wasted little time in promoting Wentz to first sergeant—a position also known as orderly sergeant—on February 10. Now the highest-ranking non-commissioned officer in the company, Wentz was the key link between the captain and the rest of his command.[35]

In a manual for Civil War reenactors, R. B. Hanson describes the duties of first sergeant in an artillery unit:

> The ranking staff NCO worked for, and answered to, the captain only. He carried out all details desired by the captain that pertained to the company.... He assisted the captain in the supervision of the company's operations and was responsible for the administrati[ve] work of the battery. He prepared reports, called roll, maintained the fatigue and duty rosters, and made recommendations on personnel actions. He also assigned, assisted, supervised, and checked the various details such as: posting guards, equipment repair, stable call, and horse grooming. He was the overseer of training and discipline, and instructed the sergeants on their NCO duties. During battle he had no combat station but stayed near the captain and carried out any orders issued him. If the battery happened to be short an officer due to leave, sickness, or death, the first sergeant took up

Henry Wentz was appointed to the rank of first sergeant on February 10, 1862. *www.fold3.com, Military Service Records for Henry Wentz* the duties of the chief of the line of caissons by direction of the captain.... Only in extreme necessity would the first sergeant have command of a section.[36]

Wentz and the Martinsburg gunners were repeatedly on the march during the spring and summer of 1862 but saw far less combat than other Confederate units. Even the battery's historian allowed that "the Wise Artillery always seemed to be a couple of steps behind the action." They were involved in a dustup with Union batteries near Mechanicsville on May 23 and took part in four days of sporadic fighting at Garnett's and Golding's Farm from June 25 to 28, but for the most they "did little more than tend to picket duty and march around the capital periodically without seeing battle." At one point, though, after breaking camp and trudging across the Rapidan River into Culpeper County on August 21, they managed to capture a Federal spy and hang him from "the first tree available."[37]

The lull ended in September with the battle of Antietam, near Sharpsburg, Maryland, in which the Wise Artillery, seeing its last action as a unit, proved its mettle once again. Stationed on the heights above Burnside's Bridge, the men opened "a hot and well-directed fire" at the enemy four hundred yards away. A Federal force with overwhelming numbers eventually took the hill, but not before many of their comrades were "mowed down by Brown's battery [Wise Artillery], the heroic commander of which had been wounded but a few minutes before." The grand Rebel plan to invade Maryland had been thwarted, and the army slipped back into Virginia near Shepherdstown the next night, but Robert E. Lee called the action near the bridge a "determined and brave resistance."[38]

In October Lee issued Special Orders 209, reorganizing the artillery of the Army of Northern Virginia. Small units such as the Wise Artillery were disbanded and absorbed by other commands. Henry

Wentz was one of sixty-eight men reassigned on October 8 to a battery led by Captain John Eubank. He remained in this unit through the remainder of the war, his rank listed as "Ord. Sgt." or, on one occasion, "O. Sgt." The historian Harry Pfanz, among others, suggests that Wentz had become an "ordnance sergeant"—the man in charge of surplus ordnance—by the time of the battle of Gettysburg, but the service records are inconclusive about any change in responsibility from "orderly sergeant." William Frassanito and Jim Clouse, a Gettysburg licensed battlefield guide, identify Wentz as an "orderly sergeant." Whatever his rank, the reliable Wentz was never reported as wounded or absent on furlough, appearing as "present" on every muster roll until he was captured in the final year of the war.[39]

By early December, Eubank's battery had been combined with five others in a larger unit under the command of Edward Porter Alexander, a rising star.[40] Wentz's new unit saw its first action at Fredericksburg, December 11–15. Two of Alexander's batteries were placed in a commanding position on Mayre's Heights, and four others—including Eubank's—were "in a little hollow near the brow of the hill." They did not respond to a Union artillery barrage early on the morning of December 11 but were said to have "covered the ground thoroughly" once the battle began in earnest. They were also engaged on the 13th, contributing to several bloody repulses in what Alexander described as "the easiest battle" the Confederate army ever fought.[41] The new year, however, would bring more and greater challenges.

Eight

PRELUDE TO GETTYSBURG

Bearing one of the more vivid (and accurate) nicknames of the Civil War, General William E. "Grumble" Jones led his Confederate cavalry brigade on a series of raids into western Virginia in the first half of 1863. "West Virginia" would not become a state until June 20, 1863, but pro-Union sentiment was so pervasive in the region that Jones was sent to weaken the grip of Federal power. His most crucial assignment, a thirty-day trek from Harrisonburg to Morgantown in April and May to destroy railroad bridges, cut telegraph lines, and threaten the rival "Restored Government of Virginia" at Wheeling, was a joint initiative with troops under the command of General John Imboden, famous in local military lore as the Jones-Imboden Raid.[1]

One of Jones's most dedicated and resilient troopers was a teenaged private named Wesley Atwood Hoffman. The youngest of the three fighting Hoffman brothers, seventeen-year-old Wesley enlisted in Company A of the Seventh Virginia Cavalry, which was then under the command of the legendary Fauquier County cavalier Colonel Turner Ashby, in March 1862. He got his first taste of battle when the Seventh charged Union troops during the battle of Second Manassas in August, but he did not fully experience the horrors of nineteenth-century warfare until October 9, 1862, when he was captured by Federal forces while on patrol near Leesburg, Virginia. Fortunately for young Hoffman, he was detained for less than a week at a Union prison camp at Fort McHenry in Baltimore. He was paroled on October 13 and eventually transported to Aiken's Landing, Virginia, "for exchange."[2]

It is possible that Hoffman was wounded at the time of his capture; his military service records say only that he was confined to Chimborazo Hospital in Richmond immediately following his release. According to the records of the Confederate medical director, he was treated there for an undisclosed ailment and remained at Chimborazo from October 24 to 30. Despite this early setback, Hoffman's commitment never wavered. He reported briefly to Camp Lee in nearby Petersburg and reconnected with Jones's brigade by early November 1862.[3]

"Grumble" Jones began 1863 with grandiose plans for the brigade and for himself. Profane, quick-tempered, and decidedly "prone to complaining"—hence the nickname—he knew that a series of lightning raids on Union strongholds could win him favor with the army's hierarchy and burnish his image as a dashing cavalier. Jones's attack on a Federal garrison at Moorefield, Virginia, on January 3 and 4 and a "running fight" from Woodstock to Middletown on February 26 met with only partial success, however. At one point sixty of his men were taken prisoner. The loosely-organized missions might have continued unabated were it not for a bold proposal that he sent to Robert E. Lee for a raid deep into western Virginia in April 1863.[4]

The raid's primary objective was to destroy portions of the Baltimore and Ohio Railroad, a vital Union supply line that stretched three hundred miles from Baltimore to Wheeling on the Ohio River. The plan called for "a gallant dash, with some 600 or 800 men, to accomplish the destruction of the trestle-work on the Baltimore and Ohio Railroad and the bridge over the Cheat River." Jones and the six regiments under his command, including the Seventh Virginia, would be expected to brush aside Federal resistance and incite panic among the citizens while appropriating cattle, horses, and other much-needed supplies for the Rebel army. It would be a coordinated two-pronged attack, Jones and Imboden sharing the duties and approaching their prey from different directions.[5]

The Seventh Virginia Cavalry set out from its camp at Lacey Spring, Virginia, on April 21. Wesley Hoffman was one of approximately five hundred horsemen available for duty as the raid began. We do not have individual muster roll records for troopers in the Seventh for 1863, but Hoffman's presence with the unit is established by two receipts for food and supplies that he signed in early April 1863. A more extensive collection of Hoffman's service records from 1862 and 1864–65 makes no mention of any connection to the regiment's commissary department, so we are left to assume that this was only temporary or occasional duty in the spring of 1863. Perhaps his officers and fellow soldiers detected in him the same adept business sense that distinguished his father and older brother.[6]

On April 25, the Seventh Virginia encountered its first Union resistance at Greenland Gap in the Allegheny Mountains. Fearing that an early delay to the raid "might have endangered the success of the general plan," Jones determined to "attempt carrying the place by assault." The Seventh Virginia was in the lead as the brigade charged "gallantly," forcing Union troops into a log church before eventually setting fire to the place and forcing a surrender. "They did the work assigned to them in most handsome manner," Jones wrote of the "ever-ready Seventh" in his post-action report. "We took 75

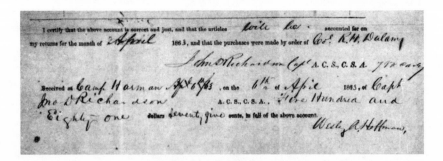

Wesley Hoffman's signature appears on this receipt from April 1863, just before the start of the raid. *www.fold3.com, Confederate Citizens File, Wesley A. Hoffman*

prisoners, 4 wagons and 1 ambulance, with their teams." But the minor victory came at a cost. The Seventh alone suffered three killed and thirteen wounded (along with nine horses killed), and Jones complained later that "we experienced an unfortunate detention of four hours here."[7]

The next day, Jones inexplicably split his command to conduct three separate attacks—two against railroad structures in eastern Maryland and a third, led by Jones himself, against the main target over the Cheat River at Rowlesburg, Virginia. It was decidedly poor generalship. Detected well in advance, Jones and three of his regiments—the Sixth, Seventh, and Eleventh Virginia—failed in their assault on the key installation after colliding with three hundred Union troops at Rowlesburg. Jones conceded in his report that "I did not succeed in destroying the bridge or trestling at Cheat River," but he complained (typically) that the failure was due to the "feebleness with which my orders were executed here."[8]

Undaunted, Jones led his men to Morgantown on April 28, facing little resistance and seizing supplies and horses, "including those of curiosity seekers who came to town to learn what the excitement was." One of the raiders was William Lyne Wilson of the Twelfth Virginia Cavalry, who would return to Morgantown twenty years later as president of West Virginia University. Crossing the Monongahela River, the Rebel horsemen proceeded to Fairmont, where on the twenty-ninth they overwhelmed a small Union home-guard force, took 260 prisoners, and destroyed a six-hundred-foot bridge, "throwing the whole magnificent structure into the water." The bridge had taken more than two years to build at a cost of five hundred thousand dollars. For good measure, they burned the personal library of Francis Pierpont, governor of the despised Restored Government of Virginia.[9]

Jones joined forces with Imboden on May 2 at Buckhannon in the Allegheny foothills. It was here that the two generals plotted their separate paths for the remaining three weeks of the raid. Moving west and north after three days of rest, Jones's brigade continued to harass Union troops and local citizenry, burning twenty thousand barrels of oil at Burning Springs (although Jones originally claimed it was 150,000 barrels) and "severely cripple[ing] production capacity" of the nearby oil fields.[10]

By the end of the raid on May 21, the combined forces under Jones and Imboden had covered seven hundred miles in thirty days, taken seven hundred prisoners, burned sixteen railroad bridges, destroyed one tunnel, captured one piece of artillery and two trains, and "secured for the Government from 1,200 to 1,500 horses and nearly 1,000 cattle." Robert E. Lee was pleased enough to declare that "General Jones displayed sagacity and boldness in his plans, and was well supported by the courage and fortitude of his officers and men," and Imboden called the raid "a splendid success, especially on General Jones' part." But the *Wheeling Intelligencer* offered an opinion that differed strikingly from the boasts of the gray-clad raiders. "The rebels have now left for Dixie with the just execrations of all loyal Virginians and most of their former sympathizers," the paper seethed. "Also, their father the devil left with them. May West Virginia never be again disgraced with such greasy Southern 'chivalry.'"[11]

The national divide was now broader and deeper than ever. Confederate forces had put on an even more extraordinary performance in the eastern half of Virginia during the first week of May. As Jones was harassing Union loyalists and burning bridges near the Pennsylvania and Ohio borders, Lee and the Army of Northern Virginia were achieving a stunning victory against overwhelming odds at a tiny crossroads on the Orange Turnpike called Chancellorsville. The Rebel tide was rolling again. Lee's blood was up, and he began to sense that a decisive blow to end the war was within his reach.

Eighteen-year-old Wesley Hoffman and his fellow soldiers in the Seventh Virginia Cavalry, flush with the success of their own raid, would have two weeks to rest and recover—and perhaps pay a quick visit home—before their next big assignment from headquarters. The feeling among many was that they soon would be heading north.

The battle of Chancellorsville, May 1–6, 1863, provided two watershed moments for Robert E. Lee and the Confederate army. It was here that the greatest Rebel general engineered his most improbable strategic victory of the war, baffling the Union high command with a series of bold maneuvers that neutralized a staggering deficit in manpower (the Federals having outnumbered him by more than two to one). But the cost of such success was enormous: Stonewall Jackson, his brilliant and virtually irreplaceable subordinate commander, was mortally wounded by his own troops.[12] "He has lost his left arm," a disconsolate Lee famously remarked, "but I have lost my right."[13]

Among the witnesses to this critical juncture in Confederate military history were Wesley Culp, Robert Hoffman, and Henry Wentz.

The three former Gettysburg residents were part of a sixty-thousand-man Rebel force sent to confront a monstrous Union army of more than 130,000 effective fighters along the banks of the Rappahannock River. There had been no significant action in this part of the country since Lee and Jackson had thrashed the hapless Ambrose Burnside at the battle of Fredericksburg in December, but the new Union commander, General Joseph Hooker, had reorganized and reinvigorated his army in the intervening four months. By late April, Hooker was itching for revenge.[14]

Strange as it seems, "Fighting Joe" stole a march on Lee. Moving out from his camp near Fredericksburg on April 27, he directed three corps to cross the Rappahannock and Rapidan Rivers and swoop east to pounce on Lee's left flank. By April 30, almost forty thousand Union troops were positioned menacingly near the crossroads of Chancellorsville. Their only opposition was a division of nine thousand men that had thrown up a thin defensive line east of the town. Hooker, known for his boasting, could not contain his glee when he addressed his officers on the eve of the battle: "My plans are perfect, and when I start to carry them out, may God have mercy on General Lee, for I will have none." In a general order to the army he reported that "the operations of the past three days have determined that our enemy must either ingloriously fly, or come out from behind his defenses and give us battle on his own ground, where certain destruction awaits him."[15]

As did many Union generals before him, however, "Fighting Joe" made the fatal error of underestimating Lee and Jackson. After leaving a small portion of his army behind at Fredericksburg to check Union forces there, Lee had ordered Jackson and three divisions of his Second Corps to Chancellorsville with all possible haste. Most of Jackson's men reached their destination by midday on May 1. Hooker had intended to attack and overwhelm the Rebel forces, but Jackson's sudden arrival on the battlefield changed the dynamic; though the fighting that day was not intense, Federal troops were unexpectedly pushed back into a defensive crouch.[16]

Most importantly, Hooker had relinquished the initiative to Lee and Jackson. Now, as evening fell on May 1, they conceived their most daring battle strategy of the war. In defiance of military doctrine, Jackson would take more than two-thirds of the available force— some thirty-three thousand men—and swing far to his left, through woods and underbrush, to strike the exposed Union right flank. It was a decidedly high-risk maneuver against massive enemy manpower.[17]

Jackson's chaplain, the Reverend Beverly Tucker Lacy, whose family owned land in the area, helped plot the course (another example of the Confederate army's use of soldiers or staffers with local ties as temporary guides). The expedition began at approximately seven o'clock in the morning, snaking its way through slender pathways on a twelve-mile march into history. Participants in "Jackson's flank march" included Wesley Culp of the Second Virginia Infantry and Henry Wentz, now of Taylor's Virginia Battery. Robert Hoffman of the Second Virginia was present for duty but likely remained behind with the staff in his new role with the commissary. The colonel of the Second Virginia, John Quincy Adams Nadenbousch, reported that "the day was very hot and the movement rapid." He was especially delighted that "not a man of the regiment straggled or fell to the rear."[18]

Most of Jackson's men had settled near the Union flank by three p.m. It took the general and his staff the better part of two hours to form a coherent battle line in the rugged terrain. The five regiments of the Stonewall Brigade, including the Second Virginia, were detached from the main force and placed on the extreme right to guard the Plank Road. Taylor's Battery, likewise, was held in reserve. But more than twenty thousand Rebel soldiers were aligned in battle formation by five o'clock, waiting anxiously for Jackson's call to action.[19]

The onslaught began at 5:30. Charging their way through trees and gnarled underbrush, scattering wild animals and livestock before them, Jackson's troopers crashed into the unsuspecting Eleventh Corps of Hooker's army just as those unfortunate souls were catching naps or cooking dinner. "The surprise was complete," wrote Shepherdstown's Henry Kyd Douglas, now serving as a lieutenant on Jackson's staff. "There was, there could be, no effective attempt at resistance.... Having no time for a formation, the retreat became a stampede."[20]

The Stonewall Brigade was in the unusual position of "watching a running fight without taking part in it." But under its latest commander, General E. Franklin "Bull" Paxton, the brigade served as the anchor on Jackson's right and the pivot point for rest of the army. Instructions finally came to make a general advance in support of the attacking force, but this was after the Federals had been routed and hastily abandoned their camps. The men resisted the temptation to plunder supplies left behind by Union soldiers, spending the rest of the evening changing positions to the right and left of the Plank Road, as ordered. The strategy of constant motion fitted well into Jackson's battle plan, but Colonel Nadenbousch of the Second Virginia complained that it deprived the brigade of the rest that was "so necessary...after the wearisome march of the morning."[21]

Elsewhere on the battlefield, however, Jackson had no intention of resting on his laurels, or resting at all. Hoping to bludgeon Hooker into submission, he directed "five fresh regiments" from a division under Ambrose Powell Hill to advance boldly in the darkness and choke off the Union escape route at the United States Ford. "General Hill, as soon as you are ready push right forward," Jackson ordered. "Allow nothing to stop you." As was his custom—one that worried his staff—Jackson rode forward himself to conduct his own scouting mission.[22]

At about nine p.m. he was somewhere in front of skirmishers from the Eighteenth North Carolina regiment. Union troops were only a short distance away. Tensions grew higher with every footstep, every snapped twig. Suddenly, a single shot rang out.[23]

Following a brief interval of startled silence, soldiers on both sides blazed away. Amid the blizzard of bullets felling men and horses in the no-man's land between the opposing armies, three bullets in particular altered the future of the Confederate States of America. Fired by Rebel soldiers who thought they were aiming at Union cavalry, they ripped into Jackson's right hand, left elbow, and upper left arm.[24]

His horrified men bore him from the field on a litter, dropping him twice on the way. The bullet that struck his arm near the shoulder had severed an artery and fractured the bone. "I am badly injured," he told the medical director on his staff, Hunter McGuire, who had hastily arranged for an ambulance. "I fear I am dying. I'm glad you have come. I think the wound in my shoulder is still bleeding."[25]

McGuire reluctantly amputated Jackson's left arm shortly after midnight. The deflating news of Jackson's wounding rippled through Confederate camps in the wee hours of May 3, but perhaps only Jackson at that point had considered that the injuries could be fatal. Lee even saw fit to dash off a note congratulating Jackson on the great success of his flank march on May 2. But he added, "Could I have directed events, I should have chosen, for the good of the country, to have been disabled in your stead."[26]

Hostilities between the armies resumed at daylight on May 3, with Southern soldiers shouting "Remember Jackson!" instead of the trademark Rebel Yell. Confederate artillery seized an excellent platform on high ground at Hazel Grove and pounded away at Federal troops below (although Taylor's Battery, with Henry Wentz, was detached from the main unit and ordered to fight on the Plank Road). Nearby, the Stonewall Brigade, including the Second Virginia and Wesley Culp, unleashed a "tumultuous leaden hail" that "hissed like darting snakes with fangs." After a vicious fight they pushed forward and captured enemy breastworks to help clear the path for more Rebel aggression. The brigade suffered mightily during three separate encounters that day and lost fifty-four men, including General Paxton.[27]

Hungry for news from the battlefield even in his impaired condition, Stonewall Jackson beamed with pride when told of the gallant charge of his old brigade. "It was just like them, just like them," he said. "They are a noble set of men. The name Stonewall ought to be attached wholly to the men of the brigade, not to me; for it was their steadfast heroism that had earned it at First Manassas." In an opinion that would later be shared by friends and loved ones of Culp and Robert Hoffman, he added, "The men of that brigade will someday be proud to say, 'I was one of the Stonewall Brigade.'"[28]

Winning a related battle at Salem Church on May 4, the Rebels pushed their frazzled opponent back across the banks of the Rappahannock by May 6. But the euphoria that came with such a stunning victory over a vastly superior force was tempered when Jackson's condition deteriorated over the next few days. He was suffering not only from his wounds but from a perplexing case of pneumonia. Despite the determined efforts of Dr. McGuire, one of the finest physicians in the army, who had been personally assigned to Jackson's care by Lee, the great Confederate warrior would never recover. Just after three o'clock on Sunday afternoon, May 10, Jackson uttered the now-famous phrase, "Let us cross over the river and rest under the shade of the trees," and then peacefully drew his last breath.[29]

The men in the Stonewall Brigade were devastated. Culp and Hoffman, among the relatively small group that had served under Jackson at three different levels of command—brigade, division, and corps—had interacted with him more often than most foot soldiers in the army. Beyond the personal grief suffered by Jackson's own troops, however, the consequences of his death for the young Confederacy were incalculable. Lee felt the loss deeply. "I am grateful to Almighty God for having given us such a man," he said, fully aware that Jackson's equal was not to be found in the army or elsewhere. He was not alone when he deemed the hole in the roster "irreparable."[30]

And yet only a few days after Jackson's death, Lee met with his remaining corps commander, General James Longstreet, to plot his next move. Even amid the national mourning, there was no time to waste. Increasingly costly victories like Chancellorsville had gained no ground and had failed to destroy the enemy. More aware than ever that he could not win a battle of attrition with the heavily-populated North, Lee determined that the best strategic option was to lead his army across the Mason-Dixon Line and force the Union into a potentially decisive showdown on its own soil.[31]

The move north would serve the dual purpose of allowing his troops to feast off the lush Pennsylvania countryside while giving war-weary Virginia farmers a chance to renew and replenish. And it would have the added psychological effect of bringing the horror of war to the doorsteps of Northern citizens for the first time.

The loss of Jackson had forced Lee to reorganize the Army of Northern Virginia in late May 1863. Jackson and James Longstreet had been the twin pillars of Lee's army to that point, each general commanding a massive corps of thirty to thirty-five thousand men. Without the great Jackson, Lee had to streamline his units for maximum efficiency on the battlefield. Instead of two corps for his sixty-thousand-plus infantry, he would now have three. Instead of eight divisions, he would have nine. Individual units were stripped, revamped, and realigned. Officers were transferred and promoted.[32] These were enormous changes—necessary, but potentially disruptive—just as Lee was putting the finishing touches on plans for his most audacious campaign of the war.

Longstreet would continue to lead the First Corps. Known since Antietam as Lee's "old war-horse," he was now unquestionably the army's senior subordinate commander. While keeping an eye on Union forces at Suffolk, Virginia, and gathering much-needed supplies for the army, Longstreet had missed Chancellorsville (as had Private Frank Hoffman of the Fauquier Artillery, who was with him). But now he was back, serving in Jackson's absence as the "staff" in Lee's right hand.[33]

Richard S. Ewell and A. P. Hill were the two new corps commanders, elevated from the division level, where both had served with distinction under Jackson. Ewell took over the bulk of Jackson's old Second Corps, and Hill was assigned to the newly-established Third Corps. There also would be four new division commanders and a slew of new regimental and brigade commanders, including James A. Walker, who replaced the fallen Paxton at the helm of the Stonewall Brigade.[34]

Looking back on the challenges of such a major reorganization, Allen Guelzo writes,

> There would necessarily be a good deal of shuffling and reshuffling.... [N]ew staffs would have to be created, old ones redistributed, colonels in command of regiments would find themselves scratching heads over the manner and personalities of new brigade commanders, and so on up the ladder—but Lee felt no unease over the ordinary soldiers' ability to adjust. "There were never such men in

an army before," Lee believed. "They will go anywhere and do anything if properly led."[35]

Of the five Gettysburg Rebels, Wesley Culp and Robert Hoffman of the Second Virginia were affected most profoundly by these changes in command structure. They suddenly had a new brigade commander (Walker), a new division commander (Edward Johnson), and a new corps commander (Ewell). Artillerist Frank Hoffman saw a modest shift in leadership as his battery was assigned to a new battalion under James Dearing (while still in Longstreet's corps). But Henry Wentz and Wesley Hoffman were largely unaffected by the changes. Wentz and his unit, Taylor's Virginia Battery, remained in E. P. Alexander's battalion of Longstreet's corps; Wesley Hoffman and the Seventh Virginia Cavalry remained in Grumble Jones's brigade of Jeb Stuart's cavalry division.[36]

Lee's move north began on June 3. Two divisions of his redesigned army left Fredericksburg that morning for Culpeper Court House, signaling the start of what would be known to history as the Gettysburg Campaign. The events of the army's first week on the march were largely uneventful ("Nothing occurred worthy of particular note," Edward Johnson wrote), but that all changed in the wee hours of June 9, when Stuart's unsuspecting horsemen were startled by a brazen attack from Union cavalry under General John Buford. A fourteen-hour rumble developed, and the ensuing battle of Brandy Station, though inconclusive, would go down as the largest cavalry battle of the war.[37]

Wesley Hoffman's unit, the Seventh Virginia Cavalry, played a key role early in the melee. Pickets from another regiment, the Sixth Virginia, had been pushed back in the initial attack by Buford's troopers and were promptly reinforced by the Seventh, which was camped two miles away at St. James Church. "Many of our men had not finished their breakfast," one soldier recalled said, "and had to mount their horses bareback and rush into the fight." The battle raged all day and into the early evening. There were more than twenty-one thousand combatants on both sides, and the losses were heavy for a cavalry fight: 856 for the Union and 433 for the Confederates. Stuart held his ground and claimed a symbolic victory, but the gallant Union horsemen made it clear that Lee's thrust toward Northern territory would not go uncontested.[38]

The Rebels dusted themselves off and proceeded without hesitation the next day. Johnson's infantry division, including the Stonewall Brigade, was among those assigned to thunder toward the crossroads town of Winchester, where a Federal force of 6,900 troops under General Robert Milroy posed an obstacle to the drive north. Milroy, it was said, "waited nervously" behind his Winchester defenses while preparing "to give the Rebs a hot reception." One of the units under his command was the Eighty-Seventh Pennsylvania regiment, including Company F from Gettysburg.[39]

The battle of Gettysburg was still more than two weeks away, but Wes Culp and the Second Virginia were about to collide in a fateful showdown with his brother and two cousins—and boyhood friend Jack Skelly—at a killing field called Carter's Woods.

Nine

BROTHER vs. BROTHER

William Culp was thirty-one years old and serving as first sergeant in the Eighty-Seventh Pennsylvania when General Robert Milroy's defiant Union division dug in to defend the forts around Winchester that June of 1863. Culp's age, experience, and position of authority made him something of a role model for the impressionable young soldiers from Gettysburg in Company F, one of whom was Private Johnston Hastings "Jack" Skelly Jr., a twenty-one-year-old family friend who had lived directly across the street from William on West Middle Street in 1861 before they both marched off to fight in the Civil War.[1]

The Culp and Skelly families had known each other since the late 1840s. Patriarchs Esaias J. Culp and Johnston H. Skelly Sr. operated tailor shops on Baltimore Street, and both families made their homes near the town square. As was the custom of the time, the boys became apprentice tailors and briefly worked for their fathers before breaking out on their own. Jack often played on Culp's Hill and splashed across Rock Creek with William's younger brother Wesley.[2]

Jack and Wes became fast friends. They were close in age and shared a love of the outdoors and adventure. Through the tight-knit Gettysburg tailoring community they also came to know a young lady named Mary Virginia "Jennie" Wade, whose father, James, had once apprenticed under Mr. Skelly and had boarded for a time in the Skelly household. James Wade had a tailor shop of his own by the mid-1840s, promising "neat, durable and fashionable" work at a new location "nearly opposite the County Jail." Advertisements for the Wade, Culp, and Skelly operations often appeared in Gettysburg's weekly newspapers, sometimes on the same page on the same day.[3]

The families grew as the town prospered. Wes Culp was born in 1839, Jack Skelly in 1841, Jennie Wade in 1843. Many of their contemporaries would recall their childhood years as idyllic. "Often do I think of the lovely groves on and around Culp's Hill," one wrote, "of the mighty boulders which there abound, upon which we often spread the picnic feast; of the now-famous Spangler's Spring, where we drank the cooling draught on those peaceful summer days.... What pleasant times were ours as we went berrying along the quiet, sodded lane that leads from the town to that now memorable hill."[4]

But Wes Culp moved to Virginia in 1856, and the advent of war shattered their small-town bliss five years later. Wes and Jack enlisted in opposing armies on the same day in April 1861. By that time, childhood friends Jack and Jennie had developed a much closer relationship, bordering on romance, and when Jack went off to fight—first with a three-month regiment, the Second Pennsylvania, and then for two more years with Company F of the Eighty-Seventh—they vowed to keep up a regular correspondence.

The few surviving letters between them make it clear that a deeper connection evolved during Jack's extended absence. The earliest letter

from Jennie to Jack, dated February 8, 1862, is signed with a somewhat detached "your true friend and well wisher," but she soon began
to insert phrases such as "With Love" or "I send my love" and at one
point declared, "I have grieved myself so much about you for the last
eighteen months, and I really think you are getting cold towards me,
but Jack never will my love change." She later told him, "you are my
only dear friend that I can tell my trouble to" and sent a poem titled,
"Friends of My Heart, Adieu." But it is striking that none of the
surviving letters contains any mention of the most intriguing aspect
of their relationship in Gettysburg legend—that Jack and Jennie were
engaged.[5]

There is in fact no evidence anywhere of an engagement. The
letters reveal occasional moments of tension—including an episode
in March 1862 when Jack's mother implied in a letter that Jennie was
being unfaithful. Members of a Union cavalry regiment from New
York, the Porter Guards, had camped in the Gettysburg area that
winter, and rumors abounded of soldiers cavorting with local ladies,
including Jennie. "The Porter Guards left today," Elizabeth Skelly
wrote to Jack on March 14. "They say there was a great time among
some of the *women* and *girls* and *tears flowed freely*."[6]

In fact, one of the Porter Guards would claim in his 1907 mem-
oir that Jennie "was well known in our regiment, and better known
to me than to any of the others, as I used to spend many pleasant
evenings with her at her home, when we were camped at Gettysburg
in '61–2." The soldier, Burton B. Porter, declared in an accompanying
passage that "my girl was Jennie Wade." But Jack brushed off the
contemporary rumors in a letter to his mother on May 4, 1862, accusing "some persons [of] interfering with us to raise a fuss between
Jennie and I, for I never heard who was going there or what all the
talk of her was, and I have not got as much faith in most of the
people of Gettysburg as I have in a worthless set of dogs, and if it was

not for the family being there I would not care whether I ever got there again."[7]

It is almost certain that some of the rumors were the result of the Wade family's deteriorating reputation in town. Jennie's biographer Cindy L. Small notes that the "social status of the Wade family was [often] a sensitive subject in the hamlet, due mostly to troubles caused by Jennie's father." James Wade ran afoul of the law on at least five occasions between 1841 and 1850, facing charges of arson, larceny, and assault and battery. He was arrested for stealing three hundred dollars in 1850 and served two years of solitary confinement at a penitentiary in Philadelphia. Upon his return to Gettysburg, he was, on his wife's petition, declared "very insane" and committed to the Adams County alms house. Mr. Wade also was alleged to have fathered a son out of wedlock (while Mrs. Wade gave birth to a son of uncertain paternity in 1855).[8]

Jack Skelly confronted Jennie about the reports of her entertaining visitors late at night. He wrote to his mother in April 1863, "About that affair with Jennie, I wrote to her and she denies part. She denies of keeping company so late, but she don't deny that she had some company.... I hope that this will be the last of it till I get home anyway, then I will settle it."[9]

Addressing his mother's concerns about the relationship, Jack added, "You should have said something to me when I first commenced going there, if you did not like it. There has somebody been trying to raise a fuss between us is my honest belief, but there is no use of trying wile [sic] I am away. I don't want you to think that I blame you at all for writing to me about it, but it is all over for the present and I hope for the future."[10]

There can be no question, however, about the affection that continued between Jack and Jennie during this difficult time apart. In the last surviving letter to her "Dearest Jack," dated February 22,

1863—Washington's birthday—Jennie recalled with fondness their time together on the same day two years earlier:

> Jack, what does the twenty second of February bring to your mind. It brings to my mind more than the birthday of Washington. I remember this day two years ago as well as if it was yesterday. I wish I could see you just half as often today as I did that day. I would be satisfied. I wish one more twenty second was over and then it would not be long till you would be home for good, but do try and get a furlough home. ... Hope to here [sic] from you or see you soon. May I ever remain your true friend and well wisher.[11]

The final letter in Jack's hand was addressed to his younger brother, Daniel, on May 11, 1863—barely a month before the Eighty-Seventh Pennsylvania met its fate at the second battle of Winchester. The contents would have been unremarkable ("Give our love to the family") had Jack not referred to the Union commander at Winchester, General Milroy, and the possibility of a Rebel attack. The Gettysburg men had just trudged twenty-two miles from Winchester to Martinsburg, there boarding railroad cars to a place called Webster in Taylor County, where gray-clad cavaliers under Grumble Jones had been tearing up tracks and tunnels. The scent of battle was in the air. "The rebels have been playing thunder here in this neighborhood," Jack wrote. "I don't know where we will go from here, but I am afraid we will have to go across the mountain again."[12]

The next phase of Lee's bold plan to invade Pennsylvania called for a probing movement north through the Shenandoah Valley.

Striking his tents on June 10, Lee assigned the revamped Second Corps, which included the Stonewall Brigade and the Second Virginia Infantry, and its new commander, Richard S. Ewell, to lead the march. These men, many of whom had grown up in the Valley and served under Stonewall Jackson, felt honored to be chosen for this task.[13]

Their immediate target was Robert Milroy's small but well-armed Federal garrison at Winchester, which Lee had been eyeing since March, when he first considered "some aggressive movements" to strike "a blow at Milroy." Ewell's men—in particular two divisions under Edward Johnson and Jubal Early—were assigned to sweep aside the 6,900 troops stationed at Winchester and reclaim the town, clearing a path for the rest of the army to roll down the Valley Turnpike toward the Potomac and Northern soil.[14]

The advance guard of Milroy's division had entered Winchester on December 24, 1862, beginning six months of tyranny and terror for the pro-secessionist population. "In this city of about 6,000 inhabitants...my will is absolute law," Milroy boasted in a letter. "The secesh here have heard many terrible stories about me before I came.... I confess I feel a strong disposition to play the tyrant among these traitors." Trained as a lawyer, well-connected politically, and openly resentful of professional soldiers from West Point ("who have ruined the country and wrecked and lost the noble institution bequeathed us by our forefathers"), he was vain, egotistical, and often disrespectful of the chain of command. One historian described him as "a man of big mouth and small talent as a soldier."[15]

At Winchester, Milroy oversaw a small division of three brigades and ten infantry regiments, including the Eighty-Seventh Pennsylvania. Confident that Milroy's force was strong enough to hold the town against small Confederate raiding parties, his superiors in Washington worried that he would be overmatched if faced with larger veteran units from the Army of Northern Virginia. Accordingly, in the second

week of June, as word reached the nation's capital that Lee was rolling northward, they advised him to pull the bulk of his troops back
to another garrison site. "Winchester is of no importance other than
as a lookout," wrote Henry Halleck, general in chief of the Union
armies. "The Winchester troops, excepting enough to serve as an
outpost, should be withdrawn to Harpers Ferry."[16]

Typically, Milroy would hear none of it. He argued that the place
was well-fortified and could be held "against any force the rebels can
afford to bring against me," seething at the prospect of being forced
to "abandon the loyal people that are in this county to the rebel
fiends." The nearly seven thousand men under his command, spread
across three forts and supported by glowering artillery, seemed to be
as anxious for a showdown here as Milroy himself. "I am, therefore,
decidedly of the opinion," he wrote, "that every dictate of interest,
policy, humanity, patriotism and bravery requires that we should not
yield a foot of this country up to the traitors again."[17]

The Gettysburg men in Company F were among the most eager
to test themselves in battle against Lee's vaunted army. First sergeant
William Culp would help to lead the way, joined by two of his cousins, David Culp and Billy Holtzworth, two of the Skelly brothers,
Jack and Edwin, and dozens of patriotic young townsmen with such
familiar names such as Sheads, Ziegler, Little, and Myers. Many of
these men had been members of the three-month regiment, the Second Pennsylvania, that tramped proudly through the town square in
the heady days of April 1861. Though they had seen little combat in
the past two years—much of their time had been spent guarding
railroad lines or simply marching to and fro—they were veteran
campaigners now, well-drilled, schooled in tactics, and ready to challenge the Rebel menace.[18]

The chance would come soon enough. On June 12, one day
before the start of the second battle of Winchester, William Culp and

the Eighty-Seventh were part of a reconnaissance-in-force assigned by Milroy to gauge the Rebel presence in the Valley. They brushed up against two Confederate cavalry regiments near Strasburg and, according to the regimental history, succeeded in "raking them with artillery and pouring a destructive broadside fire into them...creating great confusion in their ranks." Milroy reported that "the result of this reconnaissance was entirely satisfactory to me, and it was conducted with great energy." The Eighty-Seventh inflicted fifty casualties and, amazingly, suffered none.[19]

The battle began in earnest on Saturday morning, June 13, when Edward Johnson's Confederate division rattled up the Front Royal Road to test Milroy's defenses. At eight o'clock, Wes Culp and the Second Virginia, dispatched as skirmishers, made their first contact with a small Union cavalry patrol, which they summarily scattered. Milroy sent three regiments of infantry, including the Eighty-Seventh Pennsylvania, to meet the challenge. Both sides exchanged sporadic musket fire before the showdown devolved into a "noisy, but generally harmless, artillery argument." The inconclusive skirmish, only a footnote in Civil War history, marked the first time that the Culp brothers and Wes's other friends from Gettysburg, including Jack Skelly, had faced each other on the battlefield.[20]

Confederate maneuvers continued on Sunday, June 14, as Ewell sent Jubal Early's division on a flank march to some commanding high ground on the Rebel left. Johnson considered it the perfect spot "for the main attack upon the fortifications." After waiting patiently for demonstrations from other troops, including the Stonewall Brigade, to distract Milroy's attention on the right and center, Early's artillery unleashed a surprise attack sometime after five o'clock p.m. The barrage from his batteries was followed by a charge from the Louisiana Tigers under Harry Hays, who swarmed into one of the three forts and sent the bluecoats scrambling for their lives. Additional troops from Early's other brigades helped to drive the enemy "out in great haste and confusion."[21]

Only the falling darkness prevented the Rebels from completing the liberation of Winchester that day. Cornered in the remaining forts and facing almost certain defeat, a humbled Robert Milroy finally saw the folly of his stubbornness. At nine o'clock he called a council of war in which he decided on a nighttime retreat. According to a member of his staff, "Every soldier was given instructions that the evacuation was to be conducted silently, so as not to attract the attention of the enemy, whose sentinels were not more than 200 feet from the [other] forts." They would depart on the road toward Martinsburg at one o'clock in the morning on Monday, June 15, discarding their knapsacks and leaving behind "anything of any weight to it" in a strategic mission to slink away.[22]

The plan fooled no one. Crafty Dick Ewell, guessing that Milroy would make a run for it before dawn, assigned Johnson's division to intercept the Federals on the Martinsburg Road. Two brigades were promptly ordered to "cross fields over a rough country" toward Stephenson's Depot, where "there was a railroad cut masked by a body of woods...which would afford excellent shelter for troops in case of an engagement." The Stonewall Brigade was assigned to fall into line as the third Rebel unit and bring up the rear.[23]

This was easier said than done. The brigade's new general, James A. Walker, had already sent out skirmishers as previously ordered and now had to gather the scattered elements of his command before beginning the move forward. It took valuable time. In the meantime, the first two Confederate brigades, under George H. Steuart and J. M. Williams, fell suddenly on Milroy's retreating forces. Firing blindly in the darkness, both sides delivered "heavy volleys" until Union troops in superior numbers attacked on the flanks and threatened the Rebel position.[24]

At this "exceedingly critical" moment for the Confederates, Walker and his men came thundering onto the field. As Johnson himself described it later, with no small amount of relief, "Nothing could have been more timely than the arrival of the Stonewall Brigade." The Second Virginia led the charge, crashing into Milroy's startled troopers on the right and pressing them "through the woods, beyond the turnpike and into a woods a half mile to the right of the Carter House, where they surrendered as prisoners of war." Within minutes, the second wave became a rout.[25]

Wes Culp worked up a lather as he scrambled to chase Union troops into Carter's Woods. He had no way of knowing, of course, that his brother and boyhood friends were among the fleeing Federal masses. The Eighty-Seventh Pennsylvania was one of at least six Union regiments under siege from the Stonewall Brigade as the battle tumbled toward the woods, and its commander, Colonel John Schall, ordered his men to fall back "amidst some confusion." Describing the scene two months later, Schall wrote that "the enemy in large numbers followed closely behind us to the edge of the woods. My command during the retreat became scattered, some going to the right and some to the left."[26]

An elusive and resourceful William Culp was one of the few lucky ones in his regiment who got away. More than two hundred men from the Eighty-Seventh alone were taken prisoner in the early morning rumble. The Stonewall Brigade captured six battle flags (including that of the Eighty-Seventh) and counted almost nine hundred prisoners. Overall, Johnson's division took a staggering 2,500 prisoners from Milroy's command.[27]

It was not until Union captives were herded through the ranks toward a makeshift prison camp, however, that Wes realized his opponents that day had included family and friends from Gettysburg. The first hint came when his distant cousin Billy Holtzworth came trudging past under guard with other members of the Eighty-Seventh Pennsylvania. Wes and Billy were both great-grandsons of Christophel Culp, with family connections to the Culp farm and Culp's Hill. Wes's father, Esaias Culp, and Billy's mother, Anna Maria Culp Holtzworth, were first cousins, making Wes and Billy first cousins once removed.

"Hello, Billy," Wes said. "Prisoner are you? Sorry for you. What can I do for you?"

"Nothing, Wes," Holtzworth replied. "But Jack Skelly is back there at the edge of the woods, badly wounded. I'd like you to have something done for him."[28]

For a long moment, Wes was stunned into silence by the news that a boyhood friend had been gunned down by Rebel troops. Three Gettysburg men—Skelly, Holtzworth, and Billy Ziegler—had dashed out of the woods in a frantic attempt to evade capture when a Confederate Minié ball, perhaps fired by Wes's own Second Virginia, ripped into Skelly's upper arm.[29]

"What?" Wes cried out. "Jack Skelly here and wounded? I'll do it, Billy."[30]

Wes found a bleeding Skelly near the edge of the woods and arranged for Confederate troops to carry him to the Taylor House Hospital, where he was left in the care of Federal surgeons. In a brief exchange that has been shrouded in mystery for more than 150 years, Jack gave Wes a message for a loved one back in Gettysburg. In the most common version of the story, the message was a letter for Jennie Wade—perhaps about an engagement—but those details are absent from the oldest report of the incident. Writing in the *Pittsburgh Gazette Times* in 1913 and relying on second-hand sources, George T. Fleming quoted Culp as saying, "He gave me a message for his folks, which I am to tell his mother." Fleming did not identify all his sources, but it is known that he interviewed several surviving members of the Second Virginia and Eighty-Seventh Pennsylvania and, most likely, several descendants of the Culp and Skelly families. No direct evidence of Skelly's message has ever been found, and it is unclear whether it was written or merely oral.[31]

News traveled slowly in the mid-nineteenth century, and it was not until a small band of surviving soldiers made their way home to Gettysburg on foot—a distance of roughly eighty miles—that residents learned of the defeat of the Eighty-Seventh Pennsylvania at Winchester. The eyewitness accounts were stark and unsettling. Gettysburgians had been fretting for some time about an invasion by the Confederate army, and fresh reports that hometown troops had been thrashed so handily by the Rebels sent ripples of panic through the town.[32]

Salome "Sallie" Myers, who lived at the time on West High Street (and whose aunt had married William Culp), wrote in her diary on Friday, June 19:

> The excitement is intense. Some of our boys from the 87th P.V. who were in the battle of Winchester, Va., last Sunday, came home today. Among them were Uncle William Culp & Cousin David Myers, of my other two Uncles and cousins they know nothing. The boys retreated. Their ammunition gave out and they "made for home!" Poor fellows! They have been on the road since Monday evening. Dear me! What times![33]

On the same day, Sarah Broadhead, who lived on Chambersburg Street, wrote:

> Another excitement to-day. The 87th Pennsylvania Volunteers is composed of men from this and adjacent counties,

one company from our town being of that number. Word came that the captain, both lieutenants, and nearly all the officers and men had been killed or captured. Such a time as we had with those having friends in the regiment! At 10 o'clock it was rumored that some of the men were coming in on the Chambersburg Pike, and not long after about a dozen of those who lived in town came in, and their report and presence relieved some and agonized others. Those whose friends were not of the party were in a heart-rending plight, for these returned ones could not tell of the others; some would say, This one was killed or taken prisoner, and others, We saw him at such a place, and the Rebels may have taken him; and so they were kept in suspense.[34]

With no word of Jack, Jennie Wade and Elizabeth Skelly were left to agonize over his fate. By contrast, William Culp's wife and sisters were among the "relieved," because for now at least he was home and safe, but the effects of defeat at Winchester must have been painfully evident in his eyes and face.[35]

For all of them, the war had come home in ways they never imagined.

One of Lee's biggest challenges in the spring and summer of 1863 was gathering food and supplies for his army while it prepared to move north. As early as April he had complained in a letter to Jefferson Davis about a "scarcity of forage and provisions," in large part because the land of central Virginia where he had campaigned for the past nine months was "well-nigh exhausted." One of his engineer officers described it as a "stripped and desolate country," and a visiting European military officer wrote that it was "completely cleaned out." In Lee's mind, the subsistence of his army was now a "serious question." He needed to obtain more food, more fodder, more provisions, more equipment.[36]

In particular, he needed to find more cattle.

Beef was essential for a nineteenth-century army in the field. Men could not march or fight for long without proper nourishment. By one estimate Lee's army had "virtually run out of cattle" by the late spring, and supplies were so diminished that frenetic quartermasters went from "farm to farm" asking for meat. On June 1, working on a tip that cattle might be available in the upper Shenandoah Valley, Lee pleaded with an officer in the department of Western Virginia, "I am very anxious to secure all the cattle which can be obtained for the use of this army. I must beg you, therefore, to let me have the 1,250 head brought out…on the [latest expedition]…. It is reported to me there are already 3,000 head in Greenbriar and Monroe Counties. I hope, indeed, you will be able to spare some of these in addition to the 1,250."[37] On June 7, he told a cavalry officer who was primarily assigned to disrupt communications in northwestern Virginia that "it is important that you should obtain, for the use of the army, all the cattle that you can."[38]

Six months earlier Lee had been advised by the Confederate government to reduce meat rations for his soldiers. He refused to comply but paid a steep price for his obstinacy. By April, according to one account, the men were "forced to exist on a ration of one-fourth pound of salt meat a day." The need to obtain fresh beef and other food—including sheep, hogs, corn, onions, potatoes, radishes, clover, butter, wheat, hay, and oats—became one of the principal objectives of the movement north. It was essential, he knew, to collect fruit, vegetables, and other perishables as they crossed into Pennsylvania. "Beef we can drive with us," he wrote Ewell in June, "but bread [and other items] we cannot carry, and must secure it in the country."[39]

Against this backdrop, Private Robert N. Hoffman—transferred several months earlier from the infantry to the Second Virginia commissary department—received unexpected orders on June 14, the second day of second battle of Winchester, "to drive cattle by order of Gen. Walker."[40] That mission was an unqualified success. They found cattle, crops, and fodder aplenty. "We are now in the most splendid country I ever saw," one man declared after arriving in Pennsylvania, "everything in the way of subsistence being in the most profuse abundance." Indeed, Lee's army seized about forty-five thousand head of cattle in Pennsylvania, a thousand during the battle itself. The fighting and bloodshed didn't stop the quest for beef; the men still had to eat.[41]

About half the cattle and other farm animals were sent back to Lee's supply base in Winchester—"large herds of cattle are passing through every day," a local diarist wrote in late June—but many thousands went forward with the army, driven by Robert Hoffman and other reassigned troopers. Lee's quartermaster and subsistence trains followed along behind each division; as battle approached, they were placed in wagon parks, along with ordnance and ambulance trains, about two miles behind the front lines. Cattle, sheep, and hogs were kept in pens nearby, where the soldiers and cooks could get to them easily. Small numbers were moved even closer to the battle lines so that food was always available.[42]

The evidence that Robert Hoffman came north with the army instead of driving surplus cattle south to Winchester is a Confederate receipt that he signed "near Carlisle, Pa.," on June 30, 1863, just as Edward Johnson's division was making the turn back toward Gettysburg from Carlisle following Lee's order to concentrate his forces. The receipt for twenty-five head of "Beef Cattle" weighing more than eleven thousand pounds accounted for Hoffman's "returns for the month of June," with purchases "made by order of Major Gen. E. Johnson for the use of the Stonewall Brigade."[43]

Robert, who had at least briefly attended Dickinson Academy in Carlisle with the class of 1861, would have recognized the surroundings even before the army turned toward his hometown. The other Gettysburg Rebels would have experienced the same sense of familiarity as they drove north. Wesley Culp of the Second Virginia was with Ewell's corps in the vanguard of Lee's great gray force as it crossed the Potomac River into enemy territory. Henry Wentz, with Taylor's Virginia Battery, and Frank Hoffman, with Stribling's Fauquier Artillery, were attached to Longstreet's corps and followed closely behind. Wesley Hoffman, with the Seventh Virginia Cavalry, was among Grumble Jones's troops assigned to guard mountain passes to protect communications and supply lines and to thwart any annoying Union probes.[44]

When the first Confederate soldiers set foot on Northern soil in mid-June, an elated Lee sent a celebratory telegram to Jefferson Davis: "God has again crowned the valor of our troops with success."

Ten

WES CULP
COMES HOME

The three-day scuffle with Milroy at Winchester did little to impede Rebel plans for a foray north into Pennsylvania. Edward Johnson took one day to collect his scattered brigades, tend to his dead and wounded, and process almost 2,500 Union prisoners. But shortly after sunrise on the morning of June 16 he was on the march again.[1]

The timing of such a movement was not lost on the officers or men. The attack on Milroy's pesky little garrison in northern Virginia, they realized, had merely been a prelude to a bigger operation. Just over a day later, on the afternoon of June 17, Johnson set up camp for his division about three miles south of Shepherdstown, close to a convenient ford in the Potomac River that could ease their passage into Maryland. The purpose of the mission was no longer in doubt now, even to the lowliest foot soldier: a great invasion of the North was about to begin.[2]

This pause near Shepherdstown was a welcome respite for Wes Culp and other members of the Hamtramck Guards. They no doubt obtained passes from Johnson and their brigade commander, James Walker, to enter the town that night and renew old acquaintances. Henry Kyd Douglas, now a member of Johnson's division staff, received permission to visit his family home across the Potomac, but the joy of his reunion with loved ones soon dissolved into horror at the devastation he found: "My beautiful home was a barren waste,…and the blackened walls of the burnt barn stood up against the sky as a monument of useless and barbarous destruction. I felt that it would be hard for me, going into Pennsylvania, to put aside all idea of retaliation."[3]

Johnson had the men up early on Thursday, June 18, to march as a full division into Shepherdstown "amid the joyous shouts of its inhabitants." The troops let out "three rousing cheers" at their first glimpse of the Potomac, and Johnson arranged for Marylanders in the Stonewall Brigade to lead the trek across the river. They crossed at Boteler's Ford, previously known as Pack Horse Ford or Blackford's Ford but now named for the family of Alexander Boteler, the former U.S. congressman and current Rebel soldier who owned a cement mill nearby. One man in the Stonewall Brigade remembered being "amply compensated by a refreshing and no doubt much needed bath."[4]

Johnson set up headquarters at the Douglas home, Ferry Hill Place, and had his four brigades pitch their tents across what had been the battleground of Antietam at Sharpsburg, where gruesome sights still "haunted the field." A soldier wrote that he "saw dead yankeys [sic] in any number, just lying on top of the ground with a little dirt throwed over them and the hogs rooting them out of the ground and eating them and others lying on top of the ground with the flesh picked off and their bones bleaching."[5]

The men lingered at Sharpsburg for four full days, with the Second Virginia pulling picket duty at the now-famous Burnside Bridge, until Johnson got them moving again on the morning of Monday, June 22. Two other Confederate corps had finally closed the gap on the march north, and Lee felt the time was right to launch his "buoyant" force into Pennsylvania. Two days earlier, West Virginia had entered the Union as a separate state, so the army at all levels was marching in enemy territory. After crossing the border into Pennsylvania and pausing briefly in Greencastle on June 23, Johnson led his men an additional thirteen miles to the strategic juncture of Chambersburg, where they made their camp for the next three days.[6]

It was there, sometime between June 23 and June 26, that Wesley Culp wrote a letter—probably the last he would ever write—to his sister, Ann E. Culp Myers, in Gettysburg, which Ann's daughter Margaret described many years later:

> We have in our possession a letter to our mother from her brother Wesley Culp, written from Chambersburg…dated, I think, June 26…. In this letter he said he didn't know if he would get to see her or not, and he spoke of the future care of their little sister, Julia, who was younger than they were…asking our mother to look out for Julia, and once after the war he would look out for her. He said he had seen Jack Skelly after the Battle of Winchester—that he (Jack S.) was wounded—and he had seen that he was taken to a hospital. He said he thought Jack's arm would have to come off, but when he left him (Jack Skelly) he seemed to be comfortable and getting good care. He asked her to tell this to Mrs. Skelly, Jack's mother.[7]

Wes also acknowledged that he had fought against his brother's regiment ten days earlier at Winchester. "They did not meet," Margaret wrote, "but in the letter he said something like this: 'I heard that Brother William was at Winchester, but I did not see him. I understand they ran so fast you could not see them for dust.'"[8]

Johnson's division was marching again on Friday, June 26, leaving its camp at Chambersburg and slogging seven miles in a "hard and steady" rain to the hamlet of Green Village. The next day he pushed on to Carlisle, site of a prominent military barracks, where a number of Confederate soldiers, including corps commander Richard Ewell, had served while in the US Army. That put key elements of the Rebel army within striking distance of the state capital of Harrisburg. According to a published local legend, Wes Culp joked about calling on Pennsylvania Governor Andrew Curtin to "pay him my respects and maybe get a furlough and see my folks at home."[9] Confederate dreams of sacking Harrisburg would never be realized, however. Back in Chambersburg, Lee had received new intelligence that caused him suddenly to change his plan of attack.

"Preparations were…made to advance upon Harrisburg," Lee wrote in his official report, "but, on the night of the 28th, information was received from a scout that the Federal Army, having crossed the Potomac, was advancing northward, and that the head of the column had reached South Mountain." Troubled by this news, Lee had no choice but to change his strategy. "As our communications with the Potomac were thus menaced," he continued, "it was resolved to prevent his farther progress in that direction by concentrating our army on the east side of the mountains. Accordingly, Longstreet and Hill were directed to proceed from Chambersburg to Gettysburg, to which point General Ewell was also instructed to march from Carlisle."[10]

Much of Dick Ewell's corps, departing Carlisle on the morning of June 29, headed directly toward Gettysburg by way of Heidlersburg, but

Johnson's division was assigned a more circuitous route, escorting the corps' wagon train and reserve artillery in the direction of Chambersburg before trudging down the pike to the army's new destination. "In obedience to orders," Johnson wrote, "I countermarched my division to [Green Village], then eastwardly, via Scotland, [toward] Gettysburg." Johnson was likely fuming over the exhausting roundabout march, but his men reached the small town of Scotland on June 30 and camped in a "beautiful field" under a "silvery full moon" that caused some to "almost forget there is a war and [to] feel once more sentimental."[11] Wes Culp of the Second Virginia was now only a full day's march from his boyhood home.

―――――――

Edward Johnson had his men up and on the road from Scotland by seven o'clock the next morning, unaware that July 1, 1863, would be a momentous day in the history of the United States.[12] Including the corps' supply train and reserve artillery units, Johnson's massive line spanned fourteen miles as it turned onto the Cashtown Pike at Greenwood. Here they found the road clogged by Lafayette McLaws's division of Longstreet's corps, which had been ordered to take the same route to Gettysburg, and the two divisions found themselves in an unexpected traffic jam. Longstreet remembered that "my column was not well stretched on the road before it encountered the division of E. Johnson [Second Corps] cutting in on our front, with all of Ewell's reserve and supply trains." With each man accusing the other of holding him up, only Lee, the commanding general, could serve as traffic cop and untangle the mess. He granted Johnson the right of way.[13]

The troops did their best to hurry along toward Gettysburg, now only fifteen miles in the distance. Unaware that they were marching into the greatest battle of the Civil War, they paused for a moment of hero worship. Longstreet had ridden ahead of his own corps to check the progress of the army and examine the Pennsylvania landscape, and his presence caused a commotion when he pulled alongside the Stonewall Brigade. The Virginia soldiers in Jackson's old unit had rarely seen Longstreet up close. Some, it was said, ran a hundred yards "to take a good look at him"—an "immense compliment from any soldier on a long march," noted the British observer Arthur Fremantle, who himself had been dazzled momentarily by a glimpse of "the celebrated Stonewall Brigade."[14]

It was not long, however, before the mood and focus changed. The rumble of distant cannon and a staggering stream of wounded Confederate soldiers extinguished the morning's frivolity, recalling the men of Johnson's division to the difficult work ahead. Johnson diverted his supply trains to the relative safety of wagon parks and urged his infantry commanders to move forward with all possible haste. "Hearing that fighting was going on in the vicinity of Gettysburg," Henry Kyd Douglas wrote, "Johnson pushed on with vigor in that direction; he seemed to be spoiling for a fight with his new division—Jackson's own."[15]

Two brigades from A. P. Hill's corps had encountered lead elements of Federal cavalry and First Corps infantry shortly after daybreak on the ridges west of town. Early Rebel thrusts were stymied by Union resistance at an unfinished railroad cut and on McPherson's Ridge, but more fighting soon erupted after a brief noon lull. Hill resumed the attack with fresh troops at mid-afternoon, and two divisions of Ewell's corps under Robert Rodes and Jubal Early came crashing down on the Union flank to precipitate a rout. Panting and disoriented blue troops scrambled through Gettysburg's confusing web of streets and alleys before re-forming on a bald eminence near Evergreen Cemetery. The Rebel Yell rang out defiantly from the town square.

But Robert E. Lee wasn't finished. Seeking a decisive victory that would crush the Union army and perhaps end the war on Northern soil, he gave discretionary orders to Dick Ewell to take Cemetery Hill. Ewell, however, thought his best chance was to send Johnson's fresh division to seize the unoccupied and more dominant Culp's Hill, "on a line with and commanding Cemetery Hill." Unfortunately for Ewell and his reputation, the final brigade in Johnson's division, the Stonewall Brigade, did not even reach Gettysburg until dusk, and Ewell would later insist that darkness had fallen before the men could be properly "placed in position" for an attack. Sometime before midnight, a Rebel reconnaissance party returned with the discouraging news that the large hill on Henry Culp's farm was now occupied by Union troops.[16]

The timing is impossible to determine with precision, but it is generally accepted that Johnson's troops entered the town at about seven p.m. when daylight was starting to fade. Much of the division angled to the east side of Gettysburg along the uncompleted track of the Gettysburg & York Railroad. The Stonewall Brigade advanced erratically because of traffic congestion, and some regiments broke away to ease the approach along their own routes. At least part of the brigade came veering in on Washington Street (where the Twenty-Seventh Virginia's discovery of whiskey barrels in a cellar caused additional delays). One veteran Rebel soldier from Shepherdstown specifically remembered that Wes Culp and the Second Virginia entered on Carlisle Street before heading east through the town square.[17]

Benjamin S. Pendleton, who had served alongside Wes since their days in the Hamtramck Guards, had recently been appointed to the staff of Brigadier General James A. Walker, but even in his role as orderly during the Gettysburg campaign he managed to keep a close eye on Wes and the rest of his friends from Company B.[18] He later recalled,

When Johnson's division marched through the town on the evening of the first day it was dusk. We were not engaged that day, being the rear guard. We came in on the Carlisle road and the head of the column turned to the left at the square. There were few citizens of the town to be seen for there had been much fighting in the streets of the town before we arrived. The townspeople had made themselves scarce so that no one welcomed or recognized Wes Culp on his homecoming.[19]

Wes and the others scrambled along the railroad bed to catch up with the division in its new position on the extreme left of the Confederate army. Johnson's four brigades were posted that night on rolling and generally open farmland southeast of the York Pike, just north of the Hanover Road. The division's right flank was held by J. M. Williams's Louisiana brigade, which had been placed six hundred yards from the railroad on the George Wolf farm. The Stonewall Brigade, last in line, anchored the army on its far-left flank, near the Daniel Lady farm and at the edge of a wooded area that ran up to Brinkerhoff's Ridge.[20]

Both Walker and Colonel J. Q. A. Nadenbousch, commander of the Second Virginia, wrote in their battle reports (in virtually identical language) that they took a position "near the Hanover Road, and on the extreme left of our line, on Culp's farm," sowing confusion about the Stonewall Brigade's location on the night of July 1 that has dogged historians almost since the conclusion of the battle. Research by Troy Harman, a National Park Service ranger at Gettysburg National Military Park, has shown, however, that Walker and Nadenbousch incorrectly identified the Lady property as a farm owned by Henry Culp, which was located farther to the southwest of their position, near Rock Creek. Other than several hundred skirmishers who advanced in the falling darkness to encounter a Union detachment at Wolf Hill, the six thousand men of Johnson's division spent the rest of the night north of the Hanover Road and well to the northeast of the Culp farm.[21]

Wesley Culp was not assigned to skirmish duty on July 1. Perhaps it was because staff orderly Benjamin Pendleton had already approached General Walker to request a pass for Wes to visit his sisters, Ann and Julia, whom Pendleton knew from their visits to Shepherdstown. As Ann's daughter wrote years later, "Our mother and her sister Julia... and other Gettysburg girls, among them our mother's cousin, Mrs. Mary Culp Blessing,... knew Pendleton and some of the other boys in Shepherdstown, as they had visited Uncle Wesley there and met them. They used to tell us about the good times they had down there with these friends of Uncle Wesley."[22] She continues:

> Uncle Wesley hoped to see his home folks, but was not sure that he could get permission to do so.... Mr. Benjamin S. Pendleton, who at this time served as an orderly for Gen. James A. Walker, who commanded the "Stonewall Brigade," knew our mother and Aunt Julia intimately. Knowing it was Uncle Wesley's home, he said that Uncle Wesley came to him and asked him if he would go to Gen. Walker and get permission for him to go see his sisters, which he did.
>
> Gen. Walker asked to see him, knowing it was his hometown, and he told him he was glad he had a Penna. boy with him—and so he gave him the pass and told him

there would be fighting and, as it was his home, he could stay out of it. Wesley said he had enlisted and if there was fighting, his place was with his regiment.[23]

Armed with the unexpected pass from Walker and fully committed to battle in his hometown, Wes wasted little time in making his way from the Hanover Road on the outskirts of town to Ann's residence on West Middle Street. After two years in the army, he knew that fighting was almost certain to resume the next morning and that time allotted to visit his sisters would be brief. Wes knew that the vaguely familiar house on the south side of the first block of West Middle Street had originally been rented by his older brother, William, in the years before the war. Ann was living there now, however, at William's request, along with her husband, Jefferson Myers, her sister, Julia, then about twenty years old, and William's wife and young son, Loren.[24]

As for William Culp's whereabouts during the battle of Gettysburg, few clues are available. His niece Sallie Myers wrote in her diary that "Uncle William" and other local members of the Eighty-Seventh Pennsylvania had straggled home to Gettysburg on June 19 after being routed by Rebel troops at the second battle of Winchester, but William's military service records show that he did not rejoin his unit until July 7 at Frederick, Maryland. William no doubt spent several days at home visiting his wife and extended family, but it is doubtful that he lingered in Gettysburg for much more than a week—and surely not until July 1, when Lee's Confederate army swept like a tidal wave toward the town. Someone would have seen him. Someone would have mentioned it.[25]

Margaret Myers continues:

Our mother had told us many times of [Wesley's] coming that evening. She was living on West Middle Street, across the street from the Skelly home, in the home of the other brother, William E. Culp, who was at the time in Co. F—87th Pa. Vol.... My mother had promised her brother William that she would stay with his wife and child while he was in the army, and it was to this home that Wesley Culp came on that evening of the first day's fight at Gettysburg—July 1, 1863.[26]

Wesley's heart must have been pounding as he made his way through the familiar streets and alleys. The Confederate army held the town that night, and dust-covered Rebel soldiers were out in force—some wandering, some looting—but danger loomed around every corner for a former resident whom many considered the worst kind of traitor. "He knew they felt sore about him," Margaret Myers wrote, "and some had said they would shoot him on the spot if he ever showed his face there." At the crowded little home on West Middle Street, meanwhile, tension was high. Ann had no idea that her Rebel brother was anywhere near Gettysburg, much less on his way to pay her a visit. A knock on the door broke the silence and sent family members scurrying for cover.[27]

Twenty-eight years old and very much the matriarch of the household, Ann approached the door. Her apprehension turned to surprise, then to relief, then to elation when she saw her brother. Not even the sight of a Confederate uniform could spoil the moment. "Why, Wes!" Ann cried, "You're here!"[28]

The scene was first recounted in detail in George T. Fleming's article "The Homecoming of Wes Culp," published in the *Pittsburgh Gazette Times* on November 9, 1913, ten days before the fiftieth anniversary of the Gettysburg Address. Fleming did not identify all his sources but must have relied on Margaret Myers and her two siblings, Charles and Jessie, who would have heard it from their mother. It cannot be mere coincidence that many other aspects of

Fleming's story line up perfectly with Margaret's unpublished family history written twenty-six years later, in 1939.[29]

"That night there stepped jauntily into the Myers home a sturdy, stocky figure, sun-bronzed and weather-beaten and clad in rusty and somewhat tattered butternut, the uniform of the Army of Northern Virginia," Fleming wrote. "Brother and sister were clasped in each other's arms as though there were no such things as a war and horrors, and that deadly battle had been close at hand and would re-open with the day." The three Culp siblings had much to tell each other after more than two years apart, and Wes was fairly bursting with news for his sisters from the war's front lines. But the long-awaited family discussion could not begin in earnest until little sister Julia, on whom Wes doted, had been "duly hugged and kissed."[30]

"Naturally, there were varied feelings," Margaret wrote in her own piece years later. "Joy at seeing him, sorrow at meeting under such circumstances. He left with my mother his watch and several trinkets. I don't know...what became of them.... He said again that if our mother would take care of little Julia until war was over he would then take care of her."[31]

The visit lasted for hours, their conversation no doubt touching on the death of their father, Esaias, in June 1861, until Wes remembered he was in a war zone and had to return to his unit. Ann pleaded for him to stay until morning, but the terms of Wes's pass from General Walker did not include a family sleepover. "'No, Annie, I can't,'" he said, according to Fleming's report, "'but I'll come back in the morning...and I came near forgetting one important matter.'"[32] He continued:

> "Coming up through Winchester I ran across Billy [Holtz-worth] who was a prisoner in our hands. He told me about Jack Skelly being wounded and I hunted for poor Jack and

had him taken to the hospital where we left him in charge of Federal surgeons. He was badly shot through the arm. He gave me a message for his folks which I am to tell to his mother. It is late now and we will not disturb them, but you tell Mrs. Skelly I will be back in the morning and have her here. I want to talk to her and I'll be back for sure."

"No message from Jack for anybody else in Gettysburg, Wes?" queried his sister.

"Never mind," he replied, "you'll get all the news from Mrs. Skelly."[33]

As we see, the first published version of the story of Jack Skelly's message to Wesley Culp, a story now ensconced in Gettysburg lore, clearly describes the message as intended for Jack's mother. Could the message have been a letter, or was it merely verbal? Did it pertain to Jennie Wade? With no other evidence, we can never know for sure.

The final topic before Wes departed was a delicate one for the Culp sisters, who were by now uncomfortably aware that their older brother, William, had fought against Wes two weeks earlier at Winchester. "Brother against brother" had yet to become a Civil War cliché, but it had been a reality for the Culp family on the fields and roads around Carter's Woods in the early-morning darkness of June 16. William, it was said, never spoke his brother's name after the war. The thought of a fraternal confrontation on the battlefield horrified Ann and Julia. As Fleming wrote,

"Did you know you were fighting your brother, Will, with the other boys of the 87th at Winchester," asked Annie Myers.

"Not until Billy [Holtzworth] told me," he replied slowly.

"Oh, Wes!" exclaimed Julia Culp. "How could you shoot at poor Will?"

"I did not know it little one," answered Wes Culp. "We were fighting in the night."

Julia Culp, looking very sober, said, "I know you wouldn't have shot at Will in daylight, would you, Wes?"

What soldier brother as he stroked the distressed faced and kissed her tenderly could say aught than, "No indeed, Julia, I would not," and it was a farewell kiss at that.[34]

With that he bolted out the door and headed toward Rock Creek and the Hanover Road. Ann shouted after him, "You ought to stay with us all night, Wes. Come back. We may never see you again."[35]

Early the next morning, Thursday July 2, 1863, the second day of the battle of Gettysburg, Wesley Culp was killed while serving with the Second Virginia skirmish line.

Benjamin Pendleton, who saw Culp only "a few minutes" before the fateful action began, told Fleming in 1913 that he "was killed on Thursday morning." Pendleton remembered, "Wes returned that night and went on the skirmish line with the company in the morning. The line was being advanced when he was shot."[36]

Fleming also spoke to another Company B veteran from Shepherdstown, Daniel M. Entler. Though he had been wounded on the night of July 1, Entler learned about Culp's death from his fellow soldiers. "You have the story right as I heard it from my comrades," Entler told Fleming. "He was killed instantly, shot through the head." He said the circumstances that led to his own wounding were the same as Culp's, with "both casualties occurring in advance of our skirmish line."[37]

On July 3, Pendleton visited the Culp sisters at their home, as Margaret Myers relates in her family history. "It was in the evening that [Wes's] comrade, Ben Pendleton, who knew our mother, came to the house, sent by his captain, and told her that Uncle Wesley was killed instantly, shot through the head...the morning of July 2nd." Margaret was careful to assert on several other occasions that "Wesley Culp was killed on the morning of July 2nd" and "Wesley Culp was shot thru the head the morning of the 2nd day's fight."[38]

Such information conflicts not only with Gettysburg legend but also Confederate military service records, which declare that "John W. Culp" of the Second Virginia was "killed in battle of Gettysburg July 3, 1863." But record-keeping for an invading army in the midst of a colossal three-day battle, which it lost, cannot be relied on for precision. Daniel Entler reported that the date of his own wounding was listed incorrectly. The Gettysburg historian William Frassanito notes that "for many of the casualties of the 2nd Virginia at Gettysburg, no specific date was provided; or it was otherwise unclear whether the casualty occurred on July 2 or 3." Battlefield legend aside, the evidence that Wes was killed while advancing with his skirmish line in the early morning hours of July 2 is persuasive.[39]

But where did Culp fall? The most commonly told story is that his death took place on or near Culp's Hill, his "uncle's farm," a poetic story that tugs at the battlefield tourist's heartstrings. The problem is that the Second Virginia did not fight on Culp's Hill on July 2. Wesley's unit and the rest of the Stonewall Brigade were involved in action on the eastern side of Rock Creek, between Benner's Hill and Wolf Hill and along a rise called Brinkerhoff's Ridge.[40]

The Stonewall Brigade was still north of the Hanover Road when it set up camp on the night of July 1. Edward Johnson's entire division was stretched out in a strong line across mostly open fields near the Daniel Lady farm, just to the northwest of the imposing height of Wolf Hill, a little-known and rarely-visited battlefield landmark today, located on private property. Exercising proper caution, especially with Union troops posted nearby, General Walker had the Stonewall Brigade refuse its line to the north, at right angles to the rest of the division, so that it was now on the extreme left flank of the Confederate army. One man grumbled that such dangerous flank duty in the face of the enemy was far better suited to the "absent, truant cavalry," but Walker's veterans seemed to embrace the challenge. Some even stole a few hours of much-needed sleep.[41]

Little has been written about the fighting on this part of the field on the morning of July 2—some regimental histories ignore it altogether—but there is no doubt that skirmish action such as that described by Pendleton took place here and that it involved the Second Virginia. "Early the next morning," General Johnson wrote in his official report, "skirmishers from Walker's and [J. M.] Jones were advanced for the purpose of feeling the enemy, and desultory firing was maintained with their skirmishers until 4 p.m." Walker added a perspective from even closer to the front lines: "[A]t dawn the next morning, the enemy's skirmishers were seen in our front, and a brisk fire was opened between them and my own." Confirmation of the Second Virginia's participation came from the regiment's colonel, J. Q. A. Nadenbousch, who reported (in terms that once again parroted Walker's), "at dawn, a brisk skirmish commenced with our skirmishers and those of the enemy."[42]

During the night, several hundred skirmishers from the Stonewall Brigade had stealthily rotated to the south, crossing the Hanover Road and creeping among the rocks, trees, and fields approaching the dual humps of Wolf Hill. They were identified in this position on the original Gettysburg battlefield map drawn by the historian John Bachelder in 1863. Shortly after dawn, the Stonewall skirmishers were confronted by Twelfth Corps troops from the Twenty-Seventh Indiana, and the "brisk" action described by Walker and Nadenbousch began in earnest. It was probably the first exchange of gunfire between the massive maneuvering armies on the second day of the battle.[43]

Skirmishers from the Second Virginia soon occupied a precarious flank position east of Wolf Hill near the Ephraim Deardorff property. (The war-era Deardorff house still stands at 75 Montclair Road.) Here—just south of the Hanover Road, on land now bisected by Route 15—they became an inviting target when fresh reinforcements from the Union Fifth Corps arrived on the field by six a.m. Colonel Patrick Guiney of the Ninth Massachusetts led his men to an area south of the Deardorff buildings, where they promptly formed a skirmish line facing north and began to fire away. Given Ben Pendleton's description of Wes Culp's death and the location of the Second

The war-era Deardorff house, which still stands on Montclair Road, near both the Hanover Road and Wolf Hill. *Author photo*

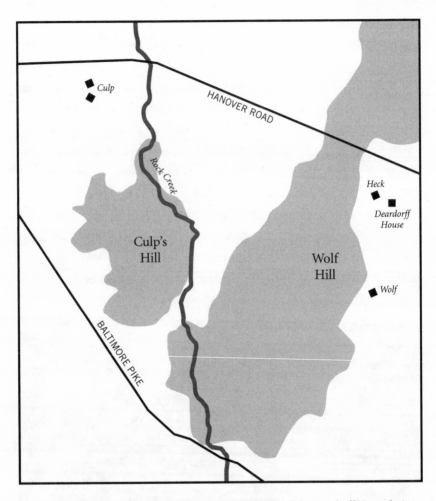

Wesley Culp was likely killed in the general area of Wolf Hill and the Deardorff House during skirmishing by the Second Virginia Infantry on the morning of July 2. *Map by Joshua Taggert*

Virginia troops on the morning of July 2, it was probably in this area—near Wolf Hill, not Culp's Hill, skirmishing against the Ninth Massachusetts or Twenty-Seventh Indiana—that Private Culp met his demise.[44]

By one account he peered carelessly over a rock and was immediately shot in the forehead, the only man from the Second Virginia killed in action during the three-day battle. "A comrade warned him not to expose himself unnecessarily," the *Shepherdstown Register* reported years later, "but he paid no attention. His friend took hold of him to pull him back, when he fell into his arms dead."[45]

———

When Benjamin Pendleton trudged down West Middle Street to the Culp house late in the evening of Friday, July 3, well after Pickett's Charge had been repelled but with Confederates still holding the town, Wes's frantic little sister, Julia, rushed forward to answer the door. Fleming describes the exchange:

> "Why, it's Mr. Pendleton," she said, "and you are in Wes' company and Wes did not come back as he promised. Something has happened to him..." and she began to cry.
>
> "Yes, Julia, Wes is dead. He was killed Thursday morning. The boys buried him where he fell and I will tell you how to find his grave, as I marked it," and Pendleton left the saddened home after minutely describing the burial spot as he had taken pains to remember it.[46]

The next day, the saddest Fourth of July in Gettysburg in memory, Julia Culp and Ann Myers led a search party that included Ann's husband, Jefferson, and other members of the family. But they were following the directions of a Virginian with no understanding of Gettysburg's topography. Pendleton had mistakenly identified the burial site as "Culp's Hill," the same error that caused Walker and Nadenbousch to identify the Lady farm as "Culp's farm." The Second Virginia did not set foot on Culp's Hill on July 2 and did not even cross that day to the west side of Rock Creek, where the Culp property was located. Wesley's body was never found.

The Culp sisters *did* come across the butt of his gun, bearing the haunting inscription "W. Culp." Perhaps they had expanded their search area after an initial lack of success, or perhaps another Confederate soldier had picked up Wes's gun and then lost or discarded it early on July 3, when the regiment was briefly posted near the base of Culp's Hill. Margaret Myers wrote only that "our mother recognized it immediately." The gun became a treasured family relic, and was even displayed in 1939 "at the New York World's Fair in the Penna. Building among the Gettysburg exhibits."[47]

———

But what became of Wesley Culp's body? It remains one of the battle of Gettysburg's enduring mysteries.

Speculation that family members actually found the body and buried it in an unmarked grave for fear of desecration is discounted by Culp descendants and seems unfounded. Visitors to the Gettysburg section of Hollywood Cemetery in Richmond, Virginia, can see a tombstone for "PVT JOHN WESLEY CULP, CO B, 2 VA INF, CSA, 1839, JUL 2 1863," but the stone is thought to be purely memorial, and there is no record that Wesley was ever buried there.[48]

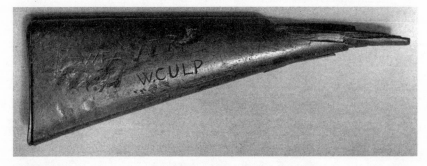

Photo of gun stock with the carving "W. Culp," found by members of the Culp family after the battle. *Gettysburg National Military Park*

Margaret Myers reported that her mother "always thought that his body was among those taken away by the Southern men and that he was buried among the 'Unknown' either at Richmond or Shepherdstown." Margaret added that an "old Shepherdstown man" once told her that Confederates from that place "brought all theirs home with them," implying that Wes may have been buried among the "Unknown" in Shepherdstown's Elmwood Cemetery, where there is a tribute plaque to Company B of the Second Virginia.[49]

"In connection with this, yet meaning nothing I suppose, I might tell you this story," Margaret wrote. "Last year [1938], two of us went to Shepherdstown for the first time, and as we went into the Cemetery and stood among the graves marked 'Unknown,' for some reason, unexplainable, we both had the feeling that Wesley Culp was

A tombstone for John Wesley Culp of the Second Virginia is located in the Gettysburg section of Hollywood Cemetery in Richmond. But Culp's body was never recovered after the battle, and its whereabouts are unknown. *Author photo*

buried there. Neither one of us spoke of it until on our way home, but we both felt it."[50]

The mystery of Wes Culp's body remains unsolvable more than 150 years later, even for descendants and Civil War historians, but perhaps George T. Fleming put it best back in 1913:

> On fame's eternal camping ground, somewhere in its vastness is spread the silent tent of Wes Culp, who came home to die in battle.[51]

Eleven

WAR AT THE WENTZ HOUSE

awn broke at 4:12 a.m. on July 2, 1863, but Robert E. Lee was up well before that, mulling over his many options and trying to assemble a battle plan.[1]

Lee was in a quandary. The superb performance of his troops on July 1 had put him in position to defeat and possibly demolish the Union army on the second day of the battle of Gettysburg, but the commanding general had little knowledge of the terrain in his immediate front and, worse, no idea of the location of the Federal left flank. "Encouraged by the successful issue of the engagement of the first day," he wrote, "and in view of the valuable results that would ensue from the defeat of [the Union army], it was thought advisable to renew the attack." But he had to determine when and where.[2]

At around four o'clock, Lee summoned several staff officers and directed them to probe "the farthest occupied point" on the Union left and survey the enemy position "toward some estimate of the ground and the best mode of attack." His elite cavalry units under

Jeb Stuart had still not met up with the army in Pennsylvania, so the task went to a group of Lee's trusted staffers, including General William N. Pendleton, his chief of artillery, and Captain Samuel Johnston, his topographical engineer.[3]

A devoted soldier and outstanding engineer, the thirty-year-old Johnston, a native of Fairfax, Virginia, had volunteered for the Confederate cavalry on the first weekend of the war. His early service had consisted of "picket duty and scouting near the enemy's line in advance of regular pickets." Stuart himself considered Johnston "sober, indefatigable and capable." Promoted to captain of engineers on Lee's staff in 1862, Johnston quickly caught the eye of James Longstreet, who called him "very energetic and untiring," acknowledging his "great courtesy and kindness in assisting me on the different battle-fields." By the summer of 1863, he had established himself as one of the army's most experienced and efficient reconnaissance officers.[4]

Departing with Pendleton and the others shortly after four o'clock, Johnston probably rode behind the safety of Seminary Ridge until breaking away from the group near Spangler's Woods. Accompanied by Longstreet's engineer, John J. Clarke, he turned toward the Emmitsburg Road and proceeded "in the direction of the round tops across the [road] and got up on the slopes of round top, where [he] had a commanding view." It was a pivotal moment for the Confederate army at Gettysburg. Convinced that he had reached the hill known to history as Little Round Top, Johnston took note that there were no Union troops in the area—a crucial discovery if true—and promptly headed back to report the news to Lee.[5]

"Did you get there?" Lee asked, pointing at Little Round Top on the headquarters map. Johnston insisted that he had.[6] Confederate battle plans for the pivotal second day of fighting at Gettysburg were thus based on flawed intelligence. Depending on how cruelly critics choose to assess his work, Johnston either made an incorrect report, misjudged his location on another hill, or simply didn't know where he was going. Many historians agree that he could not have scaled Little Round Top as he claimed because he would have seen and heard Union troops in that area—and they, in all likelihood, would have seen him. Regardless of how it happened, Lee developed his strategy for a July 2 attack on the misconception that the Union left flank did not extend much farther south than the modern-day Pennsylvania Memorial.

Harry Pfanz, a former historian at Gettysburg National Military Park, offers one of the more measured critiques of Johnston's performance: "It must be concluded that when Captain Johnston's reconnaissance party failed to detect Federal units in the area between the Peach Orchard and the Round Tops and on the lower end of Cemetery Ridge, it was somehow the victim of grave misfortune." Pfanz goes on to write that as "a result of this failure, Captain Johnston made an incorrect report to his commanding general that was to have serious consequences later in the day."[7]

Other historians have been harsher. Allen Guelzo writes:

> According to Captain Johnston's morning report, there should have been *no* Union forces of any substance anywhere south of Cemetery Hill, all of which raises the very peculiar question of what, exactly, Captain Johnston saw, or did not see, that morning.... [Records of] Federal troop movements make Johnston's claim to have ridden straight to the summit of Little Round Top unopposed with nothing to observe simply incredible—unless, of course, Johnston had not been anywhere near the Round Tops in the first place.

Another historian, Stephen Sears, concludes that "the answer to the mystery seems to be that Johnston either did not go as far as to climb Little Round Top, and, in his recollections, embellished his role rather than confess his failings; or that he unwittingly went somewhere else." But no one knows for sure.[8]

Even if we accept the theory that Johnston got lost or became disoriented on his mission, the blame should not rest solely with Johnston. Either through a breakdown in communications or a lack of knowledge about the makeup of his own army, Lee apparently was unaware that five young men who grew up in Gettysburg were part of his invading Rebel force. It was a stunning and inexplicable failure of intelligence. Any of the five could have provided valuable service as a guide for Johnston or other reconnaissance officers and could have offered crucial information about Gettysburg's roads and terrain to Lee and his senior commanders.

Wes Culp was present on the battlefield and preparing to go on the skirmish line in the wee hours of July 2, just as Lee was sending out his scouting parties. A fourth-generation Gettysburgian with two siblings and dozens of other relatives living nearby, he would have been perfect for such an assignment (which also would have saved his life).

The Shepherdstown men in Company B were well aware that Culp and Robert Hoffman had moved south from Gettysburg with Robert's father in the mid-1850s. Soldiers in the Stonewall Brigade also knew of Culp's background, and John Casler of the Thirty-Third Virginia wrote that comrades had dubbed him "Billy," for "Billy Yank." And, of course, the brigade's general, James Walker, had been informed of Wes's connection to the town on the night of July 1. His failure to pass this information up the chain of command seems like a perplexing lapse of judgement.[9]

Rebel generals, leading a notoriously understaffed army on the march, commonly sought out soldiers with local roots to serve as guides for senior officers, a practice that made even more sense during Lee's high-risk invasion of Pennsylvania. But there is no evidence that even Henry Kyd Douglas, who was serving on the staff of the division commander, Edward Johnson, and who knew Wes from their days in the Hamtramck Guards, thought to alert Johnson or his superiors. Neither Walker nor any other Rebel general mentioned Culp in his official report or post-battle letters.[10]

Nor did anyone in senior command appear to know that four other Confederate soldiers had grown up in Gettysburg. They served in different units and were stationed at varying distances from the battlefield on the morning of July 2, but Lee could have summoned them to headquarters when he decided to concentrate his army at or near Gettysburg on June 29. Even without such an order, Robert Hoffman of the Second Virginia was likely just a few miles behind the lines with the cattle of the Stonewall Brigade, and Henry Wentz of Taylor's Virginia Battery was nearing the field after an overnight march from Greenwood. Frank Hoffman's unit, the Fauquier Artillery, was twenty-five miles back in Chambersburg on July 1 (although it would arrive at Gettysburg by the morning of July 3), and Wesley Hoffman's regiment, the Seventh Virginia Cavalry, was camped for the moment in Greencastle, Pennsylvania, about thirty miles away. Certainly any of the Hoffman brothers—especially Robert, no longer in a combat role, or Wesley, whose cavalry unit was on the fringe—could have been excused from duty and assigned to serve as a scout or guide in the town where all three were born and raised.[11] It is at least possible, however, that Henry Wentz's knowledge of local hills and valleys was put to use after another bungling of directions on the afternoon of July 2.

The Confederate task that day was daunting. Lee had assigned General James Longstreet to find and assault the Union left flank with two of his three divisions, while probing the same terrain that Johnston had misidentified hours earlier. To complicate matters, division commanders John Bell Hood and Lafayette McLaws were warned to conceal themselves from a Federal signal corps stationed on Little Round Top as they maneuvered into position. With Johnston serving as a de facto guide, they marched under cover until reaching a high open hill near the Fairfield Road, where they burst into full view of the flag-waving enemy signal men. Stopped cold—"Why, this won't do!" Longstreet famously bellowed—they began a frustrating and time-consuming countermarch that delayed the Rebel attack and inflicted several more miles of wear and tear on the troops.[12]

Colonel E. P. Alexander's artillery battalion had approached the same sensitive spot a short time earlier, however, and had somehow managed to elude detection. Instructed that morning by Longstreet to reconnoiter the ground in advance, Alexander, with several unidentified couriers, had examined "all roads leading to the right and front." When his battalion approached the "high bare place" where they would have been exposed to the Federal signal crew, Alexander "avoided that part of the road by turning out to the [right], & going through fields & hollows, & getting back to the road again a quarter mile or so beyond."[13]

Alexander and his gunners, including Taylor's Virginia battery, soon paused to await the arrival of the infantry near Pitzer's Schoolhouse. They were only half a mile from the house where Henry Wentz had grown up and where, though Alexander may not have known it at the time, Henry's parents and older sister still lived. After a considerable delay, Alexander went in search of Longstreet's tardy troopers and found them in the tedious process of backtracking from the same "high bare place" and searching for another route. "I told the officers at the head of the column of the route my artillery had followed—which was easily seen," Alexander would recall, "but there was no one with authority to vary the orders they were under, & they momentarily expected the new ones for which they had sent." It took several more hours for Hood and McLaws to navigate the counter-march and file into position.[14]

Alexander never mentioned Henry Wentz in his official report or in any of his voluminous postwar writings. An outstanding engineer in his own right, he might have conceived the new route on his own, without the help of a former resident who grew up nearby. But wouldn't he at least have asked? Other members of Taylor's Virginia Battery knew of Wentz's background, and it strains credulity to suppose Wentz never said, "That was my house." One also wonders if Wentz was one of the unidentified couriers who accompanied Alexander on his morning ride to reconnoiter the ground.

Glenn Tucker, the author of the obscure book *Lee and Longstreet at Gettysburg,* is one of the few Civil War historians to have mentioned the mystery of Wentz's involvement in Alexander's approach and perhaps the first to have addressed it in depth. "One of the curious aspects of this march," Tucker writes, "was why McLaws, or Colonel J. B. Walton…the ranking artillery officer of Longstreet's Corps, or Colonel E. P. Alexander, on whom Longstreet relied more heavily, or Lee himself, did not employ Henry Wentz as a guide…." He continues:

> Wentz' home faced the Emmitsburg Road directly across the farm road (now called the Wheatfield Road) from the Peach Orchard. He had gone to Virginia…and had enlisted in the Southern army, surely without a thought that one day he would be unlimbering Confederate cannon in his own front yard. While there appears to be no record on the point, it is probable that Wentz' presence was unknown to the high command of the Confederate army.

Longstreet was ordinarily diligent in the use of scouts who knew the local country, as was evidenced at Chickamauga less than three months later. There, on reaching the field, he inquired at once about local residents who were in [General Braxton] Bragg's army. He hit on Tom Brotherton, who had farmed the land across which Longstreet attacked and, according to his brother, "knew every pig trail through these woods." Wentz would have been as well informed about his own farm and the woods west of it over which he must have wandered as a boy. Lee and Longstreet could have used the information in the absence of Stuart.[15]

Whether Sergeant Henry Wentz had anything to do with it or not, Alexander's battalion and other artillery units were settled in along the ridge well before Longstreet's panting infantry scrambled into battle formation at about four p.m. There had been additional delays when Longstreet had to adjust his attack because of unexpected changes in Federal troop positions (another outgrowth of Johnston's ill-fated morning ride), but soon they would all move forward together—the rumble of infantry, the thunder of cannon—and shatter the peace at the Wentz house up ahead.[16]

———

There was one other man in Taylor's Virginia Battery with at least some knowledge of Gettysburg roads and terrain—Sergeant Henry D. Wirt, identified in Confederate military records as a twenty-two-year-old school teacher from Martinsburg, Virginia.[17]

"Wirt" was certainly the same person as Henry D. Wirts, who had attended classes in the Preparatory Department at Pennsylvania College in Gettysburg for one school year, 1856–1857. Alumni records indicate that Wirts, a resident of Martinsburg when he enrolled in 1856, "taught at Martinsburg" from 1857 to 1861 and served in the Rebel army from 1861 to 1864.[18]

The mystery that has yet to be untangled, however, is whether Wirts was also the same person as the "Henry D. Werts" who appeared as a twelve-year-old in the 1850 federal census for Straban Township in Adams County. Their ages vary slightly—and the differences in spelling are maddening—but there is enough circumstantial evidence to raise the question whether he was another Gettysburg Rebel.[19]

According to the 1850 census, Werts, who had a much older brother named John, was the son of an elderly Straban Township farmer also named Henry Werts. William Frassanito has discovered a Civil War-era letter from a local Union soldier that mentions all three members of the Werts family of Straban. It reads, "I did not know that Hen Wertz was in the Rebel army before I received your letter do you know what Regiment he is in What does old Henry and John think of him What do they say about this war I suppose they lean a little towards the south."[20]

Here, unfortunately, the trail goes cold. "Henry D. Werts" does not appear in the Adams County census after 1850. "Henry D. Wirt" was captured by Union cavalry on July 19, 1863, sent to a prison camp at Wheeling on July 31, and released by orders of the secretary of war on September 9 upon taking the oath of allegiance. The only brief postwar reference to "Henry D. Wirts" in the Pennsylvania College Preparatory Department alumni records says that the school teacher and Confederate army veteran was "Now in the West." There is no indication in either his academic or military service records that he came from Gettysburg or had any roots in the Gettysburg area.[21]

A final footnote to the story is an 1872 letter written to the great abolitionist William Lloyd Garrison from "Henry D. Wertz," a school teacher from Peoria, Illinois—at the time regarded as "in the West"—identifying himself as a former resident of Martinsburg who participated in the John Brown raid. Wertz says he has a Sharp's rifle, taken from the engine house where Brown and his men were captured and offers to sell the rifle to Garrison for twenty-five dollars on the premise that he "perhaps would value the rifle as a relic."[22] It took two years for a response.

> In answer to your letter, I would state that I must decline the proposition contained in it, in regard to purchasing the rifle in your possession, as, for forty years, I have been avowedly a radical peace man.... I gave no sanction to John Brown's method of emancipating the slaves, though conceding to him the purest and noblest intentions. According to the theory of our government and the example of our revolutionary sires, he was a hero and a martyr, and so the civilized world regards him. That you should have had a hand in his capture and death, however true to your sense of duty at the time, is now, I trust, a matter of deep regret on your part—seeing that while he remembered those in bonds as bound with them, you took sides with their cruel oppressors.
>
> Yours for the reign of universal freedom and peace.
>
> Wm. Lloyd Garrison[23]

The Garrison narrative lines up with the 1870 Federal Census for Peoria County, Illinois, which lists a school teacher named H. D. Wertz. Moreover, a Henry D. Wertz married Mary Phillips in Peoria on November 2, 1872.[24] A "school teacher" of the same name was listed in the Peoria City Directory in 1879 (1507 South Water Street) but had moved to Joliet in Will County for the 1880 census.[25]

Spelling aside, there can be little doubt that Henry D. Wertz, the former Martinsburg resident who was teaching school in Peoria in the 1870s and wrote to William Lloyd Garrison is the same person as "Henry D. Wirts" of Martinsburg who attended the Pennsylvania College Preparatory Department in 1856–1857, and as "Henry D. Wirt" of Martinsburg who served in the Confederate army and fought with Taylor's Virginia Battery at the battle of Gettysburg. Nevertheless, his birthplace is given as Virginia, not Pennsylvania, in both the 1870 and 1880 census reports.[26]

At this point, beyond a vague reference in the 1863 letter obtained by Frassanito, no direct evidence has been found to confirm that Wirt/Wirts/Wertz was the same person as "Henry D. Werts" the twelve-year-old who appeared in the Adams County census in 1850 and then mysteriously disappeared. Future research may prove otherwise.

———

Just before four o'clock on the afternoon of July 2 Captain Osmond B. Taylor's Virginia Battery rolled four bronze Napoleons into battle line along Warfield Ridge near the Millerstown Road.

Henry Wentz, Henry D. Wirt, and others fighting to preserve the institution of slavery were posted, ironically enough, about twenty yards south of the road on land owned by a free black farmer named James Warfield, who was nowhere in sight. Six hundred yards up ahead was the one-and-a-half-story log and weatherboard house where Wentz had spent his boyhood and where his elderly parents, John and Mary, still lived with his adult sister, Susan. The two women had been sent away to safety before the battle started.[27]

The Wentzes' two-acre property sat at the intersection of the Emmitsburg and Millerstown Roads. The "Wentz House" and two

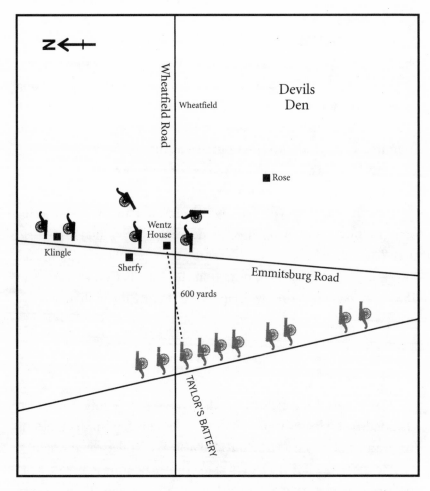

At the start of the fighting on July 2, Henry Wentz and Taylor's Battery were positioned approximately 600 yards from the house where Henry grew up, and where his parents still lived. *Map by Joshua Taggert*

outbuildings were tucked into the northeast corner of the intersection, just to the east of the Joseph Sherfy house and surrounded by Sherfy's peach orchard, most of which was directly across the lane. Family history has it that Wentz stopped by the house at least briefly on the nights of July 2 and 3, but as he never wrote about his experiences in the war, we are left to imagine what was going through his mind as he gazed upon the house and fields where he frolicked as a boy.[28]

Largely because of Johnston's faulty morning reconnaissance, the Rebel battle plan was still being cobbled together as the two massive armies pawed the turf south of Gettysburg. "I never remember hearing of any conference or discussions among our generals at this time as to the best formations & tactics in making our attacks," Colonel Alexander wrote, "& our methods on this occasion struck me as peculiar...& I don't think it was the best." Only twenty-eight years old, Alexander had been elevated to temporary command of Longstreet's artillery that morning, and he was now responsible for placing all three battalions—his own and two veteran units under Mathis Henry and Henry Cabell—in proper position without any senior command oversight. Even under those circumstances, however, and despite generally inferior Confederate equipment, he felt confident in his gunners' ability as Henry's cannons opened the attack on the far right.[29]

By Alexander's count, he had fifty-four guns available once his own battalion pulled up along the Millerstown Road. He knew he would be in action against "a heavy artillery and infantry force of the enemy, about 500 yards distant, in a peach orchard and on the Emmitsburg pike," but he was optimistic about delivering a knockout blow. "I had hoped, with my 54 guns & close range, to make it short, sharp and decisive," Alexander wrote. "At close ranges there was less inequality in our guns, & especially in our ammunition, & I thought if ever I could overwhelm & crush them it would be now." Soon after Mathis Henry started the thunder, guns were booming all along the Confederate line.[30]

Taylor's Battery, with Henry Wentz, was in the left-center of the battalion, just to the right of the Warfield buildings and within easy sight of the Wentz house and the Peach Orchard. According to Taylor, "About 4 p.m. I was ordered into position within 500 yards of the

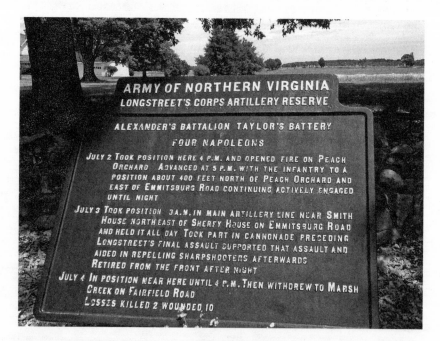

This sign marks the artillery position manned by Henry Wentz and Taylor's Battery on July 2, 1863. It is located along West Confederate Avenue, near the Longstreet Tower. *Author photo*

enemy's batteries, and to dislodge them, if possible, from a command-ing position which they held. I opened upon the batteries with my four Napoleons, firing canister and spherical case." Canister seems an odd selection for counter-battery fire in the Civil War under any circumstances, but the distance was abnormally close on the second day at Gettysburg, and Union troops, including skirmishers, were clearly visible in fields around the house and barn. Perhaps, as the historian Bert Barnett has speculated, "his supply of solid shot was exhausted, or…at that close range, he felt that the anti-personnel charges would more rapidly cripple the gun crews." Taylor did not explain the decision in his official report, and he died before the end of the war, so we cannot know for certain.[31]

Concerted Rebel efforts notwithstanding, Union artillery more than held its own in the Peach Orchard and along the Emmitsburg

Road, surprising Alexander, who admitted to being "annoyed" by Federal "obstinacy" and conceded "the fight was longer and hotter than I expected." Years after the war, assessing the fight from a broader perspective than he had on July 2, 1863, he concluded that there was never "a hotter, harder, sharper artillery afternoon than this." His grand hopes of knocking out Union guns to clear the way for Longstreet's infantry never materialized. Despite that temporary setback, however, Confederate troops under Lafayette McLaws began their ground assault in his front sometime after five o'clock, sweeping forward in two irresistible waves to attack the Union salient at the Peach Orchard and the Wentz house, as the battle moved into an even more desperate phase.[32]

The house and small corner lot that John Wentz had purchased in 1836 were dwarfed now by larger farms in the area with names about to be made famous by the battle—Sherfy, Rose, Klingle, Trostle, Rogers, and Codori. But the Wentz property, perilously close to a sharp and ill-advised salient in the Union battle line, stood out, with Joseph Sherfy's orchard at the southeast corner of the intersection, as the site most vulnerable to McLaws's attack.

Troops under General Dan Sickles held the Emmitsburg Road as far south as the Peach Orchard, at which point they angled to the southeast toward Devil's Den and Little Round Top. The odd formation made the men near the Wentz house an inviting target, susceptible to attack from two directions, with little room to maneuver or position reserve troops. Such a weakness was readily apparent to Longstreet and McLaws from their unofficial command post just six hundred yards away.

The relentless *en échelon* infantry attack that had begun with John Bell Hood's troops on the far right suddenly rumbled north as

The stone foundation is all that remains of the Wentz House today. This view faces Henry Wentz's July 2 artillery position, which was located along the tree line in the distance. *Author photo*

McLaws's men entered the fray. South Carolinians under Joseph Kershaw and Georgians under Paul Semmes moved forward on the right of Alexander's battalion, driving toward the Rose Farm and the Peach Orchard, forcing Sickles to reinforce his thin and scattered line. One of the units summoned to plug a gap was the Second New Hampshire Volunteer Infantry, which hustled forward during the artillery barrage.[33]

The regiment's first assignment was to support a New York battery under Nelson Ames that was firing from the Emmitsburg Road. Nine of its ten companies formed in two wings at right angles, with some of the men "ordered to lie down, being then parallel to and facing" the road. But according to Private Martin Haynes's regimental history, the remaining unit, Company B, was specifically posted on the Wentz property.

Company B was detached as sharpshooters and stationed near the right of the battery, about the Wentz buildings, a one-story wood farm house and two or three outbuildings on the east side of the Emmitsburg road, which at this point is intersected by the Fairfield (or Millerstown) road, running east and west. The Sherfey [sic] buildings, more often quoted in general mention of this position, were about thirty rods north, on the west side of the Emmitsburg road.[34]

It was not long before accurate fire from Alexander's and Cabell's guns compelled the Second to change its position. "The right wing of the regiment was unnecessarily exposed," Haynes wrote, "and to secure better shelter it made a change of front forward upon the color company, bringing the whole regiment to face south, with its right in the garden to the rear of the Wentz house." Amidst shrieking missiles and bursting shells, "Ames' battery was having quite a lively duel with rebel guns."[35]

In Haynes's view, the Confederate artillery, which he judged to be fifty-six pieces, had shifted its full fury to the salient near the Wentz property. "Now every gun upon that great outer circle seemed to concentrate its fire upon that little acre about the Wentz house." Muskets stirred and bayonets glistened in the tree line up ahead as exuberant Rebel commanders scurried to align their troops. Haynes and other veterans in the Second, having "learned to read the signs," knew all too well that "there was an infantry assault behind all that hubbub."[36]

It was toward six o'clock when, under cover of the artillery fire, the long-concealed infantry of McLaw's rebel division disclosed itself and moved forward for a simultaneous, converging attack upon both faces of Sickles' salient.

Kershaw's brigade, followed by Semmes', crossed to the
east side of the Emmitsburg road, and pressed forward to
get within striking distance of the peach orchard from the
south, while Barksdale's brigade, with Wofford's in support, advanced against the Emmitsburg road front.[37]

Sickles's men at the salient could not hold on for long. The Second
New Hampshire—except Company B, which was left to its "work
about the Wentz house"—briefly engaged Kershaw's brigade near the
Peach Orchard, at one point mounting a desperate charge. Soon,
however the New Hampshire men came face to face with Mississippi
troops under General William Barksdale, a fire-breathing secessionist and former U.S. congressman who was "radiant with joy" at his
chance to unhinge the Federal line. As Harry Pfanz describes it,
Barksdale's men "pressed over the Emmitsburg Road north of the
Wheatfield Road to the Wentz farm" and "overran the Wentz buildings." One by one, Sickles's besieged regiments, including the Second
New Hampshire, began to give way.[38]

But even in retreat—sometimes in a full-fledged sprint—the mis-
ery wasn't finished for the Union troops who had tried to defend the
shaky salient. Observing the carnage from six hundred yards away
and believing now that "the battle was ours," Alexander ordered all
six of his batteries to limber up and advance to support the infantry.
"They were in great spirits, cheering & straining every nerve to get
forward in the least possible time," he recalled, "all...going for the
Peach Orchard at the same time." In a matter of fifteen minutes, it
became an all-out Rebel stampede.[39]

I can recall no more splendid sight, on a small scale—and
certainly no more inspiring moment during the war—than
that of the charge of these six batteries. An artillerist's heaven

is to follow the routed enemy, after a tough resistance, and throw shells and canister into his disorganized and fleeing masses.... Now we would have our revenge.[40]

Every war scrambles the destinies of the men caught up in it, but the twists of fortune can be especially poignant in a civil war. Among the men moving forward in Alexander's charge was Sergeant Henry Wentz of Taylor's Virginia Battery, who had grown up in the house just ahead, whose parents and youngest sister still lived there, and whose father, John, was hiding in the cellar. He now charged at the retreating Yankees as a foreign invader over another patch of land *that he had personally owned since 1850.*[41]

John Wentz had purchased a nine-acre plot directly across from his own home (at the southwest corner of the intersection of the Emmitsburg and Millerstown Roads) in December 1847. He transferred it to Henry in February 1850. Although there is no record that Henry ever paid taxes on the property, there also is no evidence that he put it up for sale after moving to Martinsburg in 1852. The parcel remained in the family's possession until 1872, when Henry returned to Gettysburg to sell it following the deaths of his father, mother, and sister.

Taylor's Battery rattled across Henry's land and no doubt angled through his father's yard to take up its second position. Along the way Henry would have seen damage to his family's property, especially the barn. "The rear of the barn looked like a sieve from the numerous volleys of canister which had passed through it," remarked Private Wyman H. Holden of Company B of the Second New Hampshire, who had spent much of the day fighting nearby, "and the ground was covered with kindling wood, before it took fire from a shell and was consumed. The house escaped destruction and was not perforated by shot or shell, because, if we believe the enemy, a son of the owner was serving in the rebel ranks, and at his request they spared it."[42]

The rumor reported by Holden could not have been true, however. McLaws would not have honored such a request even if Wentz had made it, and the house, according to other observers, *did* receive some damage. It is nevertheless clear that Holden and his comrades were aware of Henry's presence on the field. Twenty-one wounded soldiers from the Second New Hampshire took refuge in the Wentz house during the second day's fight, and some of them, according to Holden's account, "scrambled down a rollway into the cellar," where they would have encountered Henry's father. Wentz family legend has it that Henry himself entered the house out of curiosity later that night. A local historian, W. C. Storrick, whose older sister married Henry's nephew in 1868 (giving him direct access to family history), wrote about it in 1932: "On the night of the second day, after Sickles' advance line at the Wentz house had been repulsed and occupied by the forces under General Lee, Henry Wentz visited his old home and was greatly surprised to find his father still there."[43]

But in the early evening hours of July 2, as Union troops fled in disarray toward the safety of another ridge, Henry and his fellow artillerists still had hard work to do. Taylor's Virginia Battery was posted "150 yards north of the Wheatfield Road and 150 yards east of the Emmitsburg Road" as Alexander spurred other batteries forward, hoping to "finish the whole war this afternoon." For a long moment he believed that "Providence was indeed 'taking the proper view.'" But Alexander did not know that Dan Sickles had ordered his corps forward to the Emmitsburg Road that day in defiance of orders and that the main Union battle line, now being reinforced in pieces, was actually back on Cemetery Ridge. "When I got to take in all the topography I was very much disappointed," he said. "It was not the enemy's main line we had broken.... [W]e only had a moderately good time with Sickles' retreating corps after all."[44]

For the remainder of the day, Rebel infantry continued its attack to the left toward the Klingle and Codori farms—making inroads, gaining ground, wreaking havoc, but never quite able to push the Federals off the far ridge. Georgia troops under Ambrose "Rans" Wright momentarily pierced the Union center at what would be the site of Pickett's Charge on the third day, but reinforcements never arrived, and they were hurled back. Alexander remembered "pell-mell fighting" that lasted until nightfall, when "the fuses of flying shells looked like little meteors in the air." But both musketry and artillery fire began to slacken out of necessity in the darkness, Alexander said, and by nine o'clock the field had fallen eerily silent:

> It was evident that we had not finished the job, and would have to make a fresh effort in the morning. The firing had hardly ceased when my faithful little darkey, Charlie, came up hunting for me, with a fresh horse, affectionate congratulations on my safety, and, what was equally acceptable, something to eat. Negro servants hunting for their masters were a feature of the landscape that night. I then found General Longstreet, learned what I could of the fortunes of the day on other parts of the field, and got orders for the morning.[45]

At one o'clock, the young colonel made a bed of fence rails at the Peach Orchard, not far from the house where one of his soldiers had grown up, and went to sleep.[46]

Twelve

CONFEDERATE HIGH TIDE

olonel E. P. Alexander slept for two hours on the morning of July 3 before rising in the "very early dimness." The work load he faced did not allow for much more. Though Confederate battle plans were still not fully developed as daylight approached, Lee had proposed an attack with fresh troops under George Pickett that would break and, he hoped, crush the Union line on Cemetery Ridge. Alexander's guns would play a crucial role.[1]

He set about his work shortly after three a.m., guided only by a "glorious moonlight" that facilitated "all the necessary moving about." Starting at the Peach Orchard, he dutifully placed his batteries, including Henry Wentz and Taylor's Virginia Battery, in a long line to the left along the Emmitsburg Road. The problem was that it was all just educated guesswork. Amid the smoke and confusion of the previous afternoon and evening, Alexander had failed to detect the precise location of the Union battle line. With the sunrise, he realized the extent of his near-fatal tactical error.[2]

Alexander was horrified. "As daylight came," he recalled, "I found I had placed about twenty guns so that the enemy's batteries on Cemetery Hill enfiladed the line, and had a panic, almost, for fear that the enemy would discover my blunder and open before I could rectify it." He allowed that it "scared me awfully." Several batteries, including those in the Washington Artillery under Major B. F. Eshelman, were promptly unlimbered, "thrown a little to the rear," and posted a safer distance from the west side of the road. Taylor's Battery remained in its position across from the Klingle house, but the Rebel line now took a northwest angle from the Peach Orchard toward Spangler's Woods so as not to present such a "good target" for probing Union guns.[3]

Alexander did not know it at the time, but he was preparing the great cannonade that preceded Pickett's Charge. By mid-morning, Lee had settled on a brazen frontal assault against the heart of the Union position on Cemetery Ridge. It called for careful planning and a grander strategic vision that involved even more artillery. Alexander later explained:

> This necessitated a good many changes of our positions, which the enemy did not altogether approve of, and they took occasional shots at us, though we shifted about, as inoffensively as possible, and carefully avoided getting into bunches. But we stood it all meekly, and by 10 o'clock, Dearing having come up, we had seventy five guns in what was virtually one battery, so disposed as to fire on Cemetery Hill and the batteries south of it.[4]

The timely arrival of James Dearing's artillery battalion added weight and depth to Alexander's impending attack. It also brought another Gettysburg Rebel, Francis W. "Frank" Hoffman, formerly of Chambersburg Street, onto the field at last.

Private Hoffman and the Fauquier Artillery were rousted in the wee hours of July 3, covering the final few miles of a twenty-five-mile trek from Chambersburg that began early on July 2. Attached to Pickett's division with other members of Dearing's battalion, they spent two days guarding the rear of the army and were one of the final Confederate units to reach the Gettysburg battlefield.[5]

It had been an eventful and not altogether pleasant year for the Fauquier County men and their captain, Robert M. Stribling. Reorganized in February as Company A of the Thirty-Eighth Battalion, they were part of Longstreet's expedition to the Suffolk, Virginia, region from February to May to gather much-needed supplies for the summer campaign while keeping an eye on troublesome Union troops nearby.

The mission turned tense when Longstreet moved to capture Suffolk in mid-April, placing Stribling's small unit at an old fort overlooking the Nansemond River to prevent Union gunboats from passing upstream. The Fauquier gunners promptly attacked and sank an offending vessel on April 17, thrilling a Southern diarist, who wrote that he "watched a fight between a gunboat and one of our batteries which was in an old fort built during the war of 1812. Was a pretty sight." But Federal troops, less charmed by Company A's performance, responded with "an incessant fire…kept up on the battery by the gunboats above and below."[6]

Stribling and his men were now the enemy's prime target for revenge. Holding an exposed position "on a neck running out into a bend" of the river, they were protected only by two small companies of Alabama infantry. Union troops took a day to rest and reorganize, then stormed the fort from above and behind, overrunning the smaller Rebel force and taking 137 prisoners, fifty-five of them from the Fauquier Artillery. Longstreet called it "the only occurrence of

serious moment while we had our forces about Suffolk." The unidentified captives were paroled two days later and allowed to rejoin their
units, but memories of the disaster lingered as they crossed the Appomattox River and headed toward Richmond in early May.[7]

The Fauquier Artillery was re-fitted with new equipment—"six
new 'Richmond model' 12-pounder Napoleons with caissons and new
harnesses"—just before receiving the order to move north on the Gettysburg campaign. The men enjoyed a brief homecoming on June 17
at Markham, Virginia, where most of them, including Frank Hoffman, had enlisted with such high hopes two years earlier. After ford-
ing the Potomac on June 26 at Williamsport, Maryland, they crossed
into Pennsylvania, passed one night at Greencastle, and spent the
better part of a week at Chambersburg while awaiting further orders.[8]

At this point, Dearing decided to make mischief during this "idle"
time. Stribling, writing thirty-five years later, recalled that Dearing

> armed and mounted on battery horses a squad of men and
> went into the mountains in search of fresh horses, and was
> successful. The party had a lively time. They were bush-
> whacked, driven back from gaps by militia, and made
> narrow escapes from capture. Dearing achieved this by
> building extensive camp fires at about eleven o'clock at
> night to deceive the enemy, and then making a hurried
> march to a gap some fifteen miles distant, and slipping
> through without being observed.[9]

The order to end such silliness and advance on the Chambersburg
Pike toward Gettysburg came on the morning of July 2. "On that
day," Dearing wrote in his report, "we marched to within a few miles
of the battle-field...and went into camp, after a very long and tiresome march to both men and horses." They bivouacked briefly behind

Longstreet's corps before reporting to Alexander on the Rebel front lines.[10]

Aside from Frank Hoffman, Dearing was the only man in the battalion who was even vaguely familiar with the battleground. He had ridden ahead on his own on July 2 and volunteered his services during the afternoon attack on the Peach Orchard. Alexander placed him in temporary command of two batteries under T. C. Jordan and Pichegru Woolfolk Jr., but the young major did not make his presence felt until a series of stubborn farm fences impeded their charge. Spotting Union prisoners nearby, Dearing brandished his sword and bellowed, "God damn you pull down those fences!" It was said that the fences "literally flew into the air."[11]

Dearing's arrival with his own battalion just before ten o'clock on July 3 allowed Alexander to extend his line northward past the Rogers house on the west side of the Emmitsburg Road. The Fauquier Artillery was placed on the far right of the battalion near the Rogers property (marked today only by a painted white fence). They were menaced almost immediately by a strong line of Union skirmishers in their front—a severe challenge in the absence of infantry. But Dearing assigned Stribling's men to "deploy and drive the venturesome Yankees back," and he proudly reported that the mission was accomplished by firing only "about a dozen rounds."[12]

Other Rebel units off to the right also were harassed by skirmishers, but the threat was diminished when Eshelman's guns, "with those of Captain Taylor, opened upon them moderately with evident effect."[13]

By a quirk of fate, Henry Wentz and Taylor's Battery were posted several hundred yards to the south of Frank Hoffman and the Fauquier Artillery.[14] It is not known if Hoffman or Wentz realized that the other was on the battlefield or if they even knew one another. It is possible they had not met. They were fifteen years apart in age, and

Frank was only ten years old when Henry left Gettysburg for Martinsburg in 1852. But modern-day Hoffman descendants report that C. W. Hoffman's sister (Frank's aunt) lived as a tenant on the Wentz property for several years in the late 1840s, so perhaps the two men had at least crossed paths on a family visit.[15] For now, however, they were merely two of the thousands of Confederate artillerists focused on driving Union guns off a small rise near a clump of trees.

The cannonade began at 1:07 p.m. Signal shots came from the Washington Artillery, followed by a thunderous symphony of 150 guns roaring in unison along the Rebel line.[16] When Union gunners responded, the ground began to shake beneath the feet of terrified soldiers on both sides. "The atmosphere was broken by the rushing solid shot, and shrieking shell," wrote Major Walter Harrison of Pickett's staff.

> The sky, just now so bright, was at the same moment lurid with flame and murky with smoke. The sun in his noontide ray was obscured by clouds of sulphurous mist, eclipsing his light, and shadowing the earth as with a funeral pall; while through this sable panoply, ever descending and wrapping this field of blood in the darkness of death, shot the fiery fuses, like wild meteors of a heavenly wrath; hurtled discordantly screaming shell, bearing mangled death and mutilation in its most horrible form.[17]

In other words, all hell broke loose.

The Fauquier Artillery and Taylor's Virginia Battery were in the thick of the action, pounding away at enemy positions, but stubborn

Union resistance made their task more difficult. With smoke blanketing the field, many Rebel guns were overshooting their targets. One shell even struck the tombstone of Wesley Culp's father, Esaias, in Evergreen Cemetery (the damage is still visible today). A wild-eyed Dearing—described by Captain Stribling as one of the most "conspicuous figures on the field"—rode from right to left along his line, waving a battle flag, encouraging his troops. But Union fire soon killed the horse of Dearing's courier, which, according to Stribling, "ended the flag-waving business, much to the delight of the men, who did not desire any more special attention than they were then receiving from the enemy's guns."[18]

Longstreet, in a stunning lapse of responsibility, had assigned Alexander to inform the infantry when to attack, but only "if the

The tombstone of Wesley Culp's father, Esaias, was struck by Confederate artillery fire during the battle. *Author photo*

artillery has the desired effect of driving the enemy's off." Alexander, understandably, tried to resist. "If...there is any alternative to this attack," he wrote in a panicked response, "it should be carefully considered before opening our fire." There were several such exchanges between the two men, but both knew it was inevitable that the attack would go forward. "When the moment arrives," Longstreet told Alexander in a final note, "advise Gen. Pickett, and of course advance such artillery as you can use in aiding the attack."[19]

The original expectation was that Pickett would advance fifteen to twenty minutes after the guns opened. A number of Dearing's batteries, including the Fauquier Artillery, were assigned to move forward *en échelon* to support the infantry, and Stribling himself had gone ahead to reconnoiter the ground. But the stoutness of Union batteries on the ridge compelled Alexander to delay the order. Finally, at 1:25 p.m., with ammunition already starting to run low in some units, he wrote to Pickett, "If you are coming at all you must come at once, or I cannot give you support, but the enemy's fire has not slackened at all." Ten minutes later, after misreading some Union maneuvers on the ridge, he pleaded, "For God's sake come quick. The 18 guns are gone. Come quick or I can't support you."[20]

Pickett readied his men at once, as did two other Rebel commanders, J. Johnston Pettigrew and Isaac Trimble, and it was not long before they stepped off in magnificent style across the open farm fields. But the grand plan already was starting to go awry. "When the time came," Stribling wrote, "through no fault of [Dearing's]...all the ammunition had been exhausted, and no more was in reach, and the advance of the artillery was consequently abandoned." This same problem—a chronic lack of ordnance—plagued various other Rebel batteries up and down the line.[21]

And so the most famous infantry attack ever conducted on U.S. soil went forward virtually on its own—uphill, over fences, against a fortified position across open ground with little chance of success. The slaughter was ghastly. Pickett's division alone suffered fifty-three-percent casualties, including the gallant brigadier, Lewis Armistead, who led a small group over the stone wall at the Angle to establish the unofficial "High Water Mark of the Confederacy." Also among the dead was General Richard Garnett, who had been humiliated by Stonewall Jackson following the battle of Kernstown in 1862, and who no doubt planned to restore his honor here.[22]

Alexander had kept some of his guns firing during the charge, even as ammunition dwindled, but the effect on Union troops was minimal. Soon he could do little more than sit and watch the carnage as Pickett's men at the wall were "swallowed up in smoke" and simply melted away.[23]

"From the position of our guns, the sight of this conflict was grand and thrilling," Alexander wrote,

> and we watched it as men with a life-and-death interest in the result. If it should be favorable to us, the war was nearly over; if against us, we each had the risks of many battles yet to go through. And the event culminated with fearful rapidity....
>
> As soon as it appeared that the assault had failed, we ceased firing in order to save ammunition in case the enemy should advance. But we held our ground as boldly as possible, though we were entirely without support and very low in ammunition. The enemy gave us an occasional shot for a while and then, to our great relief, let us rest. About that time, General Lee, entirely alone, rode up and remained with me for a long time. He then probably first appreciated the full extent of the disaster as the disorganized stragglers made their way back past us.... [I]t was

certainly a momentous thing to him to see that superb attack end in such a bloody repulse.[24]

There still were several cavalry actions to be fought that afternoon, including one involving Wesley Hoffman's unit, the Seventh Virginia Cavalry, but the battle essentially ended with the colossal failure of Pickett's Charge. Rebel artillery units remained in exposed positions for several more hours out of fear that the Union would mount its own countercharge, but an unspoken and unofficial truce soon settled over the bloody field as darkness fell on one of the most consequential days in American history.[25]

Sometime after ten o'clock, and probably close to midnight, Alexander's last two batteries, commanded by Lieutenant James Woolfolk and Captain Osmond B. Taylor, withdrew from their advanced positions to the safety of a reformed Rebel line near Willoughby Run, making Henry Wentz, whose house was still visible in the moonlight off in the distance, one of the last soldiers to leave the Gettysburg battlefield.[26]

Wesley Hoffman's regiment had opened the Gettysburg campaign as part of the battle of Brandy Station on June 9, and now those same Virginia troopers would close the proceedings at a place called Fairfield, eight miles to the southwest of his old hometown.

Part of William "Grumble" Jones's brigade, the Seventh had spent most of the past month guarding mountain passes, protecting the rear of the army. In a spirited and mildly costly clash with Union cavalry near Upperville, Virginia, on June 21, the regiment had suffered twenty-two casualties and lost forty-eight horses killed or wounded, but it would see no further combat action until it was summoned forward from its camp near Chambersburg at one o'clock in the morning on July 3.[27]

The men must have wondered what was in store for them as the third day of the battle approached. They paused briefly for breakfast at Cashtown, about eight miles west of Gettysburg on the Chambersburg Pike, then received word in the late morning that Robert E. Lee himself had ordered that "a force of cavalry...be sent at once to the vicinity of Fairfield, to form a line to the right and rear of our line of battle." In addition to protecting supply trains, Lee wanted to ensure that two key passes at Jack's Mountain, near Fairfield, remained open to his army if disaster struck. Two brigades under Jones and Beverly Robertson moved out at about one p.m., just as the great Rebel cannonade was getting underway.[28]

The sounds up ahead were harsh and unmistakable. An artillerist accompanying the cavalry, who observed the action from a high distant hill, recalled that

> at one point...we saw nothing but a vast bank of thick battle smoke with thousands of shells exploding above the surface of the white, smoking sea. Our line looked to me from our point of observation to be about three miles long and enveloped in thick smoke, from which there came a fearful roar and clash of musketry accompanied with a deep continuous roll of booming artillery, such as an American soldier never heard before on this continent. The artillery fire at one time was so heavy that the hills shook and the air trembled, and the deep thunder rolled through the sky in one incessant roar as if giants of war where hurling thunderbolts at each other.[29]

As the gunfire fell silent by mid-afternoon, rumors spread among Jones's troopers that a great victory had been achieved and their role would now be to chase and capture "retreating Federals." They were momentarily ecstatic. But the perspective changed a few hours later, probably at about five o'clock, when a force of Union cavalry began to probe near Fairfield in hot pursuit of the division wagon train.[30]

These were the men of the Sixth U.S. Cavalry regiment, and the timing was lucky for the Confederates. As Jones described it later, the supply train would have "fallen an easy prey but for our timely arrival. Many wagons in quest of forage were already within a few hundred yards of the enemy." Under duress and still unaware of what had taken place on Cemetery Ridge, he changed tactics to go on the offensive. "I at once ordered the Seventh Regiment, which was in front, to charge."[31]

Although Jones and the Rebels eventually prevailed in the little-known battle of Fairfield, the day went down as one of the worst in the annals of the Seventh Virginia Cavalry. The men in front of the charging regiment hesitated, then halted, then—worse—retreated. The unusually poor performance rankled Jones, who had once served as colonel of the Seventh and knew about its origins from the great Turner Ashby, onetime leader of the Fauquier County Rangers. "A failure to rally promptly and renew the fight is a blemish in the bright history of this regiment," he wrote in his report. Even the Seventh's own lieutenant colonel, Thomas Marshall, allowed that "the regiment did not at this place and time close up as promptly as it should."[32]

Fortunately for Jones and the Rebels, it was at this point that the Sixth Virginia Cavalry, backed by effective fire from Roger Preston Chew's artillery, swept in to turn the momentum. Scattered elements of the Seventh *did* manage to rally and assist. Jones credited these men with "assailing and completely routing one of the best United States regiments," which, though inconsequential for the overall battle, at least spared the regiment the additional ignominy of losing the division's supply train. The Confederate army, as the men would soon learn, had already lost enough on July 3, 1863.[33]

Jones later noted with some pleasure that the Seventh performed well and "cleared its reputation" during further clashes on the retreat back to Virginia, but its action closest to the Gettysburg battlefield would always remain an open wound.[34]

———

Sometime before ten o'clock on the night of July 3, Confederate artillery sergeant Henry Wentz slipped across the Emmitsburg Road under cover of darkness to pay an emotional farewell visit to his father. Fanciful as it sounds, the story was recorded by the local historian W. C. Storrick, a lifelong Gettysburg resident who was alive at the time of the battle and whose older sister married Henry Wentz's nephew in 1868.[35] Storrick later served as superintendent of Gettysburg's battlefield guides and spent more than twenty years with the Gettysburg National Park Commission. Although he incorrectly identifies Wentz as a Rebel lieutenant, he provides other information that almost certainly was obtained from his sister, her husband, and other family sources. Storrick notes, for instance, that John Wentz "kept to the cellar" during the July 3 cannonade and Pickett's Charge and "singularly, passed through it all unharmed." He continues:

> During the night of the third day, Henry was anxious to know whether or not his father was still safe. He therefore went over to the house and found him fast asleep and unhurt in a corner of the cellar. Not wishing to disturb his much-needed rest, he found a stump of a candle, lit it, and wrote, "Good-bye and God bless you!" This message he pinned on the lapel of his father's coat and returned to his command preparatory to the retreat to Virginia.

Early on the morning of the 4th, the father awoke from his much-needed sleep and found that all the soldiers had departed. He then walked back to the ridge and saw Lee's army making hurried preparations for the retreat.[36]

Questions about Storrick's account linger, including how Henry could have sidestepped the twenty-one wounded soldiers from the Second New Hampshire who were still in the house (perhaps under a flag of truce). But as E. P. Alexander reported that Taylor's Virginia Battery was one of the last Rebel units to leave the field, it is plausible that Sergeant Wentz had an opportunity to make the visit from his position a few hundred yards away on the west side of the road.[37]

It also is worth noting that Wentz's nephew, Henry H. Beamer, son of Ann Maria Wentz Beamer, never refuted Storrick's account. Young Beamer had a unique perspective on the battle, having served in the Union army with the First Pennsylvania Reserves and fought nearby in the Wheatfield–Little Round Top area on July 2. Despite his proximity to the Wentz family property, however, he apparently never thought to check in on his grandfather during or immediately after the battle.[38]

Even before Storrick's report, the Wentz-Beamer connection was mentioned in one rambling paragraph of the 516-page *History of Adams County, Pennsylvania*, published in 1886:

Jacob Beamer was married to Ann M. Wentz, of German descent, born in York County, Penn., May 24 1815, daughter of John Wentz, who came here from York County, and died, aged eighty-four, near the famous peach orchard where he resided during the battle of Gettysburg, his own son being an officer of a Confederate battery that was stationed at the head of the lot, his nephew facing the battery in the Union army.[39]

Adding confusion to the story of Henry Wentz were two other contemporary accounts, which indicated that he was killed in the battle near his boyhood home and that his indignant parents refused to accept or even view his body. Charles H. Keener, superintendent of the Maryland Institution for the Instruction of the Blind, arrived in Gettysburg with the United States Christian Commission on July 5 and remained through August. He recounted finding wounded soldiers after the battle

> at the home of Mr. Bentz [Wentz], whose son had been South for 16 years [eleven years is a more accurate figure], and came home on the day before the battle as a captain of a Rebel battery. His guns, during the fight, drew the fire of our batteries directly across his father's house, and some of his own shot struck the house and barn. The son was killed, but the father was so good a Union man that he would not consent either to look on the corpse or the grave of his miscreant son.[40]

The other account was that of Lieutenant Rufus W. Jacklin of the Sixteenth Michigan, who fought on Little Round Top on July 2 and was ordered to help bury Confederates near the Peach Orchard on July 5. In his diary, discovered many years later, Jacklin recorded:

> On Sunday morning, July 5th, I was ordered to take a detail of men from my regiment and proceed to that part of the field near the Emmitsburg Road in the direction of the peach orchard, for the purpose of burying the Confederate dead. I took up my work near the [Wentz] house. I ordered the men to dig a trench in the garden to the left and in front of the house near the road. Later, I looked up

and saw an old man and an old woman approaching. They were the owners of the house.

They turned into the yard, but instead of noticing the partial destruction, at least, of their home, barn, out-houses, fences, etc., they busied themselves gathering the tender branches of the mulberry tree or bush—for what purpose, I could not determine, until they entered the house, which was a 1½ story log building literally perforated by shot and shell, and climbed the stairway to the attic where, suspended from the rafters, were hammocks filled with silkworms, which they commenced to feed. I engaged them in conversation. They told me of their work, etc. In a short time we descended to the front of their house. The bodies of the dead were being hauled in from the field to the trench and among the number was an artillery officer.

Papers were found on the body indicating the same name as the family. I called their attention to it. They replied, "Yes, we had a son who left our home and went to Virginia. The last we heard of him he was in the Confederate service. But we disowned our son and will have nothing to do with the body if it is he."

I buried the remains in the trench with others. Think of this incident for a moment. This disowned son, a Rebel, killed and buried in the door yard where he was brought up—how pathetic.[41]

Henry Wentz, of course, was not killed at Gettysburg. He was listed as "present" on the first muster roll after the battle and continued to serve honorably for the remainder of the war until being taken prisoner at Harper's Farm on April 6, 1865. He appeared in the 1870 federal census as a "house plasterer" residing in Martinsburg (now

West Virginia), and his obituary was published in the *Martinsburg Statesman* on December 14, 1875, four days after his death.[42]

Although anti-Rebel sentiment may have fueled rumors that Henry was "disowned" by his family, there is no evidence that they did any such thing. Storrick never mentioned it, and John Wentz's 1870 will did not specifically exclude Henry from his inheritance. The elder Wentz arranged for his spinster daughter Susan to receive "all my real estate on the death of my beloved wife, Mary," but directed that the proceeds from the sale of his personal property should be "equally distributed among my surviving children." In 1872, after Mary and Susan had died, Henry returned to Gettysburg to join his brothers, Abraham and Peter, in selling the family property with the assistance of their brother-in-law, the attorney Jacob Beamer. Henry appeared to take the lead in the proceedings and is listed first on the deed for the sale of the Wentz house and outbuildings. It hardly seems that he was "disowned."[43]

A wayside exhibit titled "Henry Wentz Comes Home" was located for many years near the Wentz property along the Emmitsburg Road. Sadly, it no longer exists. The Wentz house itself underwent so many postwar renovations that it was eventually declared non-historic by the National Park Service and torn down in 1960. Only the stone foundation remains, identified by an iron tablet with the simple inscription "Wentz House," a haunting and appropriately understated tribute to the story of a little-known Gettysburg Rebel who came home to fight in his own front yard.[44]

Not until the last sounds of gunfire were muffled by darkness did word began to spread that one of Gettysburg's own was a casualty, the only local citizen killed during three days of raging warfare.

Jennie Wade had been up early on the morning of July 3, caring for her sister and newborn nephew—and baking biscuits for nearby Union soldiers—when a Rebel bullet tore through a door of her sister's Baltimore Street home and struck her just below the left shoulder blade. It pierced her heart, exited her chest, and lodged in her corset.[45]

Jennie died without ever learning that her childhood friend Wesley Culp had been killed a few miles away, near Wolf Hill, the day before. She died without knowing that her dearer friend and love interest, Jack Skelly, was himself dying in a Rebel hospital at Winchester, Virginia. The Union soldiers who wrapped her body in a quilt and carried it to the cellar for the remainder of the battle would later find Skelly's photograph placed tenderly in her apron pocket. Skelly died on July 12.[46]

Thirteen

PRISONERS OF WAR

More than sixty men deserted from the ranks of the Second Virginia Infantry within two weeks of the army's retreat from Gettysburg. Many others who remained were momentarily weakened and disillusioned. "I am too much waried down from the march that we had in the yankee states," one man wrote on July 18 from, appropriately enough, Darkesville, Virginia. "I was in good hopes that the war might soon be over, but it don't look much like it at this time."[1]

Gettysburg was a grievous blow, forcing Lee to abandon his plans for victory on Northern soil, yet it did not extinguish Southern hopes, and the army refreshed, reorganized, and renewed its war footing. The four surviving Gettysburg Rebels served through the end of the war in April 1865, by which time two of them had been wounded, three hospitalized, and all four captured and confined to Union prison camps, their fortunes mirroring that of the Confederacy itself.

Robert Hoffman drove cattle back across the Potomac and resumed his duties with the commissary department amid the desertions in his unit. He was marked "present" on the Second Virginia's muster rolls for August and September, when the Stonewall Brigade was camped at Orange Court House and then at Morton's Ford on the Rapidan River. But Robert couldn't resist taking another unsanctioned furlough in mid-October as the brigade advanced through Fauquier County in the direction of Bristoe Station, where it would clash with the Yankees on October 14. He went home to the family farm.[2]

The entry in his military records is similar to those from 1861 and 1862—"Absent without leave from Oct. 13 to Oct. 21." This time, however, he was "court martialed" and sentenced "to forfeit one month pay." Another change in assignment, perhaps a consequence of this latest violation, came in early December when the former infantryman and commissary assistant was detailed to become a "musician in the 2nd Regt. Band."[3]

We don't know which instrument Robert played or his reaction to the transfer, which was a demotion and perhaps an embarrassment. Nevertheless, military musicians played an important role in nineteenth-century warfare. Lee himself declared, "I don't think we can have an army without music." In addition to boosting morale, music "passed the time; it entertained and comforted; it brought back memories of home and family; it strengthened the bonds between comrades and helped to forge new ones. And, in the case of the Confederacy, it helped create the sense of national identity and unity so necessary to a fledgling nation."[4] Talent levels varied, of course, and one soldier compared his unit's band to the "braying of a pack of mules,"[5] but "the band of the Stonewall Brigade was considered one of the best, if not the best, in Lee's army."[6]

The life of a military musician in the Civil War was not without danger. Bands often were placed perilously close to the action by officers hoping to bolster the troops' morale, and some "did accompany their commanders onto the field and played patriotic songs while under the battle raged all around them." That may have been the case at Spotsylvania Court House on May 12, 1864, when Robert and ninety-four other members of the Second Virginia were taken prisoner during mind-numbing fighting at the "Bloody Angle." Eleven of the captives were from Robert's original unit, Company B, the Hamtramck Guards from Shepherdstown. This decidedly disastrous day for the Confederacy marked the official end of the once-proud Stonewall Brigade as a functioning army unit.[7]

The prisoners arrived at Belle Plains, Virginia, six days later, on May 18, en route to the massive Union facility at Point Lookout, Maryland.[8] Conditions were often harsh for POWs, many of them "poorly clad...some wearing but dirty underwear and having no blanket,"[9] but Robert received a new set of clothing on June 16. He did not stay at Point Lookout for long. Overcrowded conditions compelled Union officials to ship him and several thousand of his comrades to Elmira, New York, about six miles north of his native Pennsylvania.

Elmira was a former training camp recently converted into a prison, and conditions there were even harsher than at Point Lookout. Its intended capacity was five thousand prisoners, but its population had swollen to 9,600 by the time Private Hoffman and others arrived in August, and officials ran out of tents five days later. Food was scarce and cold, nutrition was virtually nonexistent, and sanitary conditions were deplorable. A 580-yard stagnant pool of water became a "festering mass of corruption, impregnating the entire atmosphere of the camp with its pestilential odors, night and day." Almost four hundred men dropped dead in September alone. "Elmira was nearer Hades than I thought any place could be," wrote an Alabama artillerist.[10]

It is no wonder that prisoners here tried to escape or that Robert, with the skills he had developed in business, was recruited for one of the plots. His daughter Ruth records in her family history, "During the winter some of the prisoners planned an escape—they were intending to tunnel out—to have outside help. My father did the letter writing—his letters were intercepted. They tried to make him tell who was implicated but he would not expose the men. He told them they could kill him but he would not tell. They put him in a dungeon and tried to starve him."[11]

This was almost certainly the same daring prison break that the historian James I. Robertson Jr. calls the "most elaborate and success-ful" plot ever attempted at the prison.

> Starting inside a tent, a determined group of prisoners dug a sixty-foot tunnel "of astonishing accuracy" underneath the wall to an open field beyond. During the nightly exca-vations, men stealthily carried dirt in blankets and dumped it noiselessly into Foster's Pond. On the night of October 6, eleven made their escape. Some went to Canada; others attempted to make the long trek southward.[12]

Robert did not make it to freedom with the others. Captured and returned to the prison camp, he was exposed to further calamities at Elmira, including scurvy, diarrhea, pneumonia, and, worst of all, smallpox. More than a hundred men contracted smallpox during one week in November.[13] Robert was among the lucky prisoners who were vaccinated, though he paid a price for the privilege: "He took cold in his arm which nearly cost him the loss of it—he would have to walk up and down in the cell trying to keep from freezing."[14]

The war was slowly grinding to an end when Robert was sent to Richmond to begin the process of exchange on May 2, 1865. First he

Robert Hoffman's oath of allegiance, including his signature. *www.fold3.com, Military Service Records for Robert N. Hoffman*

was treated at Jackson Hospital for "debilitas"—weakness or feebleness—and it was not until May 29 that he signed his oath of allegiance to the United States and was released from his year in captivity. There was some irony in that the oath was issued by the provost marshal of Harper's Ferry (now West Virginia), where he had rushed in to put down the John Brown Raid six years earlier, and where he had seen his first action of the war in April 1861.[15]

> I, Robert N. Hoffman of Co. B, 2nd Va. Infty., do solemnly swear, in the presence of Almighty God, that I will henceforth faithfully support, protect and defend the Constitution of the United States, and the Union of states thereunder; and that I will in like manner abide by and faithfully support all acts of Congress passed during the existing rebellion with reference to slaves so long and so far as not repealed, modified or held void by Congress, or by decision of the Supreme Court; and that I will in like manner abide

by and faithfully support all proclamations of the President made during the existing rebellion, having reference to slaves, so long and so far as not modified or declared void by decision of the Supreme Court—So help me God.[16]

———

There is a one-year gap in muster roll records for Company A of the Seventh Virginia Cavalry in 1863, although they resume for the three-month period January–March 1864. Private Wesley A. Hoffman is listed as being away on "horse detail" at the end of March, but one small entry confirms his presence with the unit during the raucous summer and fall of 1863: he was "last paid" for service rendered through November 1.[17]

"Horse detail" was a thankless but necessary duty for a cavalry unit in perpetual motion on the flanks of a nineteenth-century army. Notations in individual service records indicate that a soldier "had his own horse," a distinct and desirable advantage, or had lost his mount—"horse wounded," "horse lost," "horse KIA." Wesley, who was still only nineteen years old, made his way home to Fauquier County at least briefly, where his father kept and sold horses and could take advantage of local connections. Records show that C. W. Hoffman had provided horses directly to the Fauquier Mountain Rangers earlier in the war.[18]

Whatever else he did during his time away on assignment in the spring of 1864, Wesley contracted syphilis. He was diagnosed after returning to his regiment in April and underwent treatment from April 29 to May 7 at a "C.S.A. General Hospital" in Charlottesville. He returned to action only to suffer a "severe" thigh wound during a mounted charge against John B. McIntosh's Federal brigade at Ashland on June 1. Details of his injury are scarce, but he was listed as absent from his post in July and August, after which muster rolls for the Seventh Virginia again disappear.[19]

The regiment took part in various scuffles and skirmishes over the next six months, and Wesley continued to serve until February 15, 1865, when he was captured by Union troops near Upperville, about fifteen miles from the family farm in Linden. The Seventh was not involved in any action that day. It is possible that Wesley, having been assigned again to horse detail, fell into enemy hands while conducting the mission on his own. He was promptly sent to Fort McHenry, where he had been briefly imprisoned in 1862. Union General Philip Sheridan "confined him at his post" and deemed him a "guerilla not to be exchanged during the war."[20]

Wesley was held for six weeks until he signed the oath of allegiance at the provost marshal's office at Fort McHenry on May 1. At the bottom of the oath, a Union officer filled in details that give us the only known physical description of Wesley during the war: "The above named has light complexion, brown hair, hazel eyes and is 5 feet 9 inches high." Asked for a specific destination in his release documents, the now twenty-year-old Hoffman demurred, declining to give a town, county, or state. He said, simply, "home."[21]

Aside from a brief "furlough of indulgence," Private Frank Hoffman of the Fauquier Artillery had the roughest route back to Fauquier County. He and his fellow soldiers spent the nine months from June 1864 through March 1865 in the same position at the siege of Petersburg, dutifully manning the trenches and enduring "repeated bombardments and constant sniping from the Federals." Frank seems to have fallen ill at one point, being hospitalized for thirty days in December for an unspecified ailment.[22] The unit's history describes the siege as "an ordeal of tedium, hunger and death that consumed both the men's wills and lives."[23]

Petersburg was on the "verge of collapse" on March 25, 1865. Facing almost certain defeat as the Union noose tightened, Lee chose to gamble one more time and attempt to fight his way out. He ordered what would be his final offensive of the war, a desperate and almost hopeless pre-dawn assault by nearly half his command under General John B. Gordon against a Union garrison at Fort Stedman. The point of attack was directly across from the Fauquier Artillery.[24]

Gordon directed the new battalion commander, Robert Stribling, to select "two detachments" from his own unit and two men each from other batteries in the battalion. Frank Hoffman was among them. The Rebels moved forward behind Gordon's lead infantry unit at four o'clock in the morning, scattering the unsuspecting Union defenders and capturing the fort with little resistance. Stribling had been assigned to man the abandoned guns and turn them on the enemy, a goal his artillerists briefly achieved until a massive counterattack drove them back. Simultaneous Rebel attempts to capture nearby Union posts were also thwarted, and the ill-advised assault had petered out by ten o'clock, both sides still holding their original battle lines.[25]

Lee's battered forces pulled out and headed west a few days later in a desperate attempt to save the army. Private Hoffman, however, was not among them, having been wounded so terribly in the March 25 attack that he was carried "in an unconscious condition" back to Petersburg, where the surgeon in charge believed he "could not possibly recover." The details of Frank's wounds elude us after 150 years. Several accounts, including the battery history and Stribling's personal memoirs, say that he was shot "in the throat," but his military service records describe the injury as gunshot wound to the left side of the head. In any case, all accounts agree with Stribling's assessment that he was now a "complete wreck."[26]

Frank Hoffman's service records note that he had a gunshot wound (G.S.W.) to the left side of his head. *www.fold3.com, Military Service Records for Francis W. Hoffman*

Frank was not even taken prisoner until Lee moved west on April 2. Union troops officially "captured" him at a Rebel hospital in Petersburg and transferred him to their own facility on the Virginia peninsula at Hampton, where his prognosis remained grim. According to the battery history, "Hoffman's family believed him dead for six months, until they received a letter from their son explaining that he was too weak to walk or work for money enough to pay for passage home." Against all odds, he had survived.[27]

A relieved C. W. Hoffman made his way to the peninsula to retrieve his second-oldest son, who was nursed back to health among the familiar surroundings of the family farm in Linden, but it was not until the miracle of a violent coughing fit several years later that Frank made a full recovery. "He coughed up a musket ball," wrote Stribling, who must have checked in on his former soldier regularly, "and immediately a rapid recovery set in, and now he is a hale, hearty man."[28]

Frank might not have been aware that he and his fellow artillerists were acknowledged for their battlefield gallantry in dispatches from Generals Lee and Gordon. Two days after the attack on Fort Stedman, Gordon wrote of the "admirable conduct" of a "select body of officers and men, under the command of Lieutenant Colonel Stribling," who "charged the enemy's breastworks with the sharpshooters of this Corps and at one turned upon the enemy the captured guns." Lee, in turn, wrote a similarly glowing note the next day to John C. Breckenridge, the Confederate secretary of war.[29]

But the plaudits of generals and high government officials meant little now that men were home and long-broken families were reunited. For the Hoffman brothers, whose distinctly American odyssey had taken them from Chambersburg Street in Gettysburg to Shepherdstown and the Confederate army, the dreadful sacrifices of war, including battle wounds and prison camps, were now behind them. With Frank's return, C. W. Hoffman and his three sons were together for the first time since Robert marched off to Harpers Ferry in April 1861.

"What a relief it must have been to feel that this terrible war was over," Ruth Hoffman Frost wrote, "and how blessed the family must have felt that all four of the men were home once more safe, even if everything was in confusion, things wrecked and devastated."[30]

After four years of bloody conflict, the Hoffmans took their blessings as they came.

Henry Wentz was the last of the Gettysburg Rebels to serve on active duty for the Confederate army. His capture at Harper's Farm, Virginia, on April 6, 1865, three days before the surrender at Appomattox, brought an end to the unique military career of a man who had fought as an enemy soldier in his father's front yard, had charged across nine acres of his own property at the battle of Gettysburg, and—perhaps most remarkably of all—had served dutifully for four years of a bloody armed conflict and was never marked absent, never wounded, never hospitalized, and never taken prisoner until the desperate final days of the Confederacy.[31]

Though stalwart and unflinchingly dependable, Henry never stood out among his fellow soldiers after rising to first sergeant in the first nine months of the war. He was never mentioned by his commanders in an official report and was briefly mentioned in two published battery histories only because "he still had family in Gettysburg."[32] A series of seven muster roll records after the battle of Gettysburg tells the story with striking simplicity:

> September 1–December 1, 1863: Present
> January–February 1864: Present

March–April 1864: Present
May–June 1864: Present
July–August 1864: Present
September 1, 1864–January 1, 1865: Present
January–February 1865: Present[33]

Attempts at record-keeping were largely abandoned in the calamitous Confederate spring of 1865, but we know that Henry was "present" again in March–April because his unit, Taylor's Virginia Battery, ran afoul of Union troops on April 6 near Amelia Court House during Lee's westward retreat from Petersburg and his desperate attempt to connect with other Rebel forces under Joseph E. Johnston.[34]

Taylor's Battery led the way, dragging its four guns across muddy roads at Amelia Court House and uphill over marshy ground to a level field, where they encountered an imposing force of Union cavalry under the dashing General George A. Custer. The battery's captain, Osmond B. Taylor, refused to surrender despite overwhelming odds, brashly firing a few rounds at Custer until "he himself was shot dead by Union gunfire." Fifteen of his men were captured, including Sergeant Wentz, whose luck had finally run out a few days before the end of the war.[35]

Henry was taken immediately to City Point, Virginia, and transferred on April 14 to the notorious Union prison camp at Point Lookout, Maryland, where he was detained for more than two months. On June 21, he signed the oath of allegiance to the United States (and was described as being five feet, eight inches tall, with a dark complexion, black hair, and hazel eyes). The army's defiant provost marshal general in Washington, DC, listed him on a "register of refugees and rebel deserters," albeit with a conciliatory note that homebound transportation was being "furnished to Martinsburg, Va."[36]

Thus did the war come to a stumbling, crushing end for four young men from Gettysburg who stood against the United States with hundreds of thousands of native Southerners in the Confederate army. However tainted the cause for which they fought, their personal fortitude was unsurpassed on any battlefield in American history. Robert Stribling, who commanded the Fauquier Artillery alongside Wentz's unit on July 3 at Gettysburg, offered a fitting tribute to the rank-and-file Rebel soldier:

> In this War, all reward a Confederate Soldier expected was that his manhood should be recognized, for love of home and of Country was his inspiration. Though he marched and fought with bare feet and tattered clothes, and with nothing but a small ration of corn meal and coarse pork for his diet, and with worthless money for his scant pay, he wrote, in the record of his acts, with what bravery and fortitude it is possible for manhood to assert itself.[37]

Now, finally, it was time to move on.

Fourteen

RECONSTRUCTION

enry Wentz returned in late June 1865 to a Martinsburg he barely recognized. It had been caught in the crossfire of two rampaging armies, control of the town changing hands thirty-seven times during four years of civil war.[1] Shops and small factories were shuttered; mills for making flour were ransacked or destroyed. A local history describes the troubled postwar situation:

> Farms were neglected because the men had been in the army, the slaves were gone, and there was no one there to work them. Many a home was fatherless, and many a home had a vacant place in the family circle. Those adhering to the Southern cause were the worst off, as they had to face defeat and were still considered enemies by those who had adhered to the North. The Confederate money was worthless, and those who had sold what few commodities they could spare from their own use and who had accepted

Confederate money in lieu thereof were in a bad way indeed, for they had lost commodities and money too.... Before the war many slaves had been owned by the people of the county, and these, of course, were now free, hence, each slave represented so much loss to the Southern soldier in money and in production.[2]

There is no record of Henry's activities in the years immediately following the war, but when he reappeared in the federal census in 1870, he had resumed his career as a "house plasterer." There is little additional documentation of his life, because he never married, never fathered any children, and never owned property in Martinsburg or Berkeley County. The modest success he had enjoyed in the Confederate military did not carry over into civilian life, where he appears to have been a misfit or at least a loner.[3]

His residence in 1870 was the Shenandoah House on North Queen Street near the railroad, whose proprietor, John Feller, advertised it as "the best Hotel in the State East of the Alleghanies [sic]. It is furnished in the most modern and elegant style, and in every respect compares with the best city Hotels."[4] Henry shared the boardinghouse with five other adult tenants—including a "cigar-maker" and "private school teacher"—and seven members of Feller's family,[5] and they were also joined by "travelers and sojourners."[6]

We do not know how often, if ever, Henry returned to visit his parents in Gettysburg after the war. There were occasions for family gatherings following the deaths of his father, John, in April 1870, his mother, Mary, in April 1871, and his sister, Susan, in January 1872. But it is almost certain that he made his final appearance in the Gettysburg area in March 1872, when, as "one of the heirs of Susan Wentz," he joined his brothers, Abraham and Peter, and their attorney, Jacob Beamer, to sell the family property.[7]

On July 1, 1873, the tenth anniversary of the start of the battle of Gettysburg, Henry invested fifty dollars—a substantial sum for a man of modest means—in the new Martinsburg Gas Company. As far as we know, it was the only such investment he ever made. He was one of eight investors, but there are no other records of his involvement in the venture.[8]

Sometime in the first half of the 1870s, Henry moved to the Everett House at 105 South Queen Street, where Stonewall Jackson had once made his headquarters during the war.[9] Here he died on December 10, 1875, apparently of complications from heart disease. The *Martinsburg Statesman* reported his death two days later:

Sudden Death—On last Friday night, Mr. Henry Wentz, a plasterer by trade, of this city, died very suddenly at the Everett House. He had been unwell for some weeks but appeared to be recovering. The day of his death he seemed as well as usual, ate a hearty supper, and at an early hour retired. Not being able to sleep, he arose and came down into the hotel sitting room and remained until about 11 p.m., when he again retired. Mr. C. Rice assisted him to his room, and was in the act of removing his boots when Mr. W. fell over and expired. Mr. W. was a brave Confederate soldier, and a good citizen. He was a native of Gettysburg, Pa., his father being the owner of the field on which that memorable battle was fought, in which Mr. W. was a participant. He was 47 years of age, and a member of the K[nights] of P[ythias] and Odd Fellows, which Orders escorted his remains to Greenhill Cemetery.[10]

Having no immediate family and no other kin in the Martinsburg area, Henry was buried in a plot owned by George Toup, who had

Henry Wentz's tombstone sits in relative obscurity at Green Hill Cemetery in Martinsburg. *Author photo*

been his employer and landlord in the years before the war, only a few feet from his old military commander, E. G. Alburtis. The solitary grave was largely forgotten until the 1990s, when Jim Clouse, a Gettysburg Licensed Battlefield Guide, with assistance from the Berkeley County Historical Society, discovered the weathered tombstone near the back of Green Hill Cemetery, on a gentle slope beyond the old mausoleum.[11]

Henry's will confirms the simple nature of his life after the war. Many items of his personal property were connected to his work as a plasterer—five buckets, four barrels, three shovels, two hoes, a pick, 140 feet of lumber, a hatchet, two screens, "sand," a pointing tool, and at least five boxes. The rest of his property consisted of the five shares in the fledgling gas company, a gold coin, a silver coin, and a fishing rod.[12] His possessions were sold in February 1876 at a public auction in Martinsburg, where one of the bidders was J. Q. A. Nadenbousch, the commander of Wesley's Culp's regiment at the battle of Gettysburg.[13]

———

C. W. Hoffman endured more of the hardships of war than most Virginia civilians, sending three of his sons into harm's way and serving hard time himself in a Union army prison. But he was an enterprising businessman even under the most brutal conditions, and he somehow managed to expand his holdings before the war ended, acquiring large swaths of farmland at nearby Crooked Run and in Orange County. Whatever his flaws, Hoffman was devoted to his family and used his wealth to give his sons a running start in their postwar business careers. His granddaughter Ruth Hoffman Frost writes in her family history:

> They now had to make a start to begin life over. I am sure it was no easy thing to do, and the country was years getting back to normal. Grandpa began to place the boys where they could try to get started in life. There was the farm of 600 acres at Crooked Run—here he placed Uncle Frank.... Uncle Wesley had his home at the farm at Linden—he farmed some but studied law.... Grandpa had another large farm in Orange County. Here my father [Robert] went to live. This was just at the close of the war.[14]

Despite these advantages, times were tough for all three Hoff-man sons. They struggled to make a living as fledgling farmers. In the late 1860s, C. W., probably under financial stress, tried to sell the Linden farm. He filed a lawsuit when the prospective buyer backed out—the opposing attorney was John Mosby, the "Gray Ghost" of Confederate cavalry fame—but the case slogged its way through various appeals, and in the mid-1870s, the final judgement went against him.[15] By that time, however, C. W.'s fortunes had changed dramatically.

"The farm at Linden began to look more prosperous after the long siege of war and neglect," Ruth Hoffman Frost writes.

> They had all kinds of fruit, plenty of milk and butter. Grandma would make cheese for market and would tallow candles. They had honey and preserves which she put up in stone jars. She would tie a cloth over them for it was before the time of self-sealing jars. Grandpa had a cider press and would make apple cider. We had chestnuts in the winter, and cherries dried.... Grandma would insist on having [my younger sister] take a nap in the afternoon and I would have to sit around waiting for grandma to come back downstairs. The big clock would tick lonesomely.[16]

C. W. was sixty-five years old by the time of the 1880 federal census and still ostensibly running the family farm at Linden. But his son Wesley, listed as a "merchant,"[17] was playing a larger role in the family's business interests, and it is likely that control of the farm was ceded to him by the middle of the 1880s. C. W. passed away at the age of seventy-four on November 13, 1889, having lived by all accounts a decidedly remarkable life.

The *Shenandoah Herald* briefly noted the death of Hoffman, "an aged and well-known citizen."[18] A fuller account of his life and final days appeared, curiously enough, in the *Gettysburg Compiler*. Although the Hoffman family had moved south from Gettysburg more than thirty years earlier, Wesley felt obliged to inform the citizens of his old hometown that a distinguished former resident had passed on. The newspaper's obituary and a paid memorial were printed together on November 19:

> Mr. C. W. Hoffman, a former esteemed citizen of Gettysburg, died at his residence, Linden, Va., on the 13th instant. He had many excellent traits of character and his demise is much regretted by his old friends here.
>
> IN MEMORIAM—C. W. Hoffman, for twenty five years prior to 1855 a resident of Gettysburg, departed this life at his residence in Fauquier County, Va., Nov. 13, in the 75th year of his age. He was very active and energetic up to the time of his sickness Oct. 19. He preserved his mental faculties almost unbroken, and though not able to speak much or distinctly, owing to partial paralysis of the tongue, yet he was able to indicate his trust in Christ for salvation. He was kind and indulgent as a husband and father, and faithful as a friend. W.A.H.[19]

C. W. and his wife, Sarah Ann Taylor Hoffman, who died in 1893, are buried next to each other in Prospect Hill Cemetery, Front Royal, Virginia, about seven miles west of Linden. The religious inscriptions on their tombstones are now worn away.[20]

―――

Wesley Hoffman recovered well enough from his thigh wound and wartime bout of syphilis to become a respected family man and a leading citizen in Fauquier County.

In 1869 he married Bettie Marshall, a distant relative of Chief Justice John Marshall. The 1870 census lists them as tenants of the "George Marshaw" family—probably George Marshall, Bettie's father, another Confederate veteran—in the first revenue district of Fauquier County, but it was not long before they took up permanent residence at the Hoffman family farm in Linden, where they raised their eight children. Unlike his siblings, Wesley never strayed far from Fauquier County.[21] He dabbled in local politics, like his father, and at one point was named an alternate delegate to Virginia's Democratic convention, but there is no record that he ever held elected office.

Surviving his father by only six years, Wesley was the first of the three Confederate Hoffman brothers to pass away, on December 2, 1896. He was buried near the family farm at Linden Church Hill Cemetery, where he shares a tombstone with his wife and five of his children—including "Atwood," his youngest child and namesake, Wesley Atwood Hoffman Jr.[22]

A fourth Hoffman brother, Charles William Jr., born in Gettysburg in 1849, had been too young for the war, but he found other adventures to pursue, eventually traveling to Texas and opening an iron works in Dallas. According to Ruth Hoffman Frost, "he began to write to Papa about the wonderful people, climate and prospects for business." She noted that "people in the East then looked on Texas as a wild country and not very civilized," but "Uncle Charlie pictured the country in such glowing terms—the winters were so mild we would not need a feather bed."

Meanwhile, the instability that had marked Robert Hoffman's army years continued to plague him in his postwar life. He tried farming, ran a "commission business" in Alexandria with his father, worked in a foundry, ran a store, and tried his luck as a clerk and a carpenter, among other ventures. In time, his brother Charles's enthusiastic accounts of Texas won him over, and in September 1876 he moved his growing family to Dallas.[23]

The decision, his daughter Ruth recalled, was met with folded arms and cold stares in Linden:

> Grandpa did not think so well of the venture, and mama was not very favorable to the idea of moving to a new country. She did not want to leave her mother, who was getting up in years and would not consent to leave her old home [in Shepherdstown]. There was much talking, for and against, I imagine. Usually the man, or rather the head of the house, makes the decision—mother feels she does not want to throw cold water on a venture. Mama always did her best at anything she felt was a duty, so she began to plan our clothing.... I am sure when we left our grandparents felt they would never see us again, which has certainly proved to be true.[24]

Charles tried to help his brother by arranging for a job at the foundry, but Robert changed careers several times and moved the family to multiple locations in Dallas over the next fifteen years.[25] He never seemed to find a vocation that fit. In 1891, taking advantage of a special land grant from the state, Robert moved his family 340 miles northwest to Armstrong County, in the Texas Panhandle, where he again took up farming until his health gave out. He described himself as "indigent," in "very poor health," and suffering from "paralysis" when he applied for a Confederate military pension in May 1901.[26] Robert died two months later, on July 14, and was buried in Claude Cemetery in Armstrong County.[27]

Robert's widow, Ellen Humrickhouse Hoffman, returned to Dallas shortly after his death and was living there in 1905 when she applied for a Confederate pension through the State of Texas.[28] The affidavits in support of her claim included a statement by Benjamin S. Pendleton—the same man who had informed Wes Culp's sisters of his death forty years earlier. "I first knew [Robert Hoffman] when he and his father removed from Gettysburg Penna. to live here [Shepherdstown] about 1856 or 1857," Pendleton said, "and I knew him from that time the balance of his life." He affirmed that he and Robert had enlisted in Company B in 1861 and, because the regimental band was often "near headquarters," had continued to see each other even after Pendleton was assigned as a courier on General Walker's staff.[29]

Ellen eventually received the pension, which supported her until her death in 1916. She was buried in Greenwood Cemetery in Dallas, far from her nomadic husband lying alone in his Panhandle grave.[30]

After coughing up a bullet and returning to health, Frank Hoffman married Anna Mary Hoffman, perhaps a cousin or distant relative, whose father owned a large farm next to Frank's property in Culpeper County, Virginia. They soon combined their assets into an enormous tract of prime farmland. "Uncle Frank seemed to be a successful farmer [and] had a general store with a post office," his niece wrote in her family history. "He reared quite a family, had eight children [and] kept a teacher in the house when the children were young."[31] He earned a sterling reputation as a farmer and a grocer, became postmaster of Crooked Run, and was a proud member of the local United Confederate Veterans Association.[32] He moved to Washington, DC, in the first decade of the twentieth century, living there with his unmarried daughters, Ruth and Maggie, until he died in 1920.

An obituary in the *Culpeper Exponent* offered surprisingly few details of his life and accomplishments:

> The remains of Mr. Frank W. Hoffman, formerly of Crooked Run, who died at his home in Washington, D.C., on Wednesday, Oct. 13th, will be brought to Culpeper to-day, Thursday, Oct. 14th, to be taken to Crooked Run for interment in the family burying ground at 3 o'clock at that place. The deceased is survived by 6 children, four daughters and two sons: Mrs. George Sparks and Mrs. E. C. Moser of Mitchells; Messrs. Charles W. Hoffman of Culpeper and Frank W. Hoffman Jr. of Crooked Run, and two daughters with whom the deceased made his home in Washington, Misses Ruth and Maggie Hoffman.[33]

The *Washington Times*, however, offered a more expansive account of Hoffman's life under the headline "Pennsylvania Man Who Fought for Confederacy Dead." His daughters likely provided the additional biographical details (and opinions):

> Francis W. Hoffman, veteran of the Civil War, and widely known in Culpeper County, Va., was buried Thursday in the family burying ground at Crooked Run, Va. Mr. Hoffman, who was a member of a prominent family of southern Pennsylvania, was born at Gettysburg, Pa., May 13, 1842. At the outbreak of the war he enlisted in the Confederate army, believing the cause of the South a just one.... [He] fought throughout the war and a few days prior to the surrender of Gen. Robert E. Lee at Appomattox Court House

he was wounded in an engagement at Fort Stedman. He was for many years a member of the United Confederate Veterans Association, but of recent years had been unable to participate in meetings of the organization due to infirmity. He was for many years in the grocery business at Crooked Run. Mr. Hoffman is survived by four daughters, Miss Ruth and Miss Maggie E. Hoffman, Mrs. Sparks and Mrs. E. C. Moser, and two sons, C. W. Hoffman and F. W. Hoffman.[34]

The last surviving offspring of the three Hoffman brothers who returned with the Confederate army to fight in their hometown of Gettysburg was Frank's beloved daughter Maggie, who died in July 1972 at the age of ninety-four.[35]

EPILOGUE

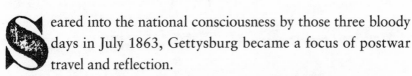eared into the national consciousness by those three bloody days in July 1863, Gettysburg became a focus of postwar travel and reflection.

As the little town's own soldiers straggled home from distant Southern battlefields to resume their lives, there was a noticeable pride among the citizens of war-torn Gettysburg. They had faced the fullest fury of the rebellion and had won.

William E. Culp returned to his wife and three young children on West Middle Street and to his prewar career as a carriage trimmer. Another veteran of the Eighty-Seventh Pennsylvania, William T. Ziegler, lived nearby and also worked in the carriage trade. Culp's brother-in-law, J. Jefferson Myers of the Thirtieth Pennsylvania, had worked as a printer before the war but now found new employment as a commissioner's clerk. Johnston H. Skelly Sr., Jack's father, who served briefly with the 101st Pennsylvania, returned to his role as one of the town's most prominent tailors.[1]

Rightfully proud of their role in the victorious Union war effort, these and other local veterans formed Post No. 9 of the Grand Army of the Republic, the national fraternal organization of Union veterans. They named it after their fallen comrade, Jack Skelly. One of the charter members was William D. "Billy" Holtzworth, who as a prisoner of war at Winchester had told his cousin Wes Culp about Skelly's wounding. The post quickly broke apart because of "political dissensions" but was re-organized in 1872 under the same name—Corporal Skelly Post No. 9 of the G.A.R.—and with Culp, Ziegler, Myers, Skelly Sr., and Holtzworth all serving terms as post commander, it occupied a position of great esteem in Gettysburg well into the twentieth century.[2]

By 1880, the post had outgrown its meeting room in a three-story building across from the Adams County Courthouse, so the trustees purchased the vacant Methodist church at 53 East Middle Street and remodeled it, pews and all, into a permanent home that still exists today.[3] A nineteenth-century chronicle of Adams County proudly described the new G.A.R. post room:

> [T]he walls...are all hung with fine pictures, comprising battle scenes, views of different battle fields, photographs of members of the post, and votes of thanks from the department of Pennsylvania G.A.R. and different posts of this and other States. The post owns a very fine collection of relics gathered from Gettysburg, and other battle fields. The commander's pedestal is made from a section of a hickory tree cut along the bank of Willoughby's Run (the scene of the first day of the battle of Gettysburg), with a Hotchkiss shell sticking in the center of it, and the top is a piece of dressed granite from the woods in front of Round Top. Another relic in the post room is a small cannon, weighing 150 pounds, with one and one-half inch bore,

made from one of the guns of Henry's North Carolina rebel batteries, which exploded during the battle of Gettysburg in front of Round Top. The post also owns the chair belonging to Gen. Ewell, and which he left in his hurry to get away from Gettysburg.[4]

There was a curious twist of fate in the conversion of the Methodist church into the G.A.R. hall that was perhaps lost on much of the post's membership. This was the same church where C. W. Hoffman had served as a trustee and had worshipped every Sunday with his family in the 1840s and 1850s. His humiliating punishment by the congregation following his assault on John Barrett had contributed to Hoffman's decision to move to Shepherdstown, Virginia, in

The Corporal Skelly GAR Post No. 9 remains a local landmark on East Middle Street in Gettysburg. It was formerly a Methodist church, where C. W. Hoffman and his family had worshipped. *Author photo*

1856—a move that resulted in his three sons' and young employee Wesley Culp's serving in the Confederate army.

In its new home on East Middle Street, the Skelly Post grew in visibility and stature. Few of its members were more passionate than William Holtzworth. One of the town's first battlefield guides, he helped shape Gettysburg's postwar image for tourists and distinguished guests, lending a soldier's credibility to his specialized personal tours. Although he was not an eyewitness—his capture at Winchester two weeks earlier had kept him out of the battle of Gettysburg—"his knowledge of the battle was widely respected and he spent many of his winters lecturing through the states. Among his guests on the battlefield were Presidents Grant, Hayes and Cleveland; [and] Generals Meade, Sheridan, Sherman, Hancock, Sickles, Warren, Slocum, Gregg, Hooker, Crawford and Longstreet...."[5]

William Culp was active in the post's early years until he moved twenty-five miles west to Chambersburg in the fall of 1874. A devoted family man and upstanding citizen, he continued to work as a carriage trimmer until he died of liver disease on October 12, 1882, at the age of fifty-one.[6] William is buried alongside his wife, Salome; his parents, Esaias and Margaret; his sister Ann and her husband, J. Jefferson Myers; his son, Loren; and Loren's son, J. Donald (who died in 1980), in the frequently visited Culp family plot at Evergreen Cemetery.[7] A nineteenth-century rumor that his younger brother Wes's body was found and secretly buried in an unmarked grave nearby was long ago refuted.

———

A house and several outbuildings stood on the John Wentz property for almost a hundred years after the battle, helping visitors understand the chaotic action on this key portion of the battlefield, but those buildings have been gone since 1960.[8] The two-acre lot near the famous Peach Orchard is all but vacant now, marked only by an iron tablet reading "Wentz House" at the northeast corner of the Emmitsburg and Wheatfield Roads and by an irregular stone foundation that likely dates to the house Henry's father purchased here in 1836; tourists flocking to the Peach Orchard today rarely give it a second look.

The history of the Wentz house, unfamiliar to all but the most ardent Gettysburg buffs, would be largely forgotten if not for the *Survey Report for Restoration and Rehabilitation of Historic Structures: Wentz Buildings*, published in 1956–1957 by Gettysburg National Military Park. The earliest known photos of the Wentz property were taken by W. H. Tipton in the 1890s, after much renovation and the erection of several regimental monuments nearby. The *Survey Report*, with its eyewitness accounts, therefore provides the most vivid and accurate descriptions we have of the structures as they existed during and immediately after the battle. It includes interviews conducted between 1938 and 1942 with five local residents who were alive at the time of the battle. Among them is Louise Weikert Bair, who reported that she visited the Wentz home often as a teenager in the 1860s:

> Mrs. Bair, 92 years old at the time her statement was given in 1938, was 17 years old at the time of the battle. She was a daughter of George Weikert and lived at the G. Weikert farm one-half mile east of the Wentz place. She stated that she was a friend of the daughter of J. Wentz (Susan), and often visited at the Wentz home. Mrs. Bair stated that the Wentz house was a small, one and one-half story structure of logs and weatherboarding, that it stood parallel to the Emmitsburg Road and on the location of the existing

house. The house, she said, had two rooms on the first floor. A dug well was located just north of the house. Mrs. Bair said the barn was located on or very near the present location, and she thought it possible that the existing barn was the original barn rebuilt.[9]

Charles Culp, a first cousin of Wesley and William Culp, who in his early teens lived with his family as tenants on the Wentz property from 1869 to 1871, agreed with Mrs. Bair's recollection that the house was "built of logs" and was a "one and one-half story structure, with rooms on the second floor." Perhaps his most intriguing description was that it was the "same shape" as the Lydia Leister house on the Taneytown Road, which served as the headquarters of Union General George Meade during the battle. Culp recalled that the house was later "remodeled and added to" by John Beecher, "who resided at the house in the 1880s. Mr. Culp said Beecher by trade was a builder of barns and covered bridges."[10]

The 1957 GNMP report says that "Beecher, upon his purchase of the house in 1877 or soon thereafter, razed the original house and built the existing two-story house of rough-sawed framing lumber, drop-siding and shingle roof. The frame lean-to on the east side may well have been added in the 1890s to serve as a kitchen,"[11] during a period when many historic features of the war-era property were lost or destroyed.

Morris E. Munshour purchased the property in 1900 and operated a grocery store in the smaller gabled structure, although he discontinued the business after two unsuccessful years and eventually lost his holdings in a 1906 sheriff's sale. The final individual deed-holder, Mrs. Mary Haller, sold the Wentz homestead to the government for $1,500 on May 18, 1908. The GNMP commission reported in December of the same year that "some of the buildings on the land, erected since the war, were taken down, others moved to a more suitable location, and the whole put in complete repair."[12]

Park officials apparently did not undertake their next detailed survey of the property until 1942. Tenants had been living there for much of the early twentieth century, and the buildings on the site, though not historic, gave visitors a clear and valuable sense of the obstacles faced by both armies along the Emmitsburg Road. Following the 1957 survey, when the house and barn were still judged to be in "fair condition," the GNMP recommended that "the buildings be maintained in their present status, but that necessary house repair and improvements be made to provide better living quarters. It is recommended also that the barn, the wood shed and the chicken house be maintained either for tenant use or for Park storage."[13]

The outlook changed dramatically over the next three years, however, and on April 29, 1960, the *Gettysburg Times* reported that the buildings on the property were to be destroyed:

> The National Park Service today announced it plans to sell the Wentz house on the battlefield for removal from its site on the Emmitsburg Rd., near the Peach Orchard....
>
> The park service has decided to dispose of the building because it is neither the original house that was on the site nor on the same location as the house around which soldiers fought in 1863.
>
> In addition...the structure, erected in 1885, has reached the point where it is no longer practical to repair it for habitation.
>
> The original Wentz house was a log cabin and located a short distance from the present structure which consists of an original house and a lean-to addition at the rear, plus several outbuildings.

Plans for the park service call for the placing of a marker showing the original site of the log cabin structure known as the Wentz House during the battle.[14]

The absence of buildings on the Wentz property since 1960 has made it difficult for tourists to grasp the challenges faced by Union artillery and the Second New Hampshire infantry as E. P. Alexander's guns pummeled them on the second day of the battle. Much of the action here is ignored. Only those visitors who park their cars at the nearby Peach Orchard and explore the ground behind the "Wentz House" sign are able to see the small stone foundation running parallel to the Emmitsburg Road, which the GNMP believes "is that of the war-period Wentz house"—the lone remnant of a long-forgotten structure that stood in the middle of some of the most confused and ferocious fighting on July 2, 1863.[15]

———

One hundred and fifty years after the battle of Gettysburg, a monument commemorating the story of Wesley and William Culp was dedicated in their hometown. In a shady patch of Steinwehr Avenue stands the unobtrusive Culp Brothers Memorial, next to a wayside marker inscribed "A Tale of Two Brothers." Its few visitors probably stumble upon it only after leaving the Gettysburg Heritage Center nearby.

Unveiled on July 6, 2013, the monument was erected by the Gettysburg-based John Wesley Culp Memorial Camp No. 1961 of the Sons of Confederate Veterans. Gary Casteel, the camp's commander and the monument's designer and sculptor, decided that William's image would face the North and Wesley's the South. The inscription salutes the "Culp brothers of Adams County, Pennsylvania, for duty, honor and sacrifice to their country, North and South."[16]

A monument to the Culp brothers was
placed in 2013 along Steinwehr Avenue in
Gettysburg. *Author photo*

The marker next to the monument is the best source in Gettysburg or anywhere on the battlefield for details of the Culp brothers' saga. It notes that "when Abraham Lincoln prophetically spoke
of a 'house divided,' he might well have referenced the sons of
Esaias Jesse and Margaret Sutherland Culp." There are inaccura-
cies, to be sure—the text asserts that Wes followed C. W. Hoffman
to Martinsburg instead of Shepherdstown in 1856, and it reinforces
the myth that he was killed "on his uncle Henry's farm...the famed
'Culp's Hill'"—but much of the information presented here aligns
with the family legacy. Noting that William is buried in the family
plot at Evergreen Cemetery, the account poignantly concludes that

This small sign marks the location of C. W. Hoffman's home and carriage-making operation on Chambersburg Street. *Author photo*

"Wesley's absence [from that plot] serves as silent witness to the personal cost of conflict."[17]

The only other public reference to the Culp story in Gettysburg is a sign between 117 and 119 Chambersburg Street reading "C. W. HOFFMAN HOUSE," marking the "last remaining building of the C. W. Hoffman carriage making complex." The text of the sign adds "Here worked Wesley Culp" and repeats the inaccuracy that he was "killed at Culp's Hill, his uncle's farm." There is no mention of William Culp, who worked at the complex with his brother, or of Hoffman's three sons, who also went south with their father and served alongside Wes in the Confederate army, the tangled family connections having been largely lost to history until now.[18]

E. P. Alexander, West Point class of 1857, returned to the military academy in 1902, the only Confederate alumnus invited to speak at its centennial celebration. Sharing the platform with various generals and President Theodore Roosevelt, the one-time Rebel artillery commander talked with passion about his vision for the future of a reunited nation. Given his role in battles against U.S. forces at Antietam, Chancellorsville, and, of course, Gettysburg, where he commanded Henry Wentz and Frank Hoffman, it was a remarkable moment in American history:

> The smoke of civil conflict has vanished forever from the sky, and the whole country, under the new conditions evolved in its four years' struggle, finds itself united in developing its vast resources in successful rivalry with the greatest nations on earth. Whose vision is now so dull that he does not recognize the blessing it is to himself and to his children to live in an undivided country? Who would today relegate his own State to the position it would hold in the world were it declared a sovereign, as are the States in Central and South America? To ask these questions is to answer them. And the answer is the acknowledgement that it was best for the South that the cause was "lost."[19]

Alexander was an astute choice to deliver such a message. A college professor and railroad executive in the years after the war, he had adjusted so well to postwar life that President Grover Cleveland chose him to resolve a border dispute between Costa Rica and Nicaragua in 1897. The onetime rebel had become a forward-thinking arbiter of national unity.

His extensive postwar writings, including *Military Memoirs of a Confederate: A Critical Narrative*, provide remarkably objective views of the war and clear-eyed assessments of Rebel commanders and battle plans.[20] And yet Alexander always had a soft spot in his heart for the common men in the ranks, whom he praised for setting "the world record for devotion" and for their valor in the face of staggering odds. "Shall I name to you at once the Confederate hero who deserves the highest pedestal, who bore the greatest privations, and contributed most freely of his blood to win every victory and resist every defeat?" Alexander asks. "I name the private soldier."[21] He continues:

> Practically without pay and on half rations, he enlisted for life or death and served out his contract. He did not look the fighting man he was. He was lean, sunburned, and bearded, often barefoot and ragged. He had neither training nor discipline, except what he acquired in the field. He had only antiquated and inferior arms until he captured better ones in battle. He had not even military ambition, but he had one incentive which was lacking to his opponents—brave and loyal as they were. Meeting him on the march, one might recognize in his eye a certain far-away look. He was fighting for his home.
>
> From the time of Greece to that of South Africa, all of history attests the stimulus of the thought of "home" to the soldier fighting for it. And if some young military scientist among your bright boys can formulate an equation to express the battle power of an army, I am sure he will find the thought of "home" to be the factor with the highest exponent.[22]

But does Alexander's description of Johnny Reb—an improbable warrior fighting in defense of his home—fit the Gettysburg Rebels, young men who grew up in the North but fought for their new homes in the South? Was their loyalty only a matter of geographical happenstance? Would Wes Culp and the three Hoffman brothers have joined the Eighty-Seventh Pennsylvania and fought to preserve the Union had C. W. Hoffman not moved his business south from Gettysburg in 1856?

They left no written records on the matter. Their reasons for enlisting in the Southern cause—slavery, independence, or simply the defense of hearth and home—can never be known for certain. But they do not appear ever to have repented for the role they played in the nation's greatest crisis, and their devotion to the Confederacy ran deep. Wes Culp's niece Margaret Myers wrote in her brief family history that Wes "had courage enough to take his stand with the South against the North."

Much of the country would never forgive the former rebels for trying to tear the United States asunder. "I am not indifferent to the claims of generous forgetfulness," Frederick Douglass wrote in 1884, "but whatever else I forget, I shall never forget the difference between those who fought for liberty and those who fought for slavery; between those who fought to save the Republic and those who fought to destroy it." Douglass would spend his life reminding his countrymen that "the armies of a gigantic rebellion came forth with broad blades and bloody hands to destroy the very foundation of American society." Any assessment of Confederate military valor, including that of the Gettysburg Rebels, must always be balanced by such a view.[23]

And yet E. P. Alexander looked at the war through a different lens when he spoke at West Point. Emotions were subsiding at the dawn of a new industrial century. Slavery had been abolished. The country was moving forward and starting to heal. His remarks were published in full by the *New York Times* and declared "decidedly the feature of Alumni Day," although, as one observer would put it, "not without controversy." Alexander referred to the rise of a "meteoric army, which over forty years ago sprang into existence, it would seem, our of space and nothingness...but, unsurpassed for brilliant fighting and lavish outpour of blood, vanished from earth as utterly as if it had been a phantom of imagination." He acknowledged the "many years of bitterness and estrangement between the sections, retarding the growth of national spirit and yielding, but slowly, even to the great daily object-lesson of the development of our country." He talked of lessons "rich in compensations" that have "proven to be only the birth-pangs of a new nation, in whose career we are proud to own and bear a part." But he always—*always*—praised the individual Confederate soldier for his unrelenting grit and verve.[24]

Alexander closed with a passage from "The Old Confederate Veteran," a haunting poetic tribute to young men who fought so passionately in four years of civil strife. The spirits of Wentz, Culp, and the three Hoffman brothers were among them as he spoke.

> The Old Confederate Veteran, we know him as he stands
> And listens for the thunder of the far-off battle lands.
> He hears the crash of musketry, the smoke rolls like a sea
> For he tramped the fields with Stonewall, and he climbed
> the heights with Lee.
>
> The Old Confederate Veteran, his life is in the past,
> And the war-cloud, like a mantle, round his rugged form
> is cast.
> He hears the bugle calling o'er the far and mystic sea,
> For he tramped the fields with Stonewall, and he climbed
> the heights with Lee.[25]

ACKNOWLEDGMENTS

Writing is the easy part. But what makes a book possible is the help, encouragement and critiques—especially the critiques—of countless people along the way.

Gettysburg Rebels was decades in the making. I visited Gettysburg with my parents as a young boy from Bellevue, Pennsylvania, and thought of becoming a history teacher in high school, but my interest in the battle was profoundly reignited by the release of the movie *Gettysburg* in 1993. It was based on the epic historical novel *The Killer Angels* by Michael Shaara, so it is only proper for me to start by thanking Shaara (and his son, Jeff, who has carried on the tradition after Michael's passing). They brought the battle and the Civil War to a new generation.

My literary agent, Uwe Stender, never blinked when I raised the seemingly crazy idea of writing a book about five young men who grew up in Gettysburg but fought for the Confederate army at the battle of Gettysburg. I had at least one other solid option for a book project, but Uwe told me, "No, I think you should do Gettysburg. You love Gettysburg." Agents are always right.

Alex Novak, associate publisher of Regnery History, believed in the concept from the start. We haggled over the subtitle for a bit (Alex won!) but otherwise were on the same page, and his expertise, support, and gentle guidance were essential and unyielding. The entire team at Regnery History has been tremendous to work with, but I owe special thanks to my diligent and tireless editor, Tom Spence, as well as Maria Ruhl, Nancy Feuerborn, John Caruso, Josh Taggert, Alyssa Cordova, Loren Long, Nicole Yeatman, Will Hudson, and others. What a phenomenal staff.

Three friends from the community of Civil War enthusiasts offered regular encouragement and much-needed critiques. Colonel Tom Vossler and Eric Wittenberg, Civil War authors who are experts on the battle, and Dru Anne Neil, a former executive at Gettysburg's Seminary Ridge Museum (and a former intern of mine!), read the manuscript and offered corrections and pointers. They devoted time on nights and weekends to keeping me on track.

Thanks also to Wayne Motts, licensed battlefield guide and CEO of the National Civil War Museum in Harrisburg, who offered advice in the early stages of my quest and volunteered helpful information on both Frank and C. W. Hoffman. Wayne and Jim Hessler, another battlefield friend, were the first historians to identify Rebel private Frank Hoffman as a Gettysburg native in *Pickett's Charge at Gettysburg: A Guide to the Most Famous Attack in American History*.

I am likewise indebted to Erik Dorr, curator of the Gettysburg Museum of History on Baltimore Street and a distant relative of Henry Wentz. Erik offered encouragement from the start and provided access to a treasure trove of Jack Skelly–Jennie Wade letters at the museum. During the late stages of the book project, Erik obtained the original photo of Wesley Culp as a Confederate soldier (copies of the photo abound, but Erik hunted down the actual photo from the early 1860s). It is now one of the many intriguing Civil War items on display at the museum.

No author can attempt such a project without standing on the shoulders of researchers who built the foundation of Gettysburg scholarship. Chief among them in my case was William Frassanito, whose books on battlefield photography—especially *Early Photography at Gettysburg*—provided unique and compellingly detailed outlines of the town and its residents. Frassanito was the first to identify Robert Hoffman as a Gettysburg native who fought for the Confederate army. *Early Photography* also offered the most complete details until now on the story of Wesley Culp and his relationship with Jack Skelly and Jennie Wade. I do not pretend to know Frassanito (although I've encountered him on occasion at the Reliance Mine Saloon in Gettysburg), but his work has had an enormous influence on mine and has contributed greatly to this project. He is a giant among Civil War researchers.

Benjamin Neely and his staff of enthusiastic volunteers at the Adams County Historical Society were most accommodating on my many visits to scour Gettysburg deeds, tax records, church records, and family files. The ACHS, of which I am a proud member, is certainly the finest small-town historical society in the country.

John Heiser, historian at Gettysburg National Military Park, provided access to park files on the Culp and Wentz families as well as photos of Wesley Culp and his gun stock. Anyone who has attended one of John's Gettysburg "battle walks" can appreciate the depth and breadth of his knowledge of the battle.

The professional and volunteer staffs at the Jefferson County Courthouse, Shepherdstown Visitor Center, Shepherd University Library, Berkeley County Courthouse, Berkeley County Historical Society, Fauquier County Administration Building, and the Library of Virginia (Richmond) were helpful and most patient with my repeated inquiries.

Brian Kennell, superintendent at Evergreen Cemetery in Gettysburg, provided the cemetery's background details on the Culp family and William Holtzworth (and sold me my own plot two rows in front of Wesley Culp's father).

Dennis Frye, chief historian at Harpers Ferry National Historical Park and author of the *2nd Virginia Infantry* regimental history, took the time to meet with me at Harpers Ferry and engaged in several informative email exchanges related to the John Brown Raid and Second Virginia research.

I had the pleasure of communicating with six Hoffman family descendants who supported my efforts. Martha Goshaw is the daughter of E. Murray Taylor, who painstakingly compiled the *Ancestral Record of Francis William Hoffman and Anna Barbara Esser*—an invaluable family resource for this project. "Dad would be so excited that his research was helpful," Martha told me. "I just wish he were still alive to see the book." Others who kindly responded to my calls and email inquiries were Lynne Ann Shalata, Joe Thompson, Karen Leeds, Marianne Grabowski, and Charlie Taylor.

And I owe a very special thanks to Michael Fahnestock, a direct descendant of William Culp, who graciously provided rare documents—two letters written by Wesley Culp in 1860, a letter that William Culp wrote in 1862 after visiting his brother as a prisoner of war, a hand-written (and extremely valuable) copy of *The Story of Wesley Culp* by Wesley's niece Margaret Myers, and assorted other archival family items.

My partner and dearest friend, Colleen Willison, helped to make it all happen with her love, support, devotion, and incomparable research assistance (she found more of the historic documents referenced in this book than I did). We now share a mutual affinity for the memory of Henry Wentz, a seemingly lonely soul who never married, never owned his own home, had no direct descendants and—sadly, in our eyes—lived out his post-war life in a Martinsburg boarding house. We count ourselves among the very few who have visited his gravesite at Green Hill Cemetery in Martinsburg.

If you ever make the trip to Green Hill and notice flowers on the hillside near Henry's tombstone, you can rest assured that Colleen planted them there.

BIBLIOGRAPHY

BOOKS

Aler, F. Vernon. *Aler's History of Martinsburg and Berkeley County, West Virginia.* Middletown: Forgotten Books, 2012.

Alexander, Edward Porter. *Fighting for the Confederacy: The Personal Recollections of General Edward Porter Alexander.* Edited by Gary W. Gallagher. Chapel Hill: The University of North Carolina Press, 1989.

Alexander, E.P. *The Great Charge and Artillery Fighting at Gettysburg.* New York: Firework Press, 1904.

Alexander, E.P. *Military Memoirs of a Confederate: A Critical Narrative.* New York: Charles Scribner's Sons, 1907.

Andrus, Michael J. *The Brooke, Fauquier, Loudoun and Alexandria Artillery.* Lynchburg: H.E. Howard, Inc., 1990.

Armstrong, Richard L. *7th Virginia Cavalry.* Lynchburg: H.E. Howard, Inc., 1992.

Black, Robert W. *Cavalry Raids of the Civil War.* Mechanicsburg: Stackpole Books, 2004.

Bradsby, H C., with Aaron Sheely and M.A. Leeson. *History of Adams County, Pennsylvania.* Chicago: Warner, Beers and Co., 1886; reprinted by the Adams County Historical Society, Gettysburg, Pa., 1992. The book was originally published in the 19th century as the *History of Cumberland and Adams Counties.* No overall author is listed, but, according to the preface, Bradsby, Sheely, and Leeson wrote and compiled the portion on Adams County.

Breidenbaugh, E.S., ed. *The Pennsylvania College Book 1832–1882.* Philadelphia: Lutheran Publication Society, 1882.

Brown, Kent Masterson. *Retreat from Gettysburg: Lee, Logistics and the Pennsylvania Campaign.* Chapel Hill: The University of North Carolina Press, 2005.

Busey, John W. and David G. Martin, *Regimental Strengths and Losses at Gettysburg.* Hightstown: Longstreet House, 1982.

Bushong, Millard Kessler. *A History of Jefferson County West Virginia 1719–1940.* Westminster: Heritage Books, 2007.

Carhart, Tom. *Sacred Ties, From West Point Brothers to Battlefield Rivals: A True Story of the Civil War.* New York: Berkley Caliber, 2010.

Casler, John O. *Four Years in the Stonewall Brigade.* Columbia: University of South Carolina Press, 1893.

Clemmer, Gregg S. *Old Alleghany: The Life and Wars of General Ed Johnson.* Staunton: The Hearthside Publishing Company, 2004.

Coco, Gregory A. *On the Bloodstained Field: 130 Human Interest Stories of the Campaign and Battle of Gettysburg.* Gettysburg: Thomas Publications, 1987.

Coddington, Edwin B. *The Gettysburg Campaign, A Study in Command.* New York: Charles Schribner's Sons, 1968.

Cullum, George Washington and Edward Singleton Holden. *Biographical Register of the Officers and Graduates of the United States Military Academy at West Point, NY, Nos. 1-1000.* Boston: Houghton, Mifflin and Company, 1891.

D'Alessandro, Enrica. *"My Country Needs Me," The Story of Corporal Johnston Hastings Skelly Jr., A Son of Gettysburg and Confidant of Jennie Wade.* Lynchburg: Schroeder Publications, 2012.

Davis, William C. *Battle at Bull Run: A History of The First Major Campaign Of The Civil War.* Baton Rouge: Louisiana State University Press, 1977.

Douglas, Henry Kyd. *I Rode with Stonewall: The War Experiences of the Youngest Member of Jackson's Staff.* Chapel Hill: The University of North Carolina Press, 1940.

Dreese, Michael A. *Torn Families: Death and Kinship at the Battle of Gettysburg.* London: McFarland and Company, Inc. Publishers, 2007.

Evans, Willis F. *History of Berkeley County West Virginia.* Westminster: Heritage Books Inc., 2007.

Field, Ron. *Avenging Angels: John Brown's Raid on Harpers Ferry 1859.* Long Island City: Osprey Publishing, 2012.

Figg, Royall W. *Where Men Only Dare to Go, or The Story of a Boy Company, C.S.A.* Baton Rouge: Louisiana State Press, 2008.

Frassanito, William A. *Early Photography at Gettysburg.* Gettysburg: Thomas Publications, 1995.

Frye, Dennis E. *2nd Virginia Infantry.* Lynchburg: H.E. Howard, Inc., 1984.

Guelzo, Allen C. *Gettysburg: The Last Invasion.* New York: Alfred A. Knopf, 2013.

Gottfried, Bradley M. *The Artillery of Gettysburg.* Nashville: Cumberland House, 2008.

———. *The Maps of Gettysburg.* New York: Savas Beatie, 2007.

Gwynne, S. C. *Rebel Yell: The Violence, Passion, and Redemption of Stonewall Jackson.* New York: Scribner, 2014.

Harpers Ferry Historical Association. *John Brown's Raid.* Virginia Beach: The Donning Company Publishers, 2009.

Hassler, William Woods. *Colonel John Pelham, Lee's Boy Artillerist.* Chapel Hill: The University of North Carolina Press, 1960.

Haynes, Martin A. *A History of the Second Regiment, New Hampshire Volunteer Infantry, in the War of the Rebellion.* Concord: Republican Press Association, 1896.

Haynes, Martin A. *History of The Second Regiment New Hampshire Volunteers: Its Camps, Marches and Battles.* Manchester: Charles F. Livingston, 1865.

Harrison, Kathy Georg, and John W. Busey, David G. Martin ed. *Nothing but Glory: Pickett's Division at Gettysburg.* Gettysburg: Thomas Publications, 1987.

Hennessey, John, *The First Battle of Manassas: An End to Innocence, July 18–21, 1861.* Lynchburg: H. E. Howard, Inc., 1989.

Hesseltine, William B., ed. *Civil War Prisons*. Kent: The Kent State University Press, 1962.

Hessler, James A. and Wayne E. Motts. *Pickett's Charge at Gettysburg: A Guide to the Most Famous Attack in American History*. El Dorado Hills: Savas Beatie, 2015.

Horwitz, Tony. *Midnight Rising: John Brown and the Raid That Sparked the Civil War*. New York: Henry Holt and Company, 2011.

Johnston, John White. *The True Story of "Jennie" Wade*. Rochester, NY: printed by author, 1917. (Reproduced by Google Books.)

Koleszar, Marilyn Brewer. *Ashland, Bedford and Taylor Virginia Light Artillery*. Lynchburg: H. E. Howard, Inc., 1994.

Krick, Robert K. *The Smoothbore Volley That Doomed the Confederacy*. Baton Rouge: Louisiana State University Press, 2002.

Laino, Philip. *Gettysburg Campaign Atlas*. Gettysburg: Gettysburg Publishing, 2014.

Maier, Larry B. *Gateway to Gettysburg: The Second Battle of Winchester*. Shippensburg: Burd Street Press, 2002.

Martin, David G. *Gettysburg July 1*. Conshohocken: Combined Publishing, 1996.

McDonald, William N. *A History of the Laurel Brigade: Originally the Ashby Cavalry of the Army of Northern Virginia and Chew's Battery*. Baltimore: The John Hopkins University Press, 2002.

Meredith, Frank, ed. *The Battle of Gettysburg As Seen by Two Teens: The Stories of Tillie Pierce and Daniel Skelly*. Schoharie: Savannah Books, Inc., 2010.

Merrill, Walter M., and Louis Ruchames. *To Rouse the Slumbering Land 1868–1879: The Letters of William Lloyd Garrison, Vol. VI.* Cambridge: The Belknap Press of Harvard University Press, 1981.

Mockenhaupt, Brian. *Three Days at Gettysburg: An Intimate Tale of Lost Love and Divided Hearts at the Battled That Defined America.* San Francisco: Byliner Inc., 2013.

Moore II, Robert H. *Miscellaneous Disbanded Virginia Light Artillery.* Lynchburg: H. E. Howard, Inc., 1997.

Murray, R. L. *E.P. Alexander and the Artillery Action in the Peach Orchard.* Wolcott: Benedum Books, 2000.

Musser, Clifford S. *Two Hundred Years' History of Shepherdstown (1730-1931).* Shepherdstown: The Independent, 1931.

Nasby, Dolly. *Images of America: Shepherdstown.* Charleston: Arcadia Publishing, 2005.

Pfanz, Harry W. *Gettysburg: Culp's Hill and Cemetery Hill.* Chapel Hill: The University of North Carolina Press, 1993.

———. *Gettysburg: The First Day.* Chapel Hill: The University of North Carolina Press, 2001.

———. *Gettysburg: The Second Day.* Chapel Hill: The University of North Carolina Press, 1987.

Porter, Burton B. *One of The People: His Own Story.* Printed by author, 1907. https://archive.org/details/onepeoplehisown00portgoog.

Prowell, George R. *History of the Eighty-Seventh Regiment Pennsylvania Volunteers.* York: Press of the York Daily, 1903; located at the Gettysburg College library.

Ramey, Emily G. and John K. Gott. *The Years of Anguish: Fauquier County, Virginia, 1861–1865.* Westminster: Heritage Books, 2008.

Redding, Nicholas A. *A History and Guide to Civil War Shepherdstown: Victory and Defeat in West Virginia's Oldest Town.* Lynchburg: Schroeder Publications, 2012.

Rodgers, Sarah Sites. *The Ties of the Past: The Gettysburg Diaries of Salome Myers Stewart 1854–1922.* Gettysburg: Thomas Publications, 1996.

Robertson, James I., Jr. *The Stonewall Brigade.* Baton Rouge: Louisiana State University Press, 1963.

Samito, Christian G. *Commanding Boston's Irish Ninth: The Civil War Letters of Colonel Patrick R. Guiney, Ninth Massachusetts Volunteer Infantry.* New York: Fordham University Press, 1998.

Schultz, David L. and Scott L. Mingus, Sr. *The Second Day at Gettysburg: The Attack and Defense of Cemetery Ridge, July 2, 1863.* El Dorada Hills: Savas Beatie, 2015.

Sears, Stephen W. *Gettysburg.* Boston: Houghton Mifflin Company, 2002.

Sheldon, George. *When the Smoke Cleared at Gettysburg: The Tragic Aftermath of the Bloodiest Battle of the Civil War.* Nashville: Cumberland House Publishing, 2003.

Speer, Lonnie L. *Portals to Hell: Military Prisons of the Civil War.* Lincoln: University of Nebraska Press, 2005.

Spruill, Matt. *Summer Thunder: A Battlefield Guide to the Artillery at Gettysburg.* Knoxville: The University of Tennessee Press, 2010.

Storrick, W. C. *Gettysburg, Battle & Battlefield*. New York: Barnes and Noble Books, 1994.

Stribling, Robert M. *Gettysburg Campaign and Campaigns of 1864–1865 in Virginia*. London: Forgotten Books, 2015.

Taylor, E. Murray. *Ancestral Record of Francis William Hoffman and Anna Barbara Esser*. Privately printed, 1980 (available at Dallas Public Library). Includes a section on Hoffman family history written by Ruth Hoffman Frost, daughter of Gettysburg native and Confederate soldier Robert N. Hoffman.

Trudeau, Noah Andrew. *Gettysburg, A Testing of Courage*. New York: HarperCollins Publishers, 2002.

United States War Department et al. *The War of the Rebellion: A Compilation of the Official Records of the Union and Confederate Armies*. Series 1, Volume 27, Parts I, II, and III. Washington, DC: Government Printing Office, 1889.

Wittenberg, Eric J. *Gettysburg's Forgotten Cavalry Actions: Farnsworth's Charge, South Cavalry Field and the Battle of Fairfield, July 3, 1863*. El Dorado Hills: Savas Beatie, 2011.

———. *"The Devil's to Pay:" John Buford at Gettysburg*. El Dorado Hills: Savas Beatie, 2014.

ARTICLES, PAPERS, AND PERIODICALS

Alexander, Edward Porter. "Letter from General E. P. Alexander, late Chief of Artillery, First Corps, A.N.V." *Southern Historical Society Papers* vol. 4. Richmond, 1877.

Barnett, Brett. "'The Severest and Bloodiest Artillery Fight I Ever Saw': Colonel E.P. Alexander and the First Corps Artillery Assail the Peach Orchard, July 2, 1863," http://npshistory.com/series/symposia/gettysburg_seminars/7/essay4.pdf.

Bellamy, Jay. "Brother Vs. Brother, Friend against Friend." National Archives.

http://www.archives.gov/publications/prologue/2013/spring/gettysburg.pdf.

Berkeley Journal, The. *Berkeley County in the Civil War*, issue 26, Berkeley County Historical Society, 2000.

———. *Martinsburg, West Virginia During the Civil War*, issue 27, Berkeley County Historical Society, 2001.

"Borough Elections." *The Adams Sentinel.* March 20, 1854.

Boteler, Alexander. "Recollections of the John Brown Raid by a Virginian Who Witnessed the Fight." http://www2.iath.virginia.edu/jbrown/boteler.html; Boteler's account originally appeared in *Century Magazine 26* (July 1883).

Broadhead, Sarah. *The Diary of a Lady from Gettysburg, Pennsylvania: From June 15 to July 15, 1863.* Not published; Sabin Americana, Print Editions 1500-1926.

Carrick, Samuel. "County Backgrounds: Wesley Culp, CSA." *The Gettysburg Times*, October 25, 1978.

Christ, Elwood W. "Charles W. Hoffman House." *Gettysburg Times*, February 15, 1988.

Collins, Darrell L. "The Jones-Imboden Raid." http://essentialcivilwarcurriculum.com/the-jones-imboden-raid.html.

"The Confederate Veteran: Address of Gen. E. Porter Alexander, Delivered on Alumni Day, West Point Military Academy Centennial,

June 9, 1902." Cleveland: Burrows Brothers Company. https:// archive.org/details/confederateveter01alex.

Culp, David A. "Gettysburg Culp Family Experience: Freedom, Civil War and The Battle of Gettysburg." *Gettysburg Magazine* 25, 94–104.

———. "Some Culp Family Members in the Civil War." *Adams County History* 4, article 3. http://cupola.gettysburg.edu/cgi/ viewcontent.cgi?article=1019&context=ach.

Fleming, George T. "The Homecoming of Wes Culp; Romance of Corporal Skelly and Jennie Wade Reads Like a Work of Fiction." *Pittsburgh Gazette Times*, November 9, 1913.

Gettysburg *Compiler.* "New Steam Mill." August 7, 1854.

Gettysburg *Star and Banner.* "Adams County Temperance Convention." February 25, 1848.

Gottfried, Bradley M. "An End to Innocence: The First Battle of Manassas." *Hallowed Ground Magazine*, Spring 2011. www. civilwar.org.

Guelzo, Allen G. "How the Town Shaped the Battle: Gettysburg 1863" *Gettysburg Magazine* no. 51, July 2014.

Haines, Joe D. "America's Civil War: Stonewall Jackson's Last Days." HistoryNet, June 12, 2006. http://www.historynet.com/stonewall-jacksons-death.htm.

Harman, Troy D. "The Gap: Meade's July 2 Offensive Plan." *The Second Day at Gettysburg.* Gettysburg National Military Park.

"The Insurrection in Virginia: Capt. Alburtis' Statement." *New York Herald.* Morning Edition, October 24, 1859, 1.

Jefferson County Historical Society Magazine. *John Brown Raid Issues 1859-2009*, Volume LXXV. October 2009.

Library of Virginia. "John Brown's Raid: Records and Resources." https://www.lva.virginia.gov/public/guides/JohnBrownBib.pdf.

Myers, Margaret E. "The Story of Wesley Culp." Unpublished. 1939. It was provided to the author by Culp descendant Michael Fahnestock. (Margaret E. Myers was the daughter of Ann E. Culp Myers and the niece of Wesley Culp. Fahnestock's collection includes a hand-written version and a typed version; much of the information is identical, but there are unique details in each.)

Nekoranec, Jacob A. "Cavalry on the Right! The Battle for Brinkerhoff's Ridge." *Gettysburg Magazine* no. 51, July 2014.

Pellechio, Vanessa. "The Culp Brothers Gettysburg Memorial Revealed, July 6, 2013. *Hanover Evening Sun* (reprinted by Baltimore Civil War Roundtable).

Smith, Karlton D. "To Consider Every Contingency: Lt. Gen. James Longstreet, Capt. Samuel R. Johnston, and the factors that affected the reconnaissance and countermarch, July 2, 1863." http://npshistory.com/series/symposia/gettysburg_seminars/11/essay4.pdf.

———. "'We drop a comrade's tear': Colonel Edward Lyon Bailey and the Second New Hampshire Infantry at Gettysburg." http://npshistory.com/series/symposia/gettysburg_seminars/9/essay5.pdf\.

Strilbing, Robert M. "From Markham to Appomattox with the Fauquier Artillery." Found in Emily G. Ramey and John K. Gott's, *The Years of Anguish: Fauquier County, Virginia 1861-1865*, 184–197.

Surkamp, Jim. "Strange Is Wes Culp's Way Home." Parts 1, 2 and 3. http://civilwarscholars.com/2013/09/videopost-strange-is-wesley-culps-way-home-part-1-of-3-by-jim-surkamp-2/.

United States Christian Commission. *Second Report of the Committee of Maryland*. Baltimore: Sherwood & Co., September 1, 1863.

Wittenberg, Eric. "Battle of Fairfield: Grumble Jones' Gettysburg Campaign Victory." http://www.historynet.com/battle-of-fairfield-grumble-jones-gettysburg-campaign-victory.htm.

There are also numerous excerpts from the Gettysburg *Star and Banner,* the Gettysburg *Compiler,* the *Adams Sentinel,* and the *Shepherdstown Register,* noted herein.

MILITARY SERVICE AND PENSION RECORDS
(National Archives and www.fold3.com unless otherwise noted)

John W. Culp, Military Service Records.

William E. Culp, Military Federal Pension Application.

William E. Culp, Military Service Records.

F. W. Hoffman, Military Service Records.

Robert N. Hoffman, Confederate Pension Application (submitted by Robert N. Hoffman).

Robert N. Hoffman, Confederate Pension Application (submitted by Ellen L. Hoffman). Alabama, Texas and Virginia Confederate Pensions, 1884-1958. www.ancestry.com,

Robert N. Hoffman, Military Service Records.

Henry Wentz, Military Service Records.

Johnston H. Skelly, Military Federal Pension Application.

OFFICIAL RECORDS OF THE UNION AND CONFEDERATE ARMIES

OFFICIAL REPORTS

Colonel E. Porter Alexander, CSA

Major James Dearing, CSA

Major B. F. Eshelman, CSA

General Edward Johnson, CSA

General Joseph E. Johnston, CSA

General William E. Jones, CSA

General Robert E. Lee, CSA

General James Longstreet, CSA

Colonel J. Q. A. Nadenbousch, CSA

General William N. Pendleton, CSA

Captain Osmond B. Taylor, CSA

General James Walker, CSA

ADAMS COUNTY HISTORICAL SOCIETY DOCUMENTS/FILES

Clouse, Jim. "Whatever Happened to Henry Wentz?" *Battlefield Dispatch* 17 no. 10. (October 1998): 6–10.

Culp, Karen. "Historical Background of Culp Family." Family File.

Gettysburg History of Town Lots (Research by Tim Smith and Randy Miller).

Letter from Charles H. Glaffelter, director, to Mr. Rollin L. Culp, May 11, 1991. Subject: Culp family.

Letter from Timothy H. Smith, research assistant, to Mr. James Lawrence, February 5, 1997. Subject: Culp family.

Memorandum from Harry W. Pfanz, Gettysburg National Military Park historian, August 11, 1961. Subject: Wesley Culp.

"Methodist Episcopal Church Records."

"Petition for the appointment of a guardian for Jacob David Hoffman by his mother, Anna Barbara Hoffman." April 30, 1834.

"Quarterly Conference Reports of the Gettysburg Circuit" (Methodist church).

Survey for Restoration and Rehabilitation of Historic Structures: *Wentz Buildings* (file also located at Gettysburg National Military Park).

RELATED DOCUMENTS

The Civil War in The Shenandoah Valley. http://www.angelfire.com/va3/valleywar/battle/61campaign.html.

Declaration of Causes of Seceding States, http://www.civilwar.org/education/history/primarysources/declarationofcauses.html.

Dickinson College, Full Text of Alumni Records (1787-1889), https://archive.org/stream/alumnirecord178700dick/alumnirecord178700dick_djvu.txt\.

"Family History of Hattie Grace Taylor-May," provided by Hoffman family descendant Joe Thompson.

"Gettysburg Borough Council Minutes, 1848-1860." Obtained from the Gettysburg Borough Office, East High Street.

"Historic Shepherdstown: A Brief History and Walking Tour." www. historicshepherdstown.com.

"History of Fauquier County Artillery." http://www.alexanders battalion.com/striblingsbattery/history.htm.

Library of Virginia, Department of Confederate Military Records, Unit Records. "Company B, 1st regiment of artillery, Wise Artillery, Alburtis' battery." Box 11, Folder 4.

Library of Virginia, Department of Confederate Military Records, John Brown's Raid Unit Records. "Alburtis Co. (Wise Artillery) 1859-1860." Box 46, Folder 2.

Library of Virginia, Department of Confederate Military Records, John Brown's Raid Unit Records, Infantry. "Regiment 55, Butler's company (Hamtramck Guards), 1859–1860." Box 46, Folder 24.

McCourtney, Donna J. "Descendants of Matthias Kolb—Ten Generations." www.genealogy.com.

McLaws, Lafayette. Southern Historical Society Papers, Volume VII.

Pennsylvania State Archives. "Commonwealth vs. Charles W. Hoffman, John Hoffman, William Graham," *Indictments presented by the Grand Jury, August Term 1854*. August 22, 1854.

Proceedings of the Pennsylvania State Temperance Convention. Harrisburg, PA, January 26-27, 1854. William F. Geddes, printer; Philadelphia, 1854. Found at www.books.google.com, via the Harvard College Library.

"Robert E. Lee's Report Concerning the Attack at Harpers Ferry." October 19, 1859. http://law2.umkc.edu/faculty/projects/ftrials/

johnbrown/leereport.html. Also included is Lee's written demand that John Brown's forces surrender.

Ware, Judy C. "Transcription of 1861 Letter to Josiah Ware from Captain E. G. Alburtis." http://www.waregenealogy.com/LetterFromAlburtis.htm.

Notes

Introduction

1. Marilyn Brewer Koleszar, *Ashland Bedford and Taylor Virginia Light Artillery*, 103; Robert H. Moore II, *Miscellaneous Disbanded Virginia Light Artillery*, 29–31, 35–39, 106; Jim Clouse, *Battlefield Dispatch*, Vol. 17. No. 10, October 1998, 9–10; author visit to Green Hill Cemetery, Martinsburg.

2. Koleszar, *Ashland, Bedford and Taylor Virginia Light Artillery*, 103; Moore, *Miscellaneous Disbanded Virginia Light Artillery*, 106. There is no record of Henry's birth, but both of these military histories list him as being forty-eight years old when he died in December 1875. That would make his birth year 1827. The inscription on his tombstone also has him dying at age forty-eight in 1875. (A newspaper obituary, however, says he was forty-seven.) Evidence that Henry was born in York County is persuasive but circumstantial. His father, John, was a native of York County and does not appear in the Adams County census until after 1830. He

did not purchase his Adams County property until 1836. At least one of Henry's siblings, Ann Maria Wentz, was "born in York County" (*History of Adams County, Pennsylvania*, 485). The same passage says John Wentz "came here from York County."

3. Adams County Historical Society (ACHS), *Survey For Restoration And Rehabilitation of Historic Structures: Wentz Buildings,* "Record of Conveyance of the Wentz farm," 9; Ibid., "Statements of War-period and Early Post-war Residents of the Wentz Property and Vicinity," 7–8; Adams County Deed Book BB, 281–82; Koleszar, *Ashland, Bedford and Taylor Light Artillery*, 103; 1860 U.S. Federal Census, Martinsburg, Berkeley, Virginia; *Martinsburg Statesman*, "Sudden Death," December 14, 1875; W.C. Storrick, *Gettysburg: Battle and Battlefield*, 90; www.fold3. com, Military Service Records (MSR) for Henry Wentz, First Regiment Virginia Light Artillery.

4. National Archives, MSR for John W. Culp, Company B, Second Virginia Infantry (Culp's given name was John Wesley Culp); as will be examined later in the text, Henry Culp, whose farm encompassed part of Culp's Hill, was not Wesley's uncle. He was actually a more distant relative—the first cousin of Wesley's father, Esaias.

5. Jefferson County (W.Va.) Deed Book 35 (1855–56), 374–75. On March 24, 1856, C. W. Hoffman purchased "a lot of ground in the town of Shepherdstown...on Princess Street and New Street," which contained "a two-story brick house, two-story shop carriage shed" and a "brick carriage house;" George T. Fleming, *Pittsburgh Gazette Times*, "The Homecoming of Wes Culp," November 9, 1913.

6. William Frassanito, *Early Photography at Gettysburg*, 370; Hessler and Motts, *Pickett's Charge at Gettysburg: A Guide to the Most Famous Attack in American History*, 61-62.

7. Edwin B. Coddington's *The Gettysburg Campaign*, which has stood for decades as the definitive history of the battle, does not mention either Culp or Wentz. Allen C. Guelzo's *Gettysburg: The Last Invasion* and Stephen W. Sears' *Gettysburg* each refer to Culp in just one sentence. Noah Trudeau's *Gettysburg: A Testing of Courage*, has two sentences on Culp. None of the latter three books mention Wentz. Harry Pfanz, in *Gettysburg: The Second Day*, referred to Wentz on 118. Pfanz also wrote four paragraphs on Culp in *Gettysburg: Culp's Hill and Cemetery Hill*, 328–29.

8. Pfanz, *Gettysburg: Culp's Hill and Cemetery Hill*, 328; Frassanito, *Early Photography at Gettysburg*, 370; excerpts from "Family History of Hattie Grace Taylor-May," provided to the author by Hoffman descendant Joe Thompson, along with other informal family history notes. C. W. Hoffman's sister, Sarah Ann, and her husband, Sampson Taylor, lived on the Wentz farm property in the late 1840s. It is mentioned that Sarah was doing housekeeping for the Wentz family (and therefore likely lived with her husband in one of the outbuildings). Her son, Charles Williams (probably named for C. W.) was born there in July 1848. Henry Wentz was still living at home in the late 1840s. It is probable that C. W. visited his sister and, therefore, was at least acquainted with Henry.

9. Margaret E. Myers, "The Story of Wesley Culp," unpublished, provided to the author by Culp descendant Michael Fahnestock; Fleming, *Pittsburgh Gazette Times*, "The Homecoming of Wes Culp," November 9, 1913.

10. Fleming, *Pittsburgh Gazette Times*, "The Homecoming of Wes Culp," November 9, 1913; www.ancestry.com, "Alabama, Texas and Virginia, Confederate Pensions, 1884–1958 for Robert N. Hoffman." Fellow soldiers Benjamin S. Pendleton and William Arthur each filed an "Affadavit of Witness" on behalf of Robert's

wife, Ellen. Pendleton wrote that "I first knew (Robert) when he and his father arrived from Gettysburg, Penna. to live here about 1856 or 1857." Arthur wrote, "I first knew him about 1857...he came here about that date to live here from Gettysburg, Penna;" Royall W. Figg, *Where Men Only Dare to Go, or The Story of a Boy Company, C.S.A.,* 142. Figg served in Parker's Virginia Battery, which fought alongside Henry Wentz and Taylor's Virginia Battery as part of Alexander's Battalion on July 2, 1863. Figg wrote in 1885 that another battery in their unit "took position near a farm-house, and one of the men went into the house and found his own father and mother crouching in the cellar." He almost certainly was talking about Wentz, who, legend has it, entered his boyhood home to find his father on the night of July 2. This story will be examined later in the book.

11. Robert K. Krick, *The Smoothbore Volley That Doomed the Confederacy* (eighteen pages excerpted at http://www.librarypoint. org/smoothbore_volley); Sears, *Gettysburg,* 141.

12. Guelzo, *Gettysburg: The Last Invasion,* 235; Karlton D. Smith, "To Consider Every Contingency: Lt. Gen. James Longstreet, Captain Samuel R. Johnston and the factors that affected the reconnaissance and countermarch, July 2, 1863," Gettysburg National Military Park, 104; Pfanz, *Gettysburg: The Second Day,* 106–7; Sears, *Gettysburg,* 253. According to Sears, "In point of fact, if Johnston's party went where he told Lee it went, there was no way it could have failed to see or hear at least some trace of the better part of two Yankee Infantry corps and two brigades of Yankee cavalry."

13. Guelzo, *Gettysburg: The Last Invasion,* 242–43; Wittenberg, *"The Devil's to Pay": John Buford at Gettysburg,* 161. Wittenberg writes, "The only reasonable conclusion is that in the darkness Johnston mistook nearby Bushman's Hill for Little Round Top."

National Park Service Ranger Karlton Smith, in "To Consider Every Contingency," 104, writes that, "It is this writer's opinion that Johnston did not get to Little Round Top as he claimed but instead was on the slopes of Big Round Top." Sears and Guelzo merely theorize that he was on some other hill.

14. Guelzo, *Gettysburg: The Last Invasion*, 238, 240; Sears, *Gettysburg*, 255, 258.

15. E.P. Alexander, *Southern Historical Society Papers, Vol. IV*, "Letter from General E.P. Alexander, late Chief of Artillery, First Corps, Army of Northern Virginia," March 17, 1877; Alexander, *Fighting for the Confederacy*, 236; Frassanito, *Early Photography at Gettysburg*, 249. Wentz has sometimes been identified as an ordnance sergeant. Frassanito was the first to correctly identify him as an orderly, or first, sergeant.

16. Storrick, *Gettysburg: Battle and Battlefield*, 90; 1860 U.S. Federal Census, Cumberland, Adams, Pennsylvania.

One: Invaders

1. Fleming, *Pittsburgh Gazette Times*, "The Homecoming of Wes Culp," November 9, 1913. Fellow soldier Benjamin Pendleton said, "We came in on the Carlisle Road and the head of the column turned left at the square;" ACHS, *Gettysburg History of Town Lots*, Lot 72E, Lot 71W. Hoffman's carriage shop and home were located on Chambersburg Street, just west of the intersection with Washington Street, which is a block from the square; David A. Culp, *Gettysburg Magazine*, "Gettysburg Culp Family Experience: Freedom, Civil War and the Battle of Gettysburg," map, 97; ACHS, Letter from Timothy H. Smith, research assistant, to Mr. James Lawrence, February 5, 1997; ACHS, Memorandum from Harry W. Pfanz, GNMP historian,

August 11, 1961. Wesley Culp's first cousin, Barbara Culp Stallsmith, lived on York Street.

2. David A. Culp, www.cupola.gettysburg.edu, "Some Culp Family Members in the Civil War," volume 4, article 3; ACHS, Memorandum from Harry W. Pfanz, GNMP historian, August 11, 1961; York County Deed Book 2N, 526–29, "Christopher Kolb to Peter Kolb," originally located in York County Grantee Index, Book K, 1749-1912. This is the deed for the 1798 transaction when Peter bought the farm from his father, but it lists every owner and sale of the farm up to that point. The farm at the time was located in York County; Adams County was not formed until 1800. "Staphael Kolb" bought the property from Robert Scott on May 6, 1787, and the original deed was recorded in York on November 13, 1787. Many family histories describe the farm as being 239 acres, but the deed describes it several times as "233 acres and two perches;" 1860 U.S. Federal Census, Gettysburg, Adams, Pennsylvania; Evergreen Cemetery tombstone inscription; Frassanito, *Early Photography at Gettysburg*, 125, 128; ACHS, "Historical Background of Culp Family" 2. "Upon the death of Peter, the farm passed into the possession of his son, Henry, he having previously leased it."

3. *War of the Rebellion, Official Records of the Union and Confederate Armies* (heretofore referred to as *OR*), Volume 27, Part II, 503–4. Although two other divisions of Richard Ewell's corps took more direct routes to Gettysburg, Johnson "countermarched my division to [Green Village], thence eastwardly, via Scotland, to Gettsyburg."

4. Donna J. McCourtney, www.genealogy.com, *Descendants of Matthias Kolb—Ten Generations*, Generation No. 2, 1-3; ACHS, "Historical Background of Culp Family," 2; York County Deed Book 2N, 525–29; Bradsby, Sheely and Leeson, *History of Adams*

County, Pennsylvania, 242. "Stophel Culp" is listed among the original taxpayers in Cumberland Township from 1799.

5. Culp, *Gettysburg Magazine,* "Gettysburg Culp Family Experience," 95; McCourtney, www.genealogy.com, *Descendants of Matthias Kolb—Ten Generations,* Generation No. 2, 1-3; www.ancestry.com, "Christophel Kolb in the U.S. and International Marriage Records" (her last name is listed as "Lintz"); ACHS, Letter from Charles H. Glatfelter to Mr. Rollin L. Culp, May 11, 1991; York County Deed Book 2N, 526–29. Samuel Gettys sold the property to Robert Scott in 1775; Bradsby, Sheely and Leeson, *History of Adams County, Pennsylvania,* 182.

6. York County Deed Book 2N, 526–29; McCourtney, www.geneaolgy.com, *Descendants of Matthias Kolb—Ten Generations,* Generation No. 2, 2; Adams County Deed Book B, "Christopher Culp to Peter Culp," 19-20.

7. ACHS, "Historical Background of Culp Family," 2; Adams County Deed Book KK, 161–63; Culp, *Gettysburg Magazine,* "Gettysburg Culp Family Experience," 95-101; McCourtney, www.genealogy.com, *Descendants of Matthias Kolb—Ten Generations,* Generations Nos. 2 and 3. Complicating matters, Wesley *did* have an Uncle Henry, but he was not the Henry Culp who owned the farm.

8. ACHS, "The Family of Christian Kolb;" McCourtney, www.genealogy.com, *Descendants of Matthias Kolb—Ten Generations,* Generation No. 3, 1–4; Bradsby, Sheely and Leeson, *History of Adams County, Pennsylvania,* 191, 242; Culp, *Gettysburg* magazine, "Gettysburg Culp Family Experience," 99; https://www.lds.org/scriptures/bd/esaias?lang+eng. "Esaias," the Greek form of Isaiah, is the version of the name used in the Authorized Version of the New Testament.

9. ACHS, "The Family of Christian Kolb," Esaias' birthdate is listed as July 12, 1807; Samuel Carrick, *Gettysburg Times*, "County Backgrounds: Wesley Culp, CSA," October 2, 1978. Carrick writes that "Esaias Jesse Culp was a class leader and a teacher in the Sabbath School of the Methodist congregation;" Frassanito, *Early Photography at Gettysburg*, 124-125. Many stories incorrectly list Wesley's birthplace as Gettysburg. Frassanito credits Elizabeth M. Tangen of the ACHS for his discovery. Wesley's exact birthdate has never been determined, but it was probably sometime in July 1839. A letter from Wesley to his sister in June 1860 references the Fourth of July and says he will be twenty-one "at about that time." He is listed as eleven years old in the 1850 census.

10. 1850 U.S. Federal Census, Gettysburg, Adams, Pennsylvania; Jay Bellamy, "Brother vs. Brother, Friend Against Friend," https://www.archives.gov/files/publications/prologue/2013/spring/gettysburg.pdf; McCourtney, *Descendants of Matthias Kolb—Ten Generations*, Generation No. 5.

11. Henry Kyd Douglas, *I Rode with Stonewall*, 251. Douglas, who was once captain of Company B of the Second Virginia, described Culp as "very little, if any, over five feet;" Bellamy, "Brother vs. Brother, Friend Against Friend."

12. Frassanito, *Early Photography at Gettysburg*, 124; Bellamy, "Brother vs. Brother, Friend Against Friend;" National Archives, Federal Pension Application for William E. Culp. William and Salome Sheads were married on September 27, 1853.

13. Clifford S. Musser, *Two Hundred Years of Shepherdstown History (1730-1931)*, 89. The unit was not renamed the Hamtramck Guards until after Hamtramck's death in 1858; Millar Kessler Bushong, *A History of Jefferson County West Virginia, 1719–1940*, 92, 290.

14. Musser, *Two Hundred Years of Shepherdstown History*, 81-84, 290; Shepherd University, Hamtramck Guards file, *Military Images*, "Antebellum Warriors," 46.

15. National Archives, MSR for John W. Culp; www.fold3.com, Civil War Pensions Index, William E. Culp; Dennis Frye, *2nd Virginia Infantry*, 1, 6.

16. Frye, *2nd Virginia Infantry*, 13-15; James I. Robertson Jr. *The Stonewall Brigade*, 39. There are various versions of this quote attributed to General Bernard Bee; S.C. Gwynne, *Rebel Yell: the Violence, Passion and Redemption of Stonewall Jackson*, 91-94.

17. Frye, *2nd Virginia Infantry*, 16-24; National Archives, MSR for John W. Culp; Fleming, *Pittsburgh Gazette Times*, "The Homecoming of Wes Culp," November 9, 1913; *OR*, Volume 27, Part II, 503.

18. *OR*, Volume 27, Part II, 503; Margaret E. Myers, "The Story of Wesley Culp." The unpublished six-page family history vignette was provided to the author by Culp family descendant Michael Fahnestock. The author first learned of its existence from Frassanito, *Early Photography at Gettysburg*, 126.

19. *OR*, Volume 27, Part II, 504; Frye *2nd Virginia Infantry*, 54.

20. Fleming, *Pittsburgh Gazette Times*, "The Homecoming of Wes Culp," November 9, 1913.

21. Ibid.

22. Alexander, *Fighting for the Confederacy*, 229, 235.

23. Koleszar, *Ashland, Bedford and Taylor Virginia Light Artillery*, 103. Wentz "moved to Martinsburg in 1852."

24. "Johan Frederick Wentz (1730–1768)," http://freepages.genealogy. rootsweb.ancestry.com/~footprintsfromthepast/wentz_varitrees_ phillip1709_frdk.htm. Another Wentz family genealogy says he arrived on the ship *Speedwell* in 1749, but both agree that he came from Germany to Philadelphia before 1750; "Family of Frederick

Wentz (1761–1824). According to the records of the St. David's/ Sherman's Church, Henry's father, John, was born on March 26, 1786 in West Manheim Township, York County (bordering modern-day Adams County); ACHS, *Survey for Restoration and Rehabilitation of Historic Structures: Wentz Buildings,* "Record of Conveyance of the Wentz Farm," 9. John Wentz purchased the property from Jacob Kefauver on April 1, 1836.

25. www.ancestry.com, U.S. Federal Census Mortality Schedules, 1850–1885, "John Vance (Wentz);" 1850 U.S. Federal Census, Cumberland, Adams, Pennsylvania; http://freepages.genealogy. rootsweb.ancestry.com/~footprintsfromthepast/wentz_varitrees_ phillip1709_frdk.htm. John had five children with his first wife, Elizabeth Sheely, who is believed to have died in 1823. He had four children, including Henry, with his second wife, Mary (no maiden name given). This information is also found at https:// alvispat.wordpress.com/wentz-john-frederick-jr/.

26. www.fold3.com, MSR for Henry Wentz, "Oath of Allegiance," Point Lookout, Md., June 21, 1865; Storrick, *Gettysburg: Battle and Battlefield,* 90; Frassanito, *Early Photography at Gettysburg,* 249, 370; *Adams Centinel* (advertisement), December 21, 1846.

27. Adams County Deed Book BB, 281. This deed is from 1872, when Henry sold the property to Joseph Smith, but it lists the chronological history of ownership. John Wentz bought the "nine acres and sixty three perches" on Dec. 28, 1847 and it was transferred "by deed of John Wentz to Henry Wentz" three years later.

28. Koleszar, *Ashland, Bedford and Taylor Virginia Light Artillery,* 103; Storrick, *Gettysburg: Battle and Battlefield,* 90; 1860 U.S. Federal Census, Martinsburg, Berkeley, Virginia.

29. Willis F. Evans, *History of Berkeley County West Virginia,* 112– 13, 119, 149–50, 274.

30. F. Vernon Aler, *Aler's History of Martinsburg and Berkeley County, West Virginia*, 210–11.

31. www.fold3.com, MSR for Henry Wentz; Moore, *Miscellaneous Disbanded Virginia Light Artillery*, 29; Evans, *History of Berkeley County West Virginia*, 113; William Woods Hassler, *Colonel John Pelham, Lee's Boy Artillerist*, 13–14; Tom Carhart, *Sacred Ties, From West Point Brothers to Battlefield Rivals: A True Story of the Civil War*, 88.

32. Hassler, *Colonel John Pelham, Lee's Boy Artillerist*, 21–24; Moore, *Miscellaneous Disbanded Virginia Light Artillery*, 30–31, 35–39; Aler, *Aler's History of Martinsburg and Berkeley County, West Virginia*, 232.

33. Moore, *Miscellaneous Disbanded Virginia Light Artillery*, 29. 34; Koleszar, *Ashland, Bedford and Taylor Virginia Light Artillery*, 5-6, 16; Aler, *Aler's History of Martinsburg and Berkeley County, West Virginia*, 233; Evans, *History of Berkeley County, West Virginia*, 157; www.fold3.com, MSR for Henry Wentz. Wentz was promoted on February 10, 1862.

34. Koleszar, *Ashland, Bedford and Taylor Virginia Light Artillery*, 6, 16, 97; www.fold3.com, MSR for Henry Wentz; Library of Virginia, http://edu.lva.virginia.gov/online_classroom/union_or_secession/doc/flegenheimer_ordinance.

35. OR, Volume 27, Part II, 429; Alexander, *Fighting for the Confederacy*, 221, 228–30, 235.

36. Ibid., 235.

37. Fleming, *Pittsburgh Gazette Times*, "The Homecoming of Wes Culp," November 9, 1913.

Two: A Man Called C. W.

1. Jefferson County, W. Va., Deed Book 35 (1855–56), 374–75. C. W. Hoffman completed his purchase of the property at the corner of Princess and New Streets in Shepherdstown on March 24, 1856; ACHS, *Gettysburg History of Town Lots*, Lots 72W, 72WN and 72E.

2. *Adams Sentinel*, advertisement, April 8, 1839; Gettysburg *Star*, advertisement, October 6, 1854.

3. Taylor, *Ancestral Record of Francis William Hoffman and Anna Barbara Esser*, First Generation. There are conflicting reports in family histories about the date of arrival, but Taylor found additional information to show that the Hoffmans' second child, Catherine Louisa, was born in Baltimore in 1817.

4. Ibid. Three other children were born in Greencastle, Pa., between 1820 and 1825; "Family History of Hattie Grace May-Taylor."

5. Taylor, *Ancestral Record of Francis William Hoffman and Anna Barbara Esser*, First Generation. The couple's eighth child, Barbara Matilda, was born in Baltimore on December 19, 1830. The Hoffmans moved to Gettysburg sometime between then and the birth of their ninth child in March 1833. The date of Francis's departure was only recently discovered to be May 25, 1833: ACHS, Hoffman family file, "Petition for the appointment of a guardian for Jacob David Hoffman by his mother, Anna Barbara Hoffman," April 30, 1834.

6. Taylor, *Ancestral Record of Francis William Hoffman and Anna Barbara Esser*, Chapter I. This is from the beginning of the section written by Ruth Hoffman Frost, granddaughter of C. W. Hoffman and daughter of Robert N. Hoffman.

7. Ibid., Second Generation; Gettysburg *Compiler*, "Marriages," September 13, 1836; Elwood W. Christ, *Gettysburg Times*, "Charles W. Hoffman House," February 15, 1988. Christ reported that "on June 26, 1837, Hoffman purchased 'Lot 2,' located on the west side of West (Washington) Street in what was known as 'Cooper's Addition.'"

8. www.livingplaces.com, "Gettysburg Borough," 12; Frassanito, *Early Photography at Gettysburg,* 2.

9. ACHS, *Gettysburg History of Town Lots,* Lots 72W, 72WN and 72E; Christ, *Gettysburg Times,* "Charles W. Hoffman House," February 15, 1988.

10. www.livingplaces.com, "Gettysburg Borough," 12; ACHS, *Gettysburg History of Town Lots,* Lots 72W, 72WN and 72E; Christ, *Gettysburg Times,* "Charles W. Hoffman House," February 15, 1988; Adams *Sentinel,* advertisement, "Valuable Real Estate at Private Sale," January 18, 1858. A note in *Gettysburg History of Town Lots,* referring to modern-day 105 Chambersburg Street, "makes it clear that this was late the residence of Charles William Hoffman."

11. Taylor, *Ancestral Record of Francis William Hoffman and Anna Barbara Esser,* Second Generation.

12. Gettysburg *Star and Banner,* "Adams County Temperance Convention," February 25, 1848. Students of history will note that two others in attendance were Johnston H. Skelly Sr. whose son, Jack would famously fight and die in the Civil War, and David Culp, the uncle of Wesley and William Culp.

13. Gettysburg *Star,* advertisement, July 24, 1846, 3; *Star,* advertisement, February 11, 1848, 4; *Star,* advertisement, February 8, 1848, 3; *Star,* advertisement, April 3, 1846, 3; Taylor, *Ancestral Record for Francis William Hoffman and Anna Barbara Esser,* Second Generation; 1850 U.S. Federal Census for Gettysburg, Adams, Pennsylvania.

14. ACHS, *Methodist Episcopal Church Records,* 17, 22, 25, 35, 36.

15. Adams *Sentinel,* "Ever Green Cemetery," April 18, 1854; www.kevintrostle.com/antebellum.html, "A Brief History of Gettysburg, Antebellum: 1835–1860."

16. Gettysburg *Star and Banner,* advertisement, April 23, 1852.

17. Adams *Sentinel*, "Borough Elections," March 20, 1854; Bradsby, Sheely and Leeson, *History of Adams County, Pennsylvania*, 192–193.

18. ACHS, *Quarterly Conference Reports of the Gettysburg Circuit*, 37.

19. Pennsylvania State Archives, *Indictments presented by the Grand Jury, August Term 1854*, "Commonwealth vs. Charles W. Hoffman, John Hoffman, William Graham," August 22, 1854.

20. Ibid.; Pennsylvania State Archives, *Indictments presented by the Grand Jury, August Term 1854*, "Commonwealth vs. Charles W. Hoffman, John Hoffman, William Graham," August 22, 1854.

21. Ibid.

22. "Gettysburg Borough Council Minutes, 1848–1860;" ACHS, *Quarterly Conference Reports of the Gettysburg Circuit*, 37.

23. ACHS, *Miscellaneous County Records*, "Retailers of Spirituous Liquors;" Gettysburg *Republican Compiler*, advertisement, April 21, 1851.

24. "Gettysburg Borough Council Minutes, 1848–1860;" Gettysburg *Star*, advertisement, "Ever Green Cemetery," October 20, 1854, 3.

25. Gettysburg *Republican Compiler*, "New Steam Mill," August 7, 1854.

26. Gettysburg *Star*, advertisement, March 23, 1855; *Star*, "Borough Account," April 6, 1855; "Gettysburg Borough Council Minutes, 1848–1860."

27. Jefferson County, W. Va., Deed Book 23, 278–79.

28. Ibid, Book 35, 373–74; Adams *Sentinel*, advertisement, January 18, 1858; Taylor, *Ancestral Record of Francis William Hoffman and Anna Barbara Esser*, Second Generation. Robert would turn sixteen on May 27, 1856.

Three: To Virginia

1. Nicholas Redding, *A History and Guide to Civil War Shepherdstown*, 14; Bushong, *A History of Jefferson County West Virginia, 1719–1940*, 15–16; www.historicshepherdstown. com, "Historic Shepherdstown: A Brief History and Walking Tour." Regarding the town's name, Bushong wrote, "The name of Mecklenberg ceased to exist officially after January 11, 1798, (but) the act merely put into statutory form what had been the practice for a number of years, as the name Shepherdstown had gradually become more popular than Mecklenberg."

2. www.inthepanhandle.com, "DAR Bee Line March Monument Rededication," October 24, 2012; www.historicshepderdstown. com, "Historic Shepherdstown: A Brief History and Walking Tour;" Bushong, *A History of Jefferson County West Virginia 1719-1840*, 27, 29; Shepherdstown wayside exhibit: "Spirit of 1775: Beeline March to Cambridge;" www. washingtonheritagetrail.org; According to a section on Morgan's Grove Park in Shepherdstown, "In 1989, the Secretary of the Army designated Morgan's Grove (where the Beeline March began) as the birthplace of the United States Army."

3. www.historicshepherdstown.com, "Historic Shepherdstown: a Brief History and Walking Tour."

4. Redding, *A History and Guide to Civil War Shepherdstown*, 16. Bushong, *A History of Jefferson County West Virginia, 1719–1940*, 82.

5. Bushong, *A History of Jefferson County West Virginia, 1719–1940*, 85–86.

6. Ibid., 97.

7. Jefferson County (W. Va.) Deed Book 35 (1855–1856), 374–75.

8. Jefferson County (W. Va.) Deed Book 35 (1855–1856), 374–75; Redding, *A History and Guide to Civil War Shepherdstown*, 62.

9. Sheffler, a native of Franklin County, Pennsylvania, would also go on to fight for the Confederacy in the Civil War. Two sources identify him as a carriage worker who traveled south with C. W. Hoffman in 1856, but no hard evidence has been found to place him in the Gettysburg area during this period. Neither tax records, census records, nor church records from the 1840s and 1850s support the notion that Sheffler or anyone from his family lived or worked in Gettysburg or Adams County. While he certainly was a native-born Pennsylvanian who moved to Shepherdstown and fought for the South, it is unlikely that he was a rebel who grew up in Gettysburg or had deep Gettysburg roots. Surkamp, *Strange Is Wesley Culp's Way Home*, Part 1 of 3, http:// civilwarscholars.com/2013/09/videopost-strange-is-wesley-culps-way-home-part-1-of-3-by-jim-surkamp-2/; 1870 U.S. Federal Census, Edinburg, Shenandoah, Virginia. Sheffler's birthplace is listed as "Franklin Co., Penn.;" Fleming, *Pittsburgh Gazette Times*, "The Homecoming of Wes Culp," November 9, 1913; Myers, "The Story of Wes Culp." Soldier Daniel Entler and Myers both identify Jerry "Shepler" as a carriage worker who traveled south from Gettysburg with C.W. Hoffman and Wes Culp. This almost certainly was the same person as Jeremiah "Jerry" Sheffler, who enlisted in Company B of the 2nd Virginia; Frassanito, *Early Photography at Gettysburg*, 369–70. Like the author, Frassanito found no reference to anyone named Sheffler or Shepler in any "local tax, census, burial and church records… in Gettysburg or Adams County during the antebellum period."

10. Musser, *Two Hundred Years of Shepherdstown History (1730-1931)*, 89.

11. Taylor, *Ancestral Record of Francis William Hoffman and Anna Barbara Esser*, Chapter I. This is from the section written by Ruth

Hoffman Frost, granddaughter of C. W. Hoffman and daughter of Robert N. Hoffman.

12. Fauquier County, Va. Deed Book 58, 257.

13. Taylor, *Ancestral Record of Francis William Hoffman and Anna Barbara Esser*, Chapter II.

14. Fauquier County, Va. Deed Book 58, 257.

15. Taylor, *Ancestral Record of Francis William Hoffman and Anna Barbara Esser*, Chapters II, III and IV. Ruth Hoffman wrote that "before the war he had his negroes, but later white help."

16. 1860 U.S. Federal Census, Southwest Revenue District, Fauquier, Virginia; Taylor, *Ancestral Record of Francis William Hoffman and Anna Barbara Esser*, Chapter I.

17. Dickinson College, "Full Text of Alumni Record (1787–1889)," https://archive.org/stream/alumnirecord178700dick/ alumnirecord178700dick_djvu.txt; Taylor, *Ancestral Record of Francis William Hoffman and Anna Barbara Esser*, Chapter I.

18. Frye, *2nd Virginia Infantry*, 107; Taylor, *Ancestral Record of Francis William Hoffman and Anna Barbara Esser*, Chapter I, Third Generation.

19. 1860 U.S. Federal Census, Martinsburg, Berkeley, Virginia. "Westly" Culp was listed as a boarder at the home of carriage maker John C. Allen. Culp's occupation was listed as "coach trimmer;" Brian Mockenhaupt, *Three Days in Gettysburg*, 24; Michael Fahnestock, Culp family collection, Wesley Culp letter, June 1860.

Four: Drumbeats of War

1. Tony Horwitz, *Midnight Rising: John Brown and The Raid That Sparked the Civil War*, 1, 24–25, 126; Harpers Ferry Historical Association, *John Brown's Raid*, 5, 32, 35. Counting Brown himself, the full group numbered 22 men. Three were left behind to guard weapons, so the attacking party was made up of 19.

2. HFHA, *John Brown's Raid*, 77; Horwitz, *Midnight Rising*, 127–29.

3. HFHA, *John Brown's Raid*, 33-37, 39; Ron Field, *Avenging Angel: John Brown's Raid on Harpers Ferry 1859*, 32.

4. Horwitz, *Midnight Rising*, 150; HFHA, *John Brown's Raid*, 42, 44.

5. Horwitz, *Midnight Rising*, 143.

6. HFHA, *John Brown's Raid*, 49–50, 79.

7. Ibid., 35.

8. Ibid., 43; http://www2.iath.virginia.edu/jbrown/boteler.html, Alexander Boteler, "Recollections of the John Brown Raid by a Virginian Who Witnessed the Fight;" http://bioguide.congress.gov/scripts/biodisplay.pl?index=B000653, "Alexander Robinson Boteler (1852-1892)."

9. http://www2.iath.virginia.edu/jbrown/boteler.html, Alexander Boteler, "Recollections of the John Brown Raid by a Virginian Who Witnessed the Fight."

10. Field, *Avenging Angel*, 45, 47.

11. HFHA, *John Brown's Raid*, 49; Special Report to the *New York Herald*, "The Insurrection in Virginia: Capt. Alburtis' Statement," Morning Edition, October 24, 1859, 1; Evans, *History of Berkeley County West Virginia*, 112–13, 149. Alburtis had commanded a local unit known as the "Martinsburg Blues" or "Independent Blues" as far back as the Mexican War; "Transcription of 1861 Letter to Josiah Ware from Captain E. G. Alburtis" by Judy C. Ware, http://www.waregenealogy.com/LetterFromAlburtis.htm. The evidence that places Wentz at Harpers Ferry in October 1859 comes from the files of the "John Brown's Raid Unit Records" at

the Library of Virginia in Richmond and from Moore, *Miscellaneous Disbanded Virginia Light Artillery*, 29, 97, 106.

12. Library of Virginia, Department of Confederate Military Records, John Brown's Raid Unit Records, Infantry, "Regiment 55, Butler's company (Hamtramck Guards), 1859–60," box 46, folder 24; Taylor, *Ancestral Record of Francis William Hoffman and Anna Barbara Esser*, Chapter I. In another passage of her family history, Robert's daughter, Ruth Hoffman Frost, wrote of "father being one of the number at the time of John Brown's Raid at Harpers Ferry."

13. Special Report to the *New York Herald*, "The Insurrection in Virginia: Capt. Alburtis' Statement," Morning Edition, October 24, 1859, 1; Field, *Avenging Angel*, 48.

14. HFHA, *John Brown's Raid*, 49–50; Special Report to the *New York Herald*: Capt. Alburtis' Statement," Morning Edition, October 24, 1859. Many accounts say that Alburtis' company numbered about thirty men. However, in his statement published in the *Herald*, Alburtis wrote, "I directed that twenty five men should proceed down the main avenue or center, that a like number should take the rear of the shops, and the remainder should proceed down through the shops the best way they could;" Field, *Avenging Angel*, 48, 52–54.

15. Special Report to the *New York Herald*, "The Insurrection in Virginia: Capt. Alburtis' Statement," Morning Edition, October 24, 1859, 1.

16. Ibid.; Horwitz, *Midnight Rising*, 166; Field, *Avenging Angel*, 49.

17. Horwitz, *Midnight Rising*, 166–72; HFHA, John Brown's Raid, 50–53; Jefferson County Historical Magazine, *John Brown Raid Issues 1859–2009*, Volume LXXV, October 2009, 26.

18. HFHA, *John Brown's Raid*, 56; Horwitz, *Midnight Rising*, 174–75.

19. http://law2.umkc.edu/faculty/projects/ftrials/johnbrown/
leereport.html, "Lee's Demand that Brown's Forces Surrender,"
October 19, 1859.

20. HFHA, *John Brown's Raid*, 57; http://law2.umkc.edu/faculty/
projects/ftrials/johnbrown/leereport.html, "Colonel Robert E.
Lee's Report Concerning the Attack at Harpers Ferry," October
19, 1859; Horwitz, *Midnight Rising*, 177–78.

21. Horwitz, *Midnight Rising*, 178; http://law2.umkc.edu/faculty/
projects/ftrials/johnbrown/leereport.html, "Colonel Robert E.
Lee's Report Concerning the Attack at Harpers Ferry," October
19, 1859.

22. HFHA, *John Brown's Raid*, 61–62; Horwitz, *Midnight Rising*,
184–86; http://law2.umkc.edu/faculty/projects/ftrials/johnbrown/
browninterview.html, "John Brown's Interview in the Charlestown
(or Charles Town) Prison, October 18, 1859."

23. HFHA, *John Brown's Raid*, 63, 68. Botts entered the Civil War
as captain of Company G of the Second Virginia Infantry (the
"Botts Greys"); Horwitz, *Midnight Rising*, 213.

24. Horwitz, *Midnight Rising*, 225–26; Field, *Avenging Angel*, 175;
Library of Virginia, Department of Confederate Military Records,
John Brown's Raid Unit Records, "Alburtis' Co. (Wise Artillery),
1859–60," box 46, folder 2.

25. HFHA, *John Brown's Raid*, 75, 100–103. Six of Brown's men
who escaped from Harpers Ferry were captured, tried, and
executed. Four of them—John Cook, John Copeland, Edwin
Coppoc, and an escaped slave named Shields Green—were hanged
on December 16. Two others, Albert Hazlett and Aaron Stevens,
went to the gallows in March 1860. Of the fifteen other men who
invaded Harpers Ferry with Brown, ten were killed or mortally
wounded during the raid (including Brown's son, Watson), and
five escaped (including Brown's son, Owen).

26. West Virginia Archives and History, www.wvculture.org/history/ jbexhibit/bbspr05-0032.html, "An Address by Frederick Douglass at the Fourteenth Anniversary of Storer College, Harpers Ferry, West Virginia, May 30, 1881."

27. HFHA, *John Brown's Raid*, 79; Field, *Avenging Angel*, 75–76.

28. Michael Fahnestock, Culp family collection, Wesley Culp letter, June 1860.

29. Ibid., Letter from Wesley Culp, August 21, 1860.

30. Gettysburg *Republican Compiler*, "Died" November 10, 1856. Mrs. Culp died on November 7, 1856, at the age of "about 48 years;" Frassanito, *Early Photography at Gettysburg*, 125. Esaias Culp married Martha G. Creager, "a woman half his age," on July 21, 1859. In the 1860 Federal Census for Gettysburg, "Jesse" is listed as fifty years old and Martha is twenty-seven. Living with them, in addition to daughters Ann and Julia, is a one-year-old male named Charles—meaning that Wesley may have had a half-brother he never met; Culp, www.cupola.gettysburg.edu, "Some Culp Family Members in the Civil War," volume 4, number 3, 12, note 22. "Julia went numerous times to Shepherdstown and Martinsburg to see him."

31. *Shepherdstown Register*, "Celebration of the Fourth of July at Shepherdstown," July 7, 1860.

32. www.findagrave.com, "Ellen L. Humrickhouse Hoffman." Ellen Louisa Humrickhouse was the daughter of Samuel Humrickhouse, who was Albert's brother; *Shepherdstown Register*, "Celebration of the Fourth of July at Shepherdstown," July 7, 1860.

33. *Shepherdstown Register*, "Celebration of the Fourth of July at Shepherdstown," July 7, 1860.

34. Ibid.

35. Ibid.

36. Bushong, *A History of Jefferson County West Virginia, 1790–1940*, 100.

37. Ibid.

38. http://uselectionatlas.org/RESULTS/national.php?year=1860, "1860 Presidential General Election Results." Lincoln received 39.65 percent of the popular vote; http://www.civilwar.org/education/history/primarysources/declarationofcauses.html, "The Declaration of Causes of Seceding States."

39. 1860 U.S. Federal Census, Gettysburg, Adams, Pennsylvania. Charles E. (Edwin) Skelly, age twenty, is listed as living with his parents, Johnston Sr. and Elizabeth. His occupation is listed as "painter," meaning carriage painter. Also living with the family was his younger brother, Johnston Jr. (known as "Jack"), age eighteen. Writing to his brother during the Civil War, Jack often referred to his brother as "Ed."

40. Fleming, *Pittsburgh Gazette Times*, "The Homecoming of Wes Culp," November 9, 1913.

Five: Confederate Recruits

1. West Virginia Archives and History, http://www.wvculture.org/history/civilwar/hfarmory02.html, "Destruction of the Harpers Ferry Armory," Extracts from Senate Rep. Comm. No. 37, 37th Congress, 2nd Session, 3.

2. Ibid.; www.virginia.org/birthplacepresidents/. The seven presidents from that time period who were born in Virginia were George Washington, Thomas Jefferson, James Madison, James Monroe, William Henry Harrison, John Tyler, and Zachary Taylor. Some, such as Taylor, were more closely connected with other states but were nonetheless natives of Virginia.

3. http://americanhistory.about.com/od/civilwarmenu/a/secession_order.htm, "Order of Secession." The seven states that had seceded

by early February were South Carolina, Mississippi, Florida, Alabama, Georgia, Louisiana, and Texas. The Confederate States of America was formed on February 8; Bushing, *A History of Jefferson County West Virginia, 1719–1940*, 102. Both delegates from Jefferson County (where both Shepherdstown and Harpers Ferry were located) were strident anti-secessionists.

4. Gwynne, *Rebel Yell*, 30.

5. Ibid., 30.

6. Ibid., 30; http://www.angelfire.com/va3/valleywar/ battle/61campaign.html, "The Civil War in the Shenandoah Valley;" West Virginia Archives and History, http://www. wvculture.org/history/civilwar/hfarmory02.html, "Destruction of the Harpers Ferry Armory," Extracts from Senate Rep. Comm. No. 37, 37th Congress, 2nd Session, 5.

7. West Virginia Archives and History, http://www.wvculture.org/ history/civilwar/hfarmory02.html, "Destruction of the Harpers Ferry Armory," Extracts from Senate Rep. Comm. No. 37, 37th Congress, 2nd Session, 4.

8. Taylor *Ancestral Record of Francis William Hoffman and Anna Barbara Esser*, Chapter II, Third Generation; 1860 U.S. Federal Census, Southwest Revenue District, Fauquier, Virginia; Surkamp, http://civilwarscholars.com/2011/06/shepherdstown-va-july-1860-drumbeats/, "Shepherdstown, Va.—July 1860," 3. Surkamp identifies John Hoffman as the proprietor of the "coachmaker shop" on Princess Street in 1860. The 1860 U.S. Federal Census for Shepherdstown lists Hoffman as the operator of a "coach factory." County records show that John did not become owner of the property until he purchased it from his brother, C. W. Hoffman, on December 30, 1867 (Jefferson County Deed Book 2, no. 66, 350)

9. National Archives, Military Service Record for Robert N. Hoffman.

10. West Virginia Archives and History, http://www.wvculture.org/history/civilwar/hfarmory02.html, "Destruction of the Harpers Ferry Armory," Extracts from Senate Rep. Comm. No. 37, 37th Congress, 2nd Session, 4.

11. Frye, *2nd Virginia Infantry*, 1–4.

12. Ibid., 4; West Virginia Archives and History, http://www.wvculture.org/history/civilwar/hfarmory02.html, "Destruction of the Harpers Ferry Armory," Extracts from Senate Rep. Comm. No. 37, 37th Congress, 2nd Session, 5.

13. Frye, *2nd Virginia Infantry*, 4–6.

14. National Archives, MSR for John W. Culp.

15. The text of a June 1860 letter from Wesley Culp to his sister in Gettysburg references the Fourth of July and says he will be twenty-one at "about that time." Assuming that he was born in late June or early July 1839, he would have been only twenty-one when he enlisted in the Confederate army in April 1861; Douglas, *I Rode with Stonewall*, 251.

16. Frye, *2nd Virginia Infantry*, 5; Douglas, *I Rode with Stonewall*, 6.

17. Frye, *2nd Virginia Infantry*, 6; Robertson, *The Stonewall Brigade*, 9.

18. Robertson, *The Stonewall Brigade*, 10–11; Gwynne, *Rebel Yell*, pp, 47–49, 52; Frye, *2nd Virginia Infantry*, 6; Taylor, *Ancestral Record of Francis William Hoffman and Anna Barbara Esser*, Chapter II; Fleming, *Pittsburgh Gazette Times*, "The Homecoming of Wes Culp," November 9, 1913. Interview with Daniel Entler.

19. Frye, *2nd Virginia Infantry*, 7–8.

20. Ibid., 9.

21. Douglas, *I Rode with Stonewall*, 6–7.

22. Frye, *2nd Virginia Infantry*, 9.

23. www.fold3.com, MSR for Henry Wentz; Evans, *History of Berkeley County West Virginia*, 157; Aler, *Aler's History of Martinsburg and Berkeley County, West Virginia*, 233.

24. Moore, *Miscellaneous Disbanded Virginia Light Artillery*, 29.

25. Hassler, *Colonel John Pelham*, 13.

26. "Transcription of 1861 Letter to Josiah Ware from Captain E. G. Alburtis" by Judy C. Ware, http://www.waregenealogy.com/LetterFromAlburtis.htm; Carhart, *Sacred Ties*, 88; Hassler, *Colonel John Pelham*, 13.

27. Carhart, *Sacred Ties*, 89; Hassler, *Colonel John Pehlham*, 14.

28. Adams *Sentinel*, April 24, 1861, 2; http://www.pacivilwar.com/cwpa02history.html, "History of the Second Regiment," originally sourced from Samuel P. Bates' *History of Pennsylvania Volunteers*, 1861–5.

29. http://www.pacivilwar.com/cwpa02history.html, "History of the Second Regiment;" Gettysburg *Compiler*, April 22, 1861, 1.

30. Adams *Sentinel*, April 17, 1861, 2.

31. Adams *Sentinel*, April 24, 1861, 2; Gettysburg *Compiler*, April 22, 1861, 2.

32. Adams *Sentinel*, April 24, 1861, 2.

33. Ibid., 2; Gettysburg *Compiler*, April 29, 1861, 2. On the same page of the *Compiler* was a story headlined, "Stand by the old Flag." It began with the first two lines of Francis Scott Key's "Star Spangled Banner" and followed with two sentences that summed up the national mood: "The darkest period in our National history has arrived, and we are now passing through the most fearful ordeal to which our experiment of popular institutions has ever been subjected;" Erica D'Alessandro, *"My Country Needs Me," the Story of Corporal Johnston Hastings Skelly Jr*,

50. The letter was addressed "May 1861" from "Camp Scott (York PA)." Copies of the hand-written Skelly letters are also found in the Johnston H. Skelly Pension Application at the National Archives, although those selected by D'Alessandro in her book are much easier to read; Gettysburg *Compiler*, May 6, 1861, 2.

34. http://www.pacivilwar.com/cwpa02history.html, "History of the Second Regiment."

35. D'Alessandro, *"My Country Needs Me,"* 52. The letter was addressed "June 16, 1861" from "Camp Spielman (MD)." Ed Skelly, who had returned to Gettysburg from Shepherdstown by 1860, was not part of the Second Pennsylvania but enlisted with his brother several months later in a new regiment, the Eighty-Seventh Pennsylvania; "Reports of General Joseph E. Johnston, commanding Confederate armies of the Shenandoah and of the Potomac, of operations from May 23 to July 22," http://www.civilwarhome.com/johnston1stmanassas.html, 2; Frye, *2nd Virginia Infantry*, 9.

36. Robertson, *The Stonewall Brigade*, 30; Gwynne, *Rebel Yell*, 49; www.battleoffallingwaters.com.

37. "Reports of General Joseph E. Johnston, commanding Confederate armies of the Shenandoah and of the Potomac, of operations from May 23 to July 22," http://www.civilwarhome. com/johnston1stmanassas.html, 2

38. National Archives, Federal Military Pension Application of Johnston H. Skelly The application included war-time letters that Elizabeth Skelly received from her sons, Jack and Ed. This letter was written by Jack on July 5, 1861 from "Martinsburg (VA), United States Forces." The spelling, grammar and punctuation in Jack's letter are corrected for reader clarity. He actually wrote, "but we where to late they had just left if we had a been fifteen minutes sooner we might had a chance at them." Earlier in the letter, referring to members of the Rebel army, he wrote, "we saw some of the secession riding around."

39. Ibid.

Six: "Like a Stone Wall"

1. Taylor, *Ancestral Record of Francis William Hoffman and Anna Barbara Esser*, Second Generation. Francis William was born on May 13, 1842. C. W. Hoffman's first-born son died at the age of five, so Francis William was the second-oldest "surviving" son.

2. Michael Andrus, *The Brooke, Fauquier, Loudoun and Alexandria Artillery*, 60; Emily G. Ramey and John K. Gott, *The Years of Anguish: Fauquier County, Virginia 1861–1865*, 184; National Archives, MSR for Francis W. Hoffman.

3. Andrus, *The Brooke, Fauquier, Loudoun and Alexandria Artillery*, 60; http://www.alexandersbattalion.com/striblingsbattery/history.htm, "History of Fauquier Artillery, C.S.A."

4. Ramy and Gott, *The Years of Anguish*, 184; Andrus, *The Brooke, Fauquier, Loudoun and Alexandria Artillery*, 60.

5. Andrus, *The Brooke, Fauquier, Loudoun and Alexandria Artillery*, 61.

6. Ibid., 61; http://www.alexandersbattalion.com/striblingsbattery/history.htm, "History of Fauquier Artillery, C.S.A.:" National Archives, MSR for Francis W. Hoffman.

7. Andrus, *The Brooke, Fauquier, Loudoun and Alexandria Artillery*, 61.

8. Gwynne, *Rebel Yell*, 63; Robertson, *The Stonewall Brigade*, 35; Bradley M. Gottfried, http://www.civilwar.org/hallowed-ground-magazine/spring-2011/an-end-to-innocence.html, *Hallowed Ground Magazine*, "An End to Innocence: The First Battle of

Manassas," Spring 2011. Union troops under Daniel Tyler confronted a Confederate force under James Longstreet.

9. Gwynne, *Rebel Yell*, 64.
10. https://www.nps.gov/mana/learn/historyculture/first-manassas. htm, "The Battle of First Manassas;" http://www.civilwarhome. com/bullruncampaign.html, Report of General P.G.T. Beauregard; Gottfried, http://www.civilwar.org/hallowed-ground-magazine/ spring-2011/an-end-to-innocence.html, *Hallowed Ground Magazine*, "An End to Innocence: The First Battle of Manassas."
11. Frye, *2nd Virginia Infantry*, 11–12.
12. https://www.nps.gov/mana/learn/historyculture/first-manassas. htm, "The Battle of First Manassas;" Gwynne, *Rebel Yell*, 79; Frye, *2nd Virginia Infantry*, 12.
13. Robertson, The Stonewall Brigade, 37; http://www.civilwarhome. com/bullruncampaign.html, Report of General P. G. T. Beauregard."
14. Robertson, *The Stonewall Brigade*, 39. This is the most commonly recounted version of Bee's cry, although others differ slightly. S. C. Gwynne, in *Rebel Yell*, used, "Yonder stands Jackson like a stone wall. Let's go to his assistance." Henry Kyd Douglas, a soldier in the Second Virginia who later served on Jackson's staff, thought Bee was referring to the brigade as a whole and not just its commander. He quoted Bee as saying, "Look, there is Jackson's brigade standing behind you like a stone wall."
15. Robertson, *The Stonewall Brigade*, 39; Gwynne, *Rebel Yell*, 88.
16. Frye, *2nd Virginia Infantry*, 14–15.
17. Douglas, *I Rode with Stonewall*, 11. Douglas admitted that "I am surprised that I cannot remember any of my sensations during that turmoil, but I have a vague recollection of personal discomfort and apprehension." Jackson had been promoted from colonel to brigadier general shortly before the battle."

18. https://www.nps.gov/mana/learn/historyculture/first-manassas. htm, "The Battle of First Manassas;" Gwynne, *Rebel Yell*, 93.

19. Gwynne, *Rebel Yell*, 97–98; Frye, *2nd Virginia Infantry*, 15.

20. Moore, *Miscellaneous Disbanded Virginia Light Artillery*, 30; Hassler, *Colonel John Pelham*, 18.

21. Hassler, *Colonel John Pelham*, 21; Moore, *Miscellaneous Disbanded Virginia Light Artillery*, 31.

22. http://www.civilwarhome.com/bullruncampaign.html, Report of General P.G.T. Beauregard;" Robertson, *The Stonewall Brigade*, 44.

23. National Archives, Federal Military Pension Application for Johnston H. Skelly, Jack Skelly letters. This letter was addressed from Bunker Hill, Virginia on July 16, 1861; Gwynne, *Rebel Yell*, 60, 63. Gwynne described Patterson's reluctance to follow orders and prevent Johnston from connecting with Beauregard as "one of the great military blunders of the Civil War. It very likely altered the course of the war and, in any case, profoundly changed the lives of Thomas J. Jackson and his Virginia brigade."

24. National Archives, Military Federal Pension Application for Johnston H. Skelly, Jack Skelly letters.

25. Gwynne, *Rebel Yell*, 60, 62–63.

26. http://www.pacivilwar.com/cwpa02e.html, "Pa. Civil War Volunteer Soldiers, Second Regiment, Company E;" National Archives, MSR for William E. Culp; http://www.pa-roots.com/ pacw/infantry/87th/87thorg.html, "87th Regiment Pennsylvania Volunteers; www.fold3.com, Civil War Pensions Index for Charles E. Skelly; http://www.pa-roots.com/pacw/ infantry/87th/87thcof.html; Culp, www.cupola.gettysburg.edu, "Some Culp Family Members in the Civil War," volume 4, article 3, 5.

27. George R. Prowell, *History of the Eighty-Seventh Regiment Pennsylvania Volunteers*, 14–16; http://www.pacivilwar.com/cwpa87history.html, "87th PA Regiment History."

28. www.fold3.com, MSR for Robert N. Hoffman. He was captured "near Spotsylvania C.H." on "May 12, 1864." He signed his oath of allegiance on May 29, 1865, identified as "R. N. Hoffman of Co. B, 2nd Va. Infantry."

29. Ibid., Company Muster Rolls for July–August and November–December, 1861. He also was listed as "absent without leave from Sept. 1 to Oct. 16, 1861" in the September–October muster roll.

30. www.fauquiercivilwar.com/history.html; www.fold3.com, Confederate Citizens File, Chas. W. Hoffman. There are numerous receipts documenting transactions between C. W. Hoffman and the Confederate army. The first is dated July 25, 1861, shortly after the First Battle of Manassas, for "services of 2 teams (2 horses) for 1 day at $3 per day and for 7 days at $2.50 per day;" Taylor, *Ancestral Record for Francis William Hoffman and Anna Barbara Esser*, Chapter II. Ruth Hoffman Frost wrote of her parents that "after they were married, he took her to his home at Linden for he knew he would be able to see her more often during the war, for both armies would be passing in that location—he would have had to cross the lines had she stayed in her hometown."

31. Frye, *2nd Virginia Infantry*, 19; www.fold3.com, MSR for Robert N. Hoffman.

32. www.fold3.com, MSR for Wesley A. Hoffman; Taylor, *Ancestral Record for Francis William Hoffman and Anna Barbara Esser*, Chapter III.

33. Ibid., Chapter III.

34. Ibid., Chapter III.

35. www.fold3.com, MSR for Robert N. Hoffman, Company Muster Roll, November–December 1862. Robert was "detailed as assistant in Commissary 2 Regt. Va. Volunteers Sept. 1862.

36. Ibid. Company Muster Roll, May–June 1863, "Detailed to Drive Cattle by order Gen. Walker June 14, 1863;" Confederate Citizens File, Robert N. Hoffman; Company Muster Roll, November–December 1863. Robert was "detailed musician in 2nd Regt. Band Dec. 9, 1863."

Seven: 1862: Year of Turmoil

1. Gwynne, *Rebel Yell*, 175.

2. John O. Casler, *Four Years in the Stonewall Brigade*, 57; Douglas, *I Rode with Stonewall*, 15.

3. Douglas, *I Rode with Stonewall*, 15–16.

4. Ibid., 16.

5. Ibid., 16–17. Douglas called the speech "the only one [Jackson] ever made during the war." In the absence of any newspaper correspondents, he thought it prudent to record the general's rare remarks. "Within fifteen minutes after the foregoing speech of General Jackson was made, it was carefully written out in my tent by Sergeant T. Harris Towner of my company and myself," Douglas said. "We wrote it out from memory, comparing our recollections of every word until we thought it absolutely accurate." Douglas then sent a copy of the speech to the *Richmond Dispatch*, and various versions have found their way into history.

6. Robertson, *The Stonewall Brigade*, 50.

7. Ibid., 50.

8. Ibid., 69–71; http://stonewall.hut.ru/reports/jackson_rep_kern. htm, "The Battle of Kernstown—Reports of Thomas J. Jackson, C.S. Army, commanding the Valley District." On Friday, March 21, Jackson received reports that made him "apprehensive that the Federals would leave this military district." On March 23, he learned "from a reliable source that the Federals were sending off their stores and troops from Winchester." He also heard "from a source which had been remarkable in its reliability that the enemy's force at Winchester did not exceed four regiments;" Frye, *2nd Virginia Infantry*, 21.

9. Frye, *2nd Virginia Infantry*, 21; http://www.kernstownbattle.org/kernstownhistory/firstbattleofkernstown.html. Jackson's force of just over 3,000 men faced a Union army that numbered more than 8,000; Gwynne, *Rebel Yell*, 219–20.

10. Robertson, *The Stonewall Brigade*, 73; Frye, *2nd Virginia Infantry*, 23; Gwynne, *Rebel Yell*, 223. Gwynne wrote of "the astounding tale of the regimental flag of the 2nd Virginia Regiment."

11. Gwynne, *Rebel Yell*, 226.

12. Robertson, *The Stonewall Brigade*, 78; http://www.encyclopediavirginia.org/garnett_richard_b_1817-1863.

13. Robertson, *The Stonewall Brigade*, 76; Frye, *2nd Virginia Infantry*, 23–24. It should be noted that Frye found different casualty totals among the soldiers' compiled military service records. Such discrepancies, often due to incomplete or inaccurate record-keeping immediately after battles, represent one of the great challenges of Civil War research.

14. Frye, *2nd Virginia Infantry*, 23.

15. National Archives, MSR for John W. Culp, Company Muster Roll, June 30 to Oct. 31, 1862. Culp was listed as "absent on furlough" on the muster roll for January-February 1862. The regiment first recorded that he was "taken prisoner while absent on furlough" in the March-April muster roll; Frye, *2nd Virginia Infantry*, 24.

16. www.fold3.com, MSR for John W. Culp. Culp signed a receipt from "The Confederate States" for "rations whilst on furlough from the 11th day of February to the 13th day of March 1862. Thirty two days at 23 (cents) per day." It was received in October 1862 (and though it was actually thirty-one days on the calendar, the receipt said "thirty two days;" Robertson, *The Stonewall Brigade*, 68; Surkamp, "Strange is Wesley Culp's Way Home, Part 2," http://civilwarscholars.com/2013/09/videopost-strange-is-wesley-culps-way-home-part-2-of-3-by-jim-surkamp/

17. Frye, *2nd Virginia Infantry*, 24; Myers, "The Story of Wesley Culp;" Fleming, *Pittsburgh Gazette Times*, "The Homecoming of Wes Culp," November 9, 1913; Cindy L. Small, *The Jennie Wade Story*, 29. The Skelly residence was on the site of modern-day 47 West Middle Street.

18. D'Alessandro, *"My Country Needs Me,"* 78.

19. Frye, *2nd Virginia Infantry*, 25, 27–28. Frye noted that the thirty-six-mile march in a single day "rated as a major highlight in the history recorded by the 2nd Virginia Infantry," and he credited the men with completing it in fourteen hours. The regiment's chaplain, Albert C. Hopkins, wrote, "I venture to say there is no military march on record, for distance and unfavorable conditions, equal to that march of Saturday of the Second Regiment of Virginia Infantry!"

20. Adams, *Sentinel*, June 3, 1862.

21. William addressed the letter to "Sister Anne." Depending on who was speaking or writing, Ann E. Culp Myers was referred to variously as "Ann," "Anne," "Anna," and "Annie." But several friends, including Mrs. Skelly, identified her as "Ann" in letters or diaries, and the inscription on her tombstone at Gettysburg's Evergreen Cemetery is "Ann Eliza Myers." To add to the confusion, her given first name was "Barbara." Numerous

published accounts refer to Wesley's older sister as "Barbara Ann"
or "Barbara Anne," but it is clear that immediate family members
did not refer to her as "Barbara."

22. Michael Fahnestock, Culp Family Collection, William Culp letter,
June 12, 1862.

23. www.fold3.com, MSR for John W. Culp. The receipt was for
rations while he was on furlough, before he was captured.

24. Frye, *2nd Virginia Infantry*, 45.

25. www.fold3.com, Confederate Citizens File for Chas. W. Hoffman.
There are twenty-five pages of documents related to C.W.'s
transactions with the Confederate army from 1861–1864.

26. National Archives, MSR for Wesley A. Hoffman; Taylor,
*Ancestral Record of Francis William Hoffman and Anna Barbara
Esser*, Chatper III.

27. Taylor, *Ancestral Record of Francis William Hoffman and Anna
Barbara Es*ser, Chapters II, III, Some of the most compelling
passages of Ruth Hoffman Frost's family history deal with the
impact of the war on the home front.

28. Gwynne, *Rebel Yell*, 299. An account in the Gettysburg *Compiler*
on June 2, 1862 identified Geary as the commanding officer of
the troops who captured Hoffman.

29. Taylor, *Ancestral Record of Francis William Hoffman and Anna
Barbara Esser*, Chapters II, III.

30. www.fold3.com, Confederate Citizens File for Chas. W. Hoffman.
Hoffman sold the horse and saddles to the Fauquier Mountain
Rangers—officially known as Company A of the Seventh Virginia
Cavalry. His son, Wesley, had joined the unit earlier in the year.

31. Richmond *Dispatch*, "Fauquier Resident sent to Castle Thunder
for refusing to take CSA currency," September 12, 1862, 1.

32. Ibid., "Released," September 13, 1862; www.fold3.com,
Confederate Citizens File for Chas. W. Hoffman.

33. www.fold3.com, MSR for Henry Wentz. He was "Appointed 1st Sergt. Feb. 10, 1862;" Moore, *Miscellaneous Disbanded Virginia Light Artillery*, 29–39. The Wise Artillery underwent multiple reorganizations, most notably in January 1862 when James S. Brown took over as captain after Ephraim Alburtis resigned due to poor health; Koleszar, *Ashland. Bedford and Taylor Virginia Light Artillery*, 16. The Wise Artillery was disbanded in October 1862 and Wentz and others were assigned to John Eubank's battery.

34. Evans, *History of Berkeley County West Virginia*, 157; www.fold3.com, MSR for Henry Wentz, Company Muster Roll. July–August, 1861; Koleszar, *Ashland, Bedford and Taylor Virginia Light Artillery*, 106.

35. Moore, *Miscellaneous Disbanded Virginia Light Artillery*, 34, 99; www.fold3.com, MSR for Henry Wentz. He was promoted to first sergeant on February 10, 1862.

36. R. B. Hanson, "Field Artillery Battery Positions and Duties," found at http://www.batteryi.org/ranks; An even more detailed description of the duties of the first sergeant can be found in August V. Katz' *The 1865 Customs of Service for Non-commissioned Officers and Soldiers*, 131–49.

37. Moore, *Miscellaneous Disbanded Virginia Light Artillery*, 34–38.

38. Ibid., 39; http://antietam.aotw.org/exhibit.php?exhibit_id=15, "General Robert E. Lee's Official Report, Operations in Maryland (1862)."

39. www.fold3.com, MSR for Henry Wentz; Pfanz, *Gettysburg, The Second Day*, 118; Frassanito, *Early Photography at Gettysburg*, 249; Jim Clouse, *Battlefield Dispatch*, Vol. 17. No. 10, October 1998, 6–10.

40. Moore, *Miscellaneous Disbanded Virginia Light Artillery*, 39; Koleszar, *Ashland, Bedford and Taylor Virginia Light Artillery*, 16–17.

41. Koleszar, *Ashland, Bedford and Taylor Virginia Light Artillery*, 17.

Eight: Prelude to Gettysburg

1. Robert W. Black, *Cavalry Raids of the Civil War*, 46–53; http://wvencyclopedia.org/articles/1059, "Jones-Imboden Raid;" http://www.wvcommerce.org/App_Media/Assets/publications/travelrec/CivilWarBrochure.pdf, "Jones-Imboden Raids 1863."

2. National Archives, MSR for Wesley A. Hoffman. Hoffman enlisted on March 26, 1862 at Woodstock, Virginia (he had been born in Gettysburg on July 18, 1844, and thus was four months shy of his eighteenth birthday when he joined the army); Armstrong, *7th Virginia Cavalry*, 41, 164; Hoffman's capture is listed under "Roll of Prisoners of War at Ft. McHenry, Md., Oct. 13, 1862."

3. National Archives, MSR for Wesley A. Hoffman. Hoffman appears on a register for "Chimborazo Hospital No. 4, Richmond, Virginia." There is a separate document with the same information listed for the "Medical Director's Office, Richmond, Virginia." It was noted that he was "sent to Camp Lee by Med. Director;" also see listing under "Regimental Return."

4. Eric Wittenberg, http://www.historynet.com/battle-of-fairfield-grumble-jones-gettysburg-campaign-victory.htm, "Battle of Fairfield: Grumble Jones' Gettysburg Campaign Victory;" Armstrong, *7th Virginia Cavalry*, 45–46.

5. Armstrong, *7th Virginia Cavalry*, 46; http://www.essentialcivilwarcurriculum.com/the-jones-imboden-raid.html,

"The Jones-Imboden Raid;" Black, *Cavalry Raids of the Civil War*, 46.

6. Armstrong, *7th Virginia Cavalry*, 47; William N. McDonald, *A History of the Laurel Brigade: Originally the Ashby Cavalry of the Army of Northern Virginia*, 19, 21, 25–26; OR, Volume 25, Part I, 114, "Headquarters Valley District, near Harrisonburg, Va., May 4, 1863;" www.fold3.com, Confederate Citizens File for Wesley A. Hoffman.

7. Black, *Cavalry Raids of the Civil War*, 48; OR Volume 25, Part I, 114; Armstrong, *7th Virginia Cavalry*, 49.

8. Armstrong, *7th Virginia Cavalry*, 49; OR, Volume 25, Part I, 105.

9. http://wvencyclopedia.org/articles/1059, "Jones-Imboden Raid;" OR, Volume 25, Part I, 115.

10. OR, Volume 25, Part I, 119–120; http://www.essentialcivilwarcurriculum.com/the-jones-imboden-raid.html, "The Jones-Imboden Raid."

11. Black, *Cavalry Raids of the Civil War*, 53; OR, Volume 25, Part I, 98, 115, 121; http://www.essentialcivilwarcurriculum.com/the-jones-imboden-raid.html, "The Jones-Imboden Raid."

12. http://www.civilwar.org/battlefields/chancellorsville/chancellorsville-history-articles/10-facts-about.html, "10 Facts About Chancellorsville." The Union had approximately 130,000 troops to the Confederates' sixty thousand.

13. http://www.eg.bucknell.edu/~hyde/jackson/stonewallArm.html.

14. http://www.civilwar.org/battlefields/chancellorsville/chancellorsville-history-articles/10-facts-about.html, "10 Facts About Chancellorsville." The numbers are estimates. S. C. Gwynne in *Rebel Yell* writes that the Confederates had fifty-five thousand men to go against 135,000 infantry, artillery and cavalry from the Union; Gwynne, *Rebel Yell*, 520.

15. Gwynne, *Rebel Yell*, 520–22.

16. Ibid., 523.

17. Ibid., 529.

18. Ibid., 529–30; Frye, *2nd Virginia Infantry*, 49. Frye wrote that "the Second Virginia and the Stonewall Brigade participated in the 12-mile venture that exposed Hooker's right;" Koleszar, *Ashland Bedford and Taylor Virginia Light Artillery*, 19.

19. Frye, *2nd Virginia Infantry*, 49; Koleszar, *Ashland, Bedford and Taylor Virginia Light Artillery*, 19; Gwynne, *Rebel Yell*, 536.

20. Gwynne, *Rebel Yell*, 536; Douglas, *I Rode with Stonewall*, 221.

21. Douglas, *I Rode with Stonewall*, 221; Robertson. *The Stonewall Brigade*, 184; Frye, *2nd Virginia Infantry*, 49.

22. Gwynne, *Rebel Yell*, 539.

23. Ibid., 540.

24. Ibid., 541.

25. Ibid., 541–42; Joe D. Haines, *America's Civil War*, "Stonewall Jackson's Last Days," http://www.historynet.com/stonewall-jacksons-death.htm.

26. Gwynne, *Rebel Yell*, 542–44.

27. Douglas, *I Rode with Stonewall*, 227; Koleszar, *Ashland, Bedford and Taylor Virginia Light Artillery*, 19–20; Frye, *2nd Virginia Infantry*, 50; Robertson, *The Stonewall Brigade*, 187, 189.

28. Robertson, *The Stonewall Brigade*, 189; Gwynne, *Rebel Yell*, 544.

29. http://www.civilwar.org/battlefields/chancellorsville/chancellorsville-history-articles/battle-of-salem-church-final.html; Gwynne, *Rebel Yell*, 547, 551. The diagnosis of Jackson's illness is still a matter of debate.

30. Gwynne, *Rebel Yell*, 554.

31. Sears, *Gettysburg*, 5.

32. Guelzo, *Gettysburg, the Last Invasion*, 20; Pfanz, *Gettysburg, the Second Day*, 5.

33. Guelzo, *Gettysburg, the Last Invasion*, 21; Jeffrey Wert, *America's Civil War*, "Robert E. Lee and James Longstreet at Odds at Gettysburg," http://www.historynet.com/americas-civil-war-robert-e-lee-and-james-longstreet-at-odds-at-gettysburg.htm; Andrus, *The Brooke, Fauquier, Loudoun and Alexandria Artillery*, 74, 77, 112. The roster section and his military service records show that Frank Hoffman was "present on all rolls through 2/65."

34. Guelzo, *Gettysburg, The Last Invasion*, 21; Sears, *Gettysburg*, 54.

35. Guelzo, *Gettysburg, The Last Invasion*, 21.

36. Andrus, *The Brooke, Fauquier, Loudoun and Alexandria Artillery*, 74.

37. Pfanz, *Gettysburg, The Second Day*, 8; OR, Volume 27, Part II, 499; Eric Wittenberg, *The Battle of Brandy Station*, 75–80, 189.

38. Wittenberg, *The Battle of Brandy Station*, 77, 79, 190; McDonald, *A History of the Laurel Brigade*, 135; Sears, *Gettysburg*, 66; http://www.civilwar.org/battlefields/brandystation/brandy-station-history-articles/ten-facts-about-brandy.html, "10 Facts About Brandy Station."

39. Frye, *2nd Virginia Infantry*, 51.

Nine: Brother vs. Brother

1. National Archives, MSR for William E. Culp. William had been promoted to first sergeant in October 1862. According to family records and his tombstone at Evergreen Cemetery, he was born on August 8, 1831—making him thirty-one years old at this point in the war. Military documents list him as five feet, six inches tall (perhaps half a foot taller than his brother Wesley), with black hair and black eyes; Myers, "The Story of Wesley Culp." It has been well-established that the Culps' sister Ann E. Culp Myers lived directly across the street from the Skelly family on West Middle Street in 1863. But the rarely-seen document written by Ann's daughter, Margaret Myers, reveals that this was actually "the home of the other brother, William E. Culp." According to Margaret, "my mother had promised her brother William that she would stay with his wife and child while he was away in the army."

2. Gettysburg *Star* and *Republican Compiler*, various advertisements. Mr. Skelly's shop was originally on Chambersburg Street; Brian Mokenhaupt, *Three Days in Gettysburg*, 21.

3. Mockenhaupt, *Three Days in Gettysburg*, 21; Frassanito, *Early Photography at Gettysburg*, 119, 123; D'Alessandro, *"My Country Needs Me,"* 23–24, 87–94. Mary Virginia apparently went by multiple nicknames, including "Gin," "Ginnie," and "Jennie." A fawning 1917 biography by J. W. Johnston, *The True Story of "Jennie" Wade*, reports that "the title 'Jennie' was a subsequent newspaper inaccuracy that has since persisted," but that is incorrect. Jack Skelly's letters in the Skelly pension file at the National Archives show that he referred to her as "Jennie." She also signed letters to him as "Jennie;" Frassanito revealed that James Wade became an apprentice for Johnston Skelly Sr. and "lived in the Skelly home 'for two or three years' while learning the tailoring trade;" *Republican Compiler*, advertisement, December 7, 1846, 2.

4. Matilda (Tillie) Pierce Alleman, *What a Girl Saw and Heard of the Battle*, 18 (from *The Battle of Gettysburg As Seen by Two Teens*, edited by Frank Meredith).

5. D'Alessandro, *"My Country Needs Me,"* 88–90.

6. Ibid., 77. Words were underscored in the original.

7. Burton B. Porter, *One of the People: His Own Story*, 113, 143, https://archive.org/details/onepeoplehisown00portgoog; National

Archives, Federal Military Pension Application, Johnston H. Skelly, Jack Skelly letters (also found in D'Alessandro, "*My Country Needs Me,*" 61).

8. Cindy L. Small, *The Jennie Wade Story*, 11; Frassanito, *Early Photography at Gettysburg*, 121–23.

9. National Archives, Federal Military Pension Application, Johnston H. Skelly; D'Alessandro, "*My Country Needs Me,*" 68.

10. Ibid., 68.

11. Ibid., 94.

12. Ibid. 70. D'Alessandro obtained this letter from the collection of Skelly family descendant Thomas O'Connor Jr.

13. Pfanz, *Gettysburg: The Second Day*, 8.

14. Guelzo, *Gettysburg: The Last Invasion*, 33, 60, 61.

15. Larry B. Maier, *Gateway to Gettysburg: the Second Battle of Winchester*, 56, 59; Guelzo, *Gettysburg: the Last Invasion*, 60.

16. Maier, *Gateway to Gettysburg*, 55; OR, Volume 27, Part II, 50.

17. Maier, *Gateway to Gettysburg*, 122; OR, Volume 27, Part II, 178.

18. McCourtney, www.genealogy.com, Descendants of Matthias Kolb—Ten Generations. David and William Culp were first cousins. Billy Holtzworth and William were first cousins once removed. They were descended from the same great-grandfather, Christophel Culp. Billy's mother and William's father were first cousins; Guelzo, *Gettysburg: the Last Invasion*, 60.

19. Maier, *Gateway to Gettysburg*, 131; George R. Prowell, *History of the Eighty-Seventh Regiment, Pennsylvania Volunteers*, 66–67.

20. Frye, *2nd Virginia Infantry*, 51–52; Maier, *Gateway to Gettysburg*, 143, 146.

21. OR, Volume 27, Part II, 500; Sears, *Gettysburg*, 78–79; Guelzo, *Gettysburg: the Last Invasion*, 61.

22. Maier, *Gateway to Gettysburg*, 214, 216; Prowell, *History of the Eighty-Seventh Regiment, Pennsylvania Volunteers*, 74.

23. OR, Volume 27, Part II, 500–501.

24. 24 ²⁴ Ibid., 501.

25. Ibid., 501–2, 517. The Stonewall Brigade had, in fact, left its original position later than ordered, but Johnson pointed out that it was "owing to a misconception of orders, for which Brigadier-General Walker was not in the slightest degree responsible;" Frye, *2nd Virginia Infantry*, 52.

26. OR, Volume 27, Part II, 520. According to Colonel J. Q. A. Nadenbousch, the Second Virginia took prisoners from the Eighty-Seventh Pennsylvania, Eighteenth Connecticut, Fifth Maryland, Twelfth (West) Virginia, 122nd Ohio, and 123rd Ohio; Prowell, *History of the Eighty-Seventh Regiment, Pennsylvania Volunteers*, 76.

27. Prowell, *History of the Eighty-Seventh Regiment, Pennsylvania Volunteers*, 76. About one hundred more were reported missing; OR, Volume 27, Part II, 502, 517.

28. Fleming, *Pittsburgh Gazette Times*, "The Homecoming of Wes Culp," November 9, 1913.

29. Ibid. Fleming incorrectly spelled Holtzworth's name as "Holdsworth."

30. Ibid.

31. Ibid.

32. Rodgers, *The Ties of the Past: The Gettysburg Diaries of Salome Myers Stewart 1854–1922*, 160.

33. Sarah Broadhead, *The Diary of a Lady of Gettysburg, Pennsylvania from June 15 to July 15, 1863*, 6.

34. Rodgers, *The Ties of the Past: The Gettysburg Diaries of Salome Myers Stewart 1854–1922*, 160.

35. Mockenhaupt, *Three Days in Gettysburg*, 45.

36. Kent Masterson Brown, *Retreat from Gettysburg: Lee, Logistics and the Pennsylvania Campaign*, 14–15.

37. Ibid., 15.

38. Ibid., 17.

39. Ibid., 13; Guelzo, *Gettysburg: The Last Invasion*, 69.

40. www.fold3.com, MSR for Robert N. Hoffman.

41. Brown, *Retreat from Gettysburg*, 25, 28.

42. Ibid., 27, 47.

43. www.fold3.com, Confederate Citizens File for Robert N. Hoffman, June 30, 1863.

44. http://chronicles.dickinson.edu/encyclo/a/alumni/alumni4.html, "Dickinson College Alumni, 1851–1875;" OR Volume 27, Part II, 296; Sears, *Gettysburg*, Confederate Order of Battle, 534–35; Brown, *Retreat from Gettysburg*, 22.

Ten: Wes Culp Comes Home

1. *OR*, Volume 27, Part II, 503; Gregg S. Clemmer, *Old Alleghany: The Life and Wars of General Ed Johnson*, 453.

2. Clemmer, *Old Alleghany*, 453.

3. Douglas, *I Rode with Stonewall*, 243.

4. Clemmer, *Old Alleghany*, 453–54; *OR*, Volume 27, Part II, 503; http://civilwarintheeast.com/things/botelers-ford/, "Boteler's Ford;" http://jeffersoncountyhlc.org/index.php/landmarks/botelers-cement-mill/; "Boteler's Cement Mill."

5. Douglas, *I Rode with Stonewall*, 243; Clemmer, *Old Alleghany*, 454.

6. Frye, *2nd Virginia Infantry*, 53; http://www.wvculture.org/history/statehood/statehood16.html, "The Creation of West Virginia;" Clemmer, *Old Alleghany*, 456; Coddington, *The Gettysburg Campaign*, 165.

7. Margaret E. Myers, "The Story of Wesley Culp," (unpublished, 1939). Two copies of Margaret's six-page family history—one hand-written, one typed—were provided to the author by Michael Fahnestock, a Culp descendant. It is not known whether Wesley Culp's letter from Chambersburg still exists.

8. Ibid.

9. Clemmer, *Old Alleghany*, 457; Coddington, *The Gettysburg Campaign*, 171; Fleming, *Pittsburgh Gazette Times*, "The Homecoming of Wes Culp." November 9, 1913.

10. *OR*, Volume 27, Part II, 307.

11. Clemmer, *Old Alleghany*, 459–60; *OR*, Volume 27, Part II, 503.

12. Clemmer, *Old Alleghany*, 460.

13. David G. Martin, *Gettysburg July 1*, 339; James Longstreet, *From Manassas to Appomattox*, 356; Coddington, *The Gettysburg Campaign*, 190.

14. Pfanz, *Gettysburg: The Second Day*, 24; Clemmer, *Old Alleghany*, 461.

15. Clemmer, *Old Alleghany*, 462; Douglas, *I Rode with Stonewall*, 246–47.

16. *OR*, Volume 27, Part II, 445-446; Pfanz, *Gettysburg: The First Day*, 346–347; Clemmer, *Old Alleghany*, 465, n. 43. George Steuart's brigade and the Stonewall Brigade were "respectively third and fourth in Johnson's advance."

17. Clemmer, *Old Alleghany*, 465 (Washington Street identified in note 43); Fleming, *Pittsburgh Gazette Times*, "The Homecoming of Wes Culp," November 9, 1913. Fleming quotes Pendleton as calling it the "Carlisle road."

18. Myers, "The Story of Wesley Culp."

19. Fleming, *Pittsburgh Gazette Times*, "The Homecoming of Wes Culp," November 9, 1913.

20. Philip Laino, *Gettysburg Campaign Atlas*, 168; OR, Volume 27, Part II, 513; Martin, *Gettysburg July 1*, 557.

21. *OR*, Volume 27, Part II, 518, 521; Troy D. Harman, "The Gap: Meade's July 2 Offensive Plan," GNMP, *The Second Day at Gettysburg*; Clemmer, *Old Alleghany*, 80; Fleming, *Pittsburgh Gazette Times*, "The Homecoming of Wes Culp," November 9, 1913. One of Culp's comrades in the Second Virginia, Daniel Entler, was wounded during skirmishing on the night of July 1.

22. Myers, "The Story of Wesley Culp."

23. Ibid. See also, Fleming, *Pittsburgh Gazette Times*, "The Homecoming of Wes Culp," November 9, 1913. According to Fleming's account, Pendleton told him, "I went to Gen. Walker and made the request. Gen. Walker told me to bring Culp to him, and I did. He shook Wes' hand and said he was glad to know he had a Pennsylvania man in his command and would give him a pass with pleasure, and Wes, elated, thanked the general and started at once for the town, a distance, I should judge, between one and two miles."

24. Myers, "The Story of Wesley Culp." Julia's age is approximate. It is believed she was born in 1842 or 1843. She is listed as seven years old in the 1850 census and eighteen in the 1860 census. According to a 1997 letter written by research assistant Tim Smith of the Adams County Historical Society, she was "apparently living with her older sister" on Middle Street at the time of the battle. GNMP historian Harry Pfanz, however, wrote in a 1961 letter that she may have been "staying at the home of their first cousin, Mrs. William Stallsmith, who lived on York Street." If Pfanz is correct, then Julia was merely visiting her sister on the nights of July 2 and 3.

25. Rodgers, *The Ties of the Past: The Gettysburg Diaries of Salome Myers Stewart, 1854–1922*; National Archives, MSR for William E. Culp.

26. Myers, "The Story of Wesley Culp."

27. Guelzo, "How the Town Shaped the Battle: Gettysburg 1863," *Gettysburg Magazine*, No. 51, July 2014, 41; Myers, "The Story of Wesley Culp."

28. The age is approximate as there is no credible listing of Ann's exact birthdate. Her tombstone says she was born in 1834. She is listed as sixteen years old in the 1850 census and twenty-five years old in the 1860 census; Fleming, *Pittsburgh Gazette Times*, "The Homecoming of Wes Culp," November 9, 1913.

29. The author came to this conclusion after comparing both documents, but it was first proposed by William Frassanito in *Early Photography at Gettysburg*, 126.

30. Fleming, *Pittsburgh Gazette Times*, "The Homecoming of Wes Culp," November 9, 1913.

31. Myers, "The Story of Wesley Culp."

32. Fleming, *Pittsburgh Gazette Times*, "The Homecoming of Wes Culp," November 9, 1913.

33. Ibid.

34. Ibid.

35. Ibid.

36. Myers, "The Story of Wesley Culp;" Fleming, *Pittsburgh Gazette Times*, "The Homecoming of Wes Culp," November 9, 1913.

37. Fleming, *Pittsburgh Gazette Times*, "The Homecoming of Wes Culp," November 9, 1913.

38. Myers, "The Story of Wesley Culp."

39. National Archives, MSR for John W. Culp; Frassanito, *Early Photography at Gettysburg*, 128.

40. OR, Volume 27, Part II, 504, 509, 513, 518, 521; Harman, "The Gap: Meade's July 2 Offensive Plan," GNMP, *The Second Day at Gettysburg*, 80–82, 84; Wittenberg, *Protecting the Flank at Gettysburg: The Battles for Brinkerhoff's Ridge and East Cavalry Field, July 2–3, 1863*, 14–16, 22, 26, 28. On the evening of July 2, long after Wesley Culp had been killed, the Second Virginia took part in the battle for Brinkerhoff's Ridge on the eastern side of Rock Creek.

41. OR, Volume 27, Part II, 504, 509, 513, 518, 521, 531; Harman, "The Gap: Meade's July 2 Offensive Plan," GNMP, The Second Day at Gettysburg, 80–81; Laino, *Gettysburg Campaign Atlas*, 168; Jacob A. Nekoranec, "Cavalry on the Right: The Battle for Brinkerhoff's Ridge," *Gettysburg Magazine*, No. 51, July 2014, 19.

42. OR, Volume 27, Part II, 504, 518, 521.

43. Harman, "The Gap: Meade's July 2 Offensive Plan," GNMP, *Second Day at Gettysburg*, 79–81, 84; "Gettysburg Battle-Field." The map was "entered according to Act of Congress in the year 1863 by Jno. B. Bachelder in the Clerk's Office of the District Court of Massachusetts." It is signed by Union Generals Meade, Slocum, Sykes, Williams and Warren, among others; OR, Volume 27, Part II, 811; Pfanz, *Gettysburg: Culp's Hill and Cemetery Hill*, 153; Nekoranec, "Cavalry on the Right! The Battle for Brinkerhoff's Ridge," *Gettysburg Magazine*, No. 51, July 2014, 19.

44. Harman, "The Gap: Meade's July 2 Offensive Plan," GNMP, *Second Day at Gettysburg*, 81, 84; Pfanz, *Gettysburg, the Second Day*, 62; Pfanz. *Gettysburg, Culp's Hill and Cemetery Hill*, 153-155, 433, n. 1; Adams County Deed Book 58, 327; Deed Book WW, 278; https://www.youtube.com/watch?v=a3grKJK1AhU, "John Deardorff Farm." The house was built by John Deardorff in 1827, but Adams County deed records show that it was owned by Ephraim Deardorff at the time of the battle in 1863. The house still stands at 75 Montclair Road; Christian Samito, *Commanding Boston's Irish Ninth: The Civil War Letters of Colonel Patrick R. Guiney, Ninth Massachusetts Volunteer Infantry*, 200.

45. *OR*, Volume 27, Part II, 341, 522. Colonel Nadenbousch of the Second Virginia reported that "I lost one man killed and 16 wounded and 3 missing." Those figures were later amended in the Official Records to one killed and thirteen wounded; H.L. Snyder, *Shepherdstown Register*, "Notes by Observer," March 18, 1926. Snyder also appears to have gotten his information from Ben Pendleton, who was the oldest surviving member of Company B. Snyder wrote that "[Culp] had been shot in the forehead the moment he had peered over the rock." Reporter McClure Moler published a similar account in the *Register* on July 6, 1922.

46. Fleming, *Pittsburgh Gazette Times*, "The Homecoming of Wes Culp." November 9, 1913.

47. Myers, "The Story of Wesley Culp;" *OR*, Volume 27, Part II, 520

48. Frassanito, *Early Photography at Gettysburg*, 127; Samuel Carrick, *Gettysburg Times*, "County Backgrounds: The Grave of Wesley Culp (?)," November 16, 1978; author visit to the Gettysburg section of Hollywood Cemetery in Richmond.

49. Myers, "The Story of Wesley Culp."

50. Ibid.

51. Fleming, *Pittsburgh Gazette Times*, "The Homecoming of Wes Culp," November 9, 1913.

Eleven: War at the Wentz House

1. Guelzo, *Gettysburg: The Last Invasion*, 236; Karlton D. Smith, http://npshistory.com/series/symposia/gettysburg_seminars/11/essay4.pdf, "To Consider Every Contingency: Lt. Gen. James

Longstreet, Capt. Samuel R. Johnston, and the factors that affected the reconnaissance and countermarch, July 2, 1863, 103.

2. Pfanz, *Gettysburg: The Second Day*, 105; OR, Volume 27, Part II, 308. Lee referred to the Union army as the "army of General Meade."

3. Smith, "To Consider Every Contingency," 102–3. Pendleton and Johnston mentioned staring "after sunrise" and at "daybreak;" Pfanz, *Gettysburg: The Second Day*, 105–6. Pfanz had Johnston starting at about four a.m.; OR, Volume 27, Part II, 350.

4. Smith, "To Consider Every Contingency," 102.

5. Ibid., 104–105; OR, Volume 27, Part II, 350.

6. Pfanz, *Gettysburg: The Second Day*, 107.

7. Ibid., 107.

8. Guelzo, *Gettysburg: The Last Invasion*, 242; Sears, *Gettysburg*, 253.

9. Benjamin Pendleton, Daniel Entler, and William Arthur were among those who knew that Wesley had come from Gettysburg. The information was found in George T. Fleming's *Pittsburgh Gazette Times* story and Robert Hoffman's Confederate pension application; Casler, *Four Years in the Stonewall Brigade*, 182; Myers, "The Story of Wesley Culp."

10. Krick, *The Smoothbore Volley that Doomed the Confederacy* (eighteen pages excerpted at http://www.librarypoint.org/smoothbore_volley).

11. Koleszar, *Ashland, Bedford and Taylor Virginia Light Artillery*, 23. The artillerists "received orders to march from the camp at Greenwood, Pennsylvania at 1 a.m." and "reached Gettysburg shortly after sunrise;" Andrus, *The Brooke, Fauquier, Loudoun and Alexandria Artillery*, 77; Armstrong, *7th Virginia Cavalry*, 55. Grumble Jones's brigade "crossed the Potomac River at Williamsport, Maryland on July 1, 1863 and went into camp near

Greencastle, Pennsylvania that night." On July 2, the Seventh Virginia was sent on a brief scouting mission to Hagerstown, Maryland, and then headed to Chambersburg.

12. *Southern Historical Society Papers*, Vol. VIII, Lafayette McLaws, 69. General McLaws told Longstreet, "Ride with me and I will show you that we can't go that route, according to instructions, without being seen by the enemy"; Alexander, *Fighting for the Confederacy*, 235. Alexander said that Longstreet cautioned him "to keep all movements carefully out of view of a signal station whose flags we could see wig-wagging on Little Round Top;" there is debate as to whether Johnston was actually assigned to lead the march or was merely ordered to accompany Longstreet's men, based on his morning reconnoiter.

13. Alexander, *Fighting for the Confederacy*, 235–36. Alexander wrote that he turned to the left, but he almost certainly turned to the right.

14. Pfanz, *Gettysburg: The Second Day*, 118; Alexander, *Fighting for the Confederacy*, 235–36. Alexander estimated that his battle line later was six hundred yards from the Union position on the Emmitsburg Road (and, therefore, the Wentz House). When he first arrived in the area, however, his battalion was a bit farther back—"down in the valley of Willoughby Run, in a few hundred yards of the schoolhouse, where I had to wait on the infantry...before going further."

15. Glenn Tucker, *Lee and Longstreet at Gettysburg*, 56–57.

16. Alexander, *Fighting for the Confederacy*, 237; Pfanz, *Gettysburg: the Second Day*, 158.

17. www.fold3.com. MSR for Henry D. Wirt, Capt. Taylor's Company, Light Artillery. Wirt enlisted in Martinsburg's Wise Artillery under E. G. Alburtis in April 1861. In a July 1863 report for Confederate prisoners of war, he was described as being twenty-two years old and standing five feet, seven inches, with fair complexion, blue eyes, and auburn hair. His occupation was listed as "teacher." The same descriptions appear in regimental histories for the Wise Artillery and Taylor's Virginia Battery.

18. E. S. Breidenbaugh, editor, *The Pennsylvania College Book 1832–1882*, 403. Wirts is listed under "Preparatorians." A hard copy of the book may be found at the Gettysburg College library. There is nothing in his biographical information to indicate that Wirts was from Gettysburg. As an aside, William Frassanito in *Early Photography at Gettysburg* (376–77) identifies four other men in Lee's army who also attended either Pennsylvania College or the Preparatory Department: Enos Dinkle (Second Virginia), Goodrich Mitchell (Forty-Ninth Virginia), James McKesson (Eleventh North Carolina), and James Crocker (Ninth Virginia). All would have had some knowledge of the town, but the focus of this study is the young men who actually grew up in Gettysburg and came home as invaders.

19. 1850 U.S. Federal Census, Straban, Adams, Pennsylvania.

20. Frassanito, *Early Photography at Gettysburg*, 370. According to Frassanito, the letter was written from Private Samuel J. Cassatt of Company K, First Pennsylvania Reserves, to George Boyer of Straban Township on August 2, 1863.

21. www.fold3.com, MSR for Henry D. Wirt. Wirt was captured by the Ringgold Cavalry at Martinsburg just sixteen days after the battle of Gettysburg, Breidbenbaugh, *The Pennsylvania College Book 1832–1882*, 403.

22. Walter M. Merrill and Louis Ruchames, editors, *To Rouse the Slumbering Land 1868–1879: The Letters of William Lloyd Garrison*, Volume VI, 303; George Birkback Norman Hill, *Talks about Autographs*, 185–86. Although Hill does not identify Wertz by name (because he is focusing only on Garrison's

autograph), his book includes the full text of the letter to Garrison that was described by Merrill and Ruchames and connects it to Garrison's response above.

23. Merrill and Ruchames, *To Rouse the Slumbering Land 1868–1879*, 303.

24. www.ancestry.com, Illinois Marriage Index, 1860–1920.

25. www.ancestry.com, "Peoria, Illinois, City Directory, 1879;" 1880 U.S. Federal Census, Joliet, Will, Illinois. Wertz is listed as a widower.

26. 1870 U.S. Federal Census for McDina, Peoria, Illinois, and 1880 U.S. Federal Census for Joliet, Will, Illinois. It should also be noted that "Henry D. Wertz" appears in the 1890 census as living with his second wife, Mary E., in nearby Tazewell County, Illinois. Again, his birthplace is listed as Virginia.

27. Guelzo, *Gettysburg: the Final Invasion*, 235; ACHS, *Survey for Restoration and Rehabilitation of Historic Structures: Wentz Buildings*, "Statements of War-Period and Early Post-War Residents of the Wentz Property and Vicinity," 7–8.

28. Storrick, *Gettysburg: Battle and Battlefield*, 90–91.

29. Alexander, *Fighting for the Confederacy*, 236–38.

30. Ibid., 239; *OR*, Volume 27, Part II, 429.

31. Matt Spruill, *Summer Thunder: A Battlefield Guide to the Artillery at Gettysburg*, 116. According to Harry Pfanz in *Gettysburg: The Second Day* (529, n. 31), Alexander later said the battery's left was twenty yards south of the road; he estimated that the center was forty yards south; *OR*, Volume 27, Part II, 432; Brett Barnett, "'The Severest and Bloodiest Artillery Fight I Ever Saw': Colonel E. P. Alexander and the First Corps Artillery Assail the Peach Orchard," July 2, 1863, http://www.npshistory.com/series/symposia/gettysburg_seminars/7/essay4.pdf.

32. OR, Volume 27, Part II, 439; Alexander, *The Great Charge and Artillery Fighting at Gettysburg*, 359–60; Alexander, *Fighting for the Confederacy*, 239.

33. Pfanz, *Gettysburg: The Second Day*, 313.

34. Martin A. Haynes, *A History of the Second Regiment, New Hampshire Volunteer Infantry, in the War of the Rebellion*, 170.

35. Ibid., 171.

36. Ibid., 175.

37. Ibid., 175.

38. Pfanz, *Gettysburg: The Second Day*, 321 (Map 13-1), 329.

39. Alexander, *Fighting for the Confederacy*, 240.

40. Alexander, *The Great Charge and Artillery Fighting at Gettysburg*, 360.

41. Adams County Deed Book BB, 218–82. John Wentz had purchased the property (nine acres and sixty-three perches) on December 28, 1847, and it was "sold and conveyed" by deed "of John Wentz to Henry Wentz" on February 2, 1850. The land was described as being on "the road leading from Gettysburg to Emmitsburg" and bordering the property of George Rose and James Warfield.

42. Haynes, *A history of the Second regiment, New Hampshire volunteers*, 187.

43. Storrick, *Gettysburg: Battle and Battlefield*, 90. See also ACHS, *Survey for Restoration and Rehabilitation of Historic Structures; Wentz Buildings*, "Statements of War-period and Early Post-war Residents of the Wentz Property and Vicinity, 7. Charles Culp, who was a teenager when he lived with his parents as tenants on the Wentz property from 1868 to 1871, acknowledged that the house was damaged during the battle, although "not badly"; Gregory A. Coco, *On the Bloodstained Field: 130 Human Interest Stories of the Campaign and Battle of Gettysburg*, 36.

Coco includes an account from a soldier in the Sixteenth Michigan who was assigned to bury dead soldiers on July 5, 1863. He described the Wentz house as being "literally perforated by shot and shell;" Smith, "'We drop a comrade's tear,' Colonel Edward Lyon Bailey and the Second New Hampshire Infantry at Gettysburg," http://npshistory.com/series/symposia/gettysburg_seminars/9/essay5.pdf. According to Smith, "On the morning of July 5, Colonel Bailey...rode out to the Peach Orchard and found an additional twenty-one wounded at the Wentz house." They had apparently remained there since July 2; Haynes, *History of the Second Regiment New Hampshire Volunteers: Its Camps, Marches and Battles*, 111 (Haynes wrote two regimental histories, this one in 1865 and the other in 1896).

44. Pfanz, *Gettysburg: The Second Day*, 337; Alexander, *Fighting for the Confederacy*, 240; Alexander, *The Great Charge and Artillery Fighting at Gettysburg*, 360.

45. Alexander, *The Great Charge and Artillery Fighting at Gettysburg*, 360.

46. Ibid., 361.

Twelve: Confederate High Tide

1. Alexander, *Fighting for the Confederacy*, 244.

2. Ibid., 244.

3. Alexander, *The Great Charge and Artillery Fighting at Gettysburg*, 361; Alexander, *Fighting for the Confederacy*, 244; OR, Volume 27, Part II, 432–34; Gottfried, *The Artillery of Gettysburg*, 181; Spruill, *Summer Thunder*, 223.

4. Alexander, *Fighting for the Confederacy*, 361–62.

5. OR, Volume 27, Part II, 388.

6. Andrus, *The Brooke, Fauquier, Loudoun and Alexandria Artillery*, 74–75.

7. Longstreet, *From Manassas to Appomattox*, 327; Ramey and Gott, *The Years of Anguish, Fauquier County, Virginia 1861-65*, 193; Andrus, *The Brooke, Fauquier, Loudoun and Alexandria Artillery*, 75–77.

8. www.alexandersbattalion.com/striblingsbattery/history.htm, "Stribling's Battery, Fauquier Artillery C.S.A., 5; Andrus, *The Brooke, Fauquier, Loudoun and Alexandria Artillery*, 77.

9. "Captain Robert M. Stribling's Letter," April 1898, *Confederate Veteran*, vol. 9, no. 5, 215.

10. OR, Volume 27, Part II, 388.

11. Pfanz, *Gettysburg: the Second Day*, 326.

12. Gottfried, *The Maps of Gettysburg*, 251–63; Spruill, *Summer Thunder*, 233; Harrison and Busey, *Nothing but Glory*, 17–19; Andrus, *The Brooke, Fauquier, Loudoun and Alexandria Artillery*, 78; OR, Volume 27, Part II, 388.

13. OR, Volume 27, Part II, 434.

14. Licensed Battlefield Guides Wayne Motts and James Hessler refer to Hoffman's Gettysburg service in their book *Pickett's Charge at Gettysburg*; Hoffman also is listed on the Fauquier Artillery roster by former GNMP Chief Historian Kathy Georg Harrison in *Northing but Glory, Pickett's Division at Gettysburg*.

15. Gottfried, *The Maps of Gettysburg*, 251–63; Spruill, *Summer Thunder*, 223; "Family History of Hattie Grace Taylor." According to this informal family history, Sarah Ann Hoffman lived on the Wentz property (probably in one of the outbuildings) with her husband, Sampson Taylor, in the late 1840s, and their son, Charles William, was born there in July 1848. She may have been doing housekeeping.

16. Earl J. Hess, *Pickett's Charge: the Last Attack at Gettysburg*, 125. The precise time was recorded by Michael Jacobs, a professor of mathematics and chemistry at Pennsylvania College. Alexander, for his part, thought it was one p.m. The number of Rebel guns is an estimate and has been debated by historians since the battle. Hessler and Motts, in *Pickett's Charge at Gettysburg* (12), say the "engaged artillery would exceed 150 and perhaps 160 field pieces;" Coddington, in *The Gettysburg Campaign* (493) wrote of "over 150 guns;" Gottfried, in *The Artillery of Gettysburg* (195), wrote of "more than 140 guns."

17. Harrison and Busey, *Nothing but Glory*, 23–24.

18. "Captain Robert M. Stribling's Letter," April 1898, *Confederate Veteran*, vol. 9, no. 5, 215.

19. Alexander, *Fighting for the Confederacy*, 254–55.

20. Alexander, *The Great Charge and Artillery Fighting at Gettysburg*, 364; "Captain Robert M. Stribling's Letter," *Confederate Veteran*, vol. 9, no.5, 215; Harrison and Busey, *Nothing but Glory*, 19–20; Alexander, *Fighting for the Confederacy*, 258–59.

21. Captain Robert M. Stribling's Letter," April 1898, *Confederate Veteran*, vol. 9, no. 5, 215.

22. John W. Busey and David G. Martin, *Regimental Strengths and Losses at Gettysburg*, 283. According to these calculations, Pickett lost 2,904 out of 5,473 men engaged.

23. Alexander, *Fighting for the Confederacy*, 264; Alexander, *The Great Charge and Artillery Fighting at Gettysburg*, 365. Despite Stribling's comments, Alexander said some guns *did* advance with the infantry.

24. Alexander, *The Great Charge and Artillery Fighting at Gettysburg*, 366.

25. *OR*, Volume 27, Part II, 430.

26. Ibid., 430. In his official report, written one month after the Battle of Gettysburg, Alexander said that Captain Taylor and Lieutenant Woolfolk withdrew at midnight. In some of his writings in later

years, he estimated that it was ten p.m.; Alexander, *The Great Charge and Artillery Fighting at Gettysburg*, 367.

27. Armstrong, *7th Virginia Cavalry*, 55; OR, Volume 27, Part II, 760.

28. Wittenberg, *Gettysburg's Forgotten Cavalry Actions*, 37; OR, Volume 27, Part II, 752.

29. Wittenberg, *Gettysburg's Forgotten Cavalry Actions*, 38.

30. Ibid., 38; McDonald, *A History of the Laurel Brigade*, 154. Most Civil War timing is based on estimates. McDonald said it was "toward evening."

31. OR, Volume 27, Part II, 752.

32. Armstrong, *7th Virginia Cavalry*, 55; OR, Volume 27, Part II, 752, 760.

33. Wittenberg, *Gettysburg's Forgotten Cavalry Actions*, 125; OR, Volume 27, Part II, 752.

34. OR, Volume 27, Part II, 752.

35. ACHS, *Survey for Restoration and Rehabilitation of Historic Structures: Wentz Buildings*, "Statements of War-Period and Early Post-War Residents of the Wentz Property and Vicinity," 7. Storrick said he was eight years old at the time of the battle; Frassanito, *Early Photography at Gettysburg*, 249.

36. Storrick, *Gettysburg: Battle and Battlefield*, inside back cover, 91.

37. Smith, "We Drop Comrade's Tear," Colonel Edward Lyon Bailey and the Second New Hampshire Infantry at Gettysburg, http://npshistory.com/series/symposia/gettysburg_seminars/9/essay5.pdf. Smith, a Park Ranger at Gettysburg, reported that Colonel Bailey found twenty-one wounded soldiers from his unit at the Wentz house on July 5.

38. Frassanito, *Early Photography at Gettysburg*, 249.

39. Bradsby, Leeson and Sheely, *History of Adams County, Pennsylvania*, 485.

40. United States Christian Commission, *Second Report of the Committee of Maryland*, September 1, 1863, 91.

41. Jacklin's diary was discovered by Gregory A. Coco, a former Licensed Battlefield Guide and National Park Service ranger, at the University of Michigan Library. Coco included the text in his 1987 booklet of Gettysburg human interest stories, *On the Bloodstained Field*, 36–37.

42. National Archives, MSR for Henry Wentz; "Confederate Prisoners of War at Point Lookout, Md.;" 1870 U.S. Federal Census, Martinsburg, Berkeley, West Virginia; Wentz file, Berkeley County Historical Society.

43. ACHS, "Will and Testament of John Wentz of Cumberland Township, Adams Co., Pennsylvania, filed April 29, 1870; Adams County Deed Book BB, 280–81, 283. Henry and Abraham Wentz both signed over power of attorney to Jacob Beamer. Jacob was married to their sister, Ann Maria Wentz.

44. Jim Clouse, *Battlefield Dispatch*, Vol. 17. No. 10, October 1998, 7 (Clouse is a Licensed Battlefield Guide); ACHS, *Survey for Restoration and Rehabilitation of Historic Structures: Wentz Buildings*, 9–10.

45. Small, *The Jennie Wade Story*, 33–34; Mockenhaupt, *Three Days in Gettysburg*, 54; John White Johnston, *The True Story of "Jennie" Wade*, 23.

46. Small, *The Jennie Wade Story*, 35–36.

Thirteen: Prisoners of War

1. Frye, *2nd Virginia Infantry*, 55.

2. www.fold3.com; MSR for Robert N. Hoffman; Frye, *2nd Virginia Infantry*, 56.

3. www.fold3.com, MSR for Robert N. Hoffman.

4. Civil War Trust, "Music of the 1860's: Patriotic Songs of the Era," http://www.civilwar.org/education/history/on-the-homefront/culture/music/music.html?authToken=3206988ef9067713671e4 af595bf203e41c03483. This posting is adapted from John S. Bowman, ed., *Encyclopedia of the Civil War* (Dorset Press, 1992), and Stephen Currie, *Music in the Civil War* (Betterway Books, 1992).

5. "Civil War Music History and Songs," AmericanCivilWar.com, http://www.americancivilwar.com/Civil_War_Music/civil_war_music.html.

6. John Nicholas, "'I don't think we can have an Army without music'—Music of the 1860's," *From the Fields of Gettysburg: The Blog of Gettysburg National Military Park*, https://npsgnmp.wordpress.com/2016/07/29/i-dont-think-we-can-have-an-army-without-music-music-of-the-1860s/ (July 29, 2016).

7. www.amerciancivilwar.com, "Civil War Music History and Songs;" Frye, *2nd Virginia Infantry*, 64.

8. www.fold3.com, MSR for Robert N. Hoffman. The private also appears on a "receipt roll for clothing."

9. Lonnie R. Speer, *Portals to Hell: Military Prisons of the Civil War*, 244.

10. Ibid., 241–45.

11. James I. Robertson, "The Scourge of Elmira," 92, found in *Civil War Prisons* (edited by William B. Hesseltine); Taylor, *Ancestral Record of Francis William Hoffman and Anna Barbara Esser*, Chapter IV.

12. James I. Robertson Jr., "The Scourge of Elmira," *Civil War History*, Vol. 8, No. 2 (June 1962), 92.

13. Speer, Portals to Hell, 244–46.

14. *Ancestral Record of Francis William Hoffman and Anna Barbara Esser*, Chapter IV.

15. www.fold3.com, MSR for Robert N. Hoffman.

16. www.fold3.com, MSR for Robert N. Hoffman.

17. www.fold3.com, MSR for Wesley A. Hoffman.

18. Frye, *2nd Virginia Infantry*, 80–142. There are various similar entries in the roster section; www.fold3.com, Confederate Citizens File for Chas. W. Hoffman.

19. www.fold3.com, MSR for Wesley A. Hoffman; Armstrong, *7th Virginia Cavalry*, 68, 164. The regimental history provides more information than the service records, which note only that he was "wounded."

20. www.fold3.com, MSR for Wesley A. Hoffman.

21. Ibid.

22. National Archives, MSR for Francis W. Hoffman.

23. Andrus, *The Brooke, Fauquier, Loudoun and Alexandria Artillery*, 84.

24. Ibid., 85.

25. Ibid., 85.

26. Robert M. Stribling, "From Markham to Appomattox, with the Fauquier Artillery," found in Ramey and Gott, *The Years of Anguish: Fauquier County, Virginia 1861–1865*, 196; National Archives, MSR for Francis W. Hoffman. The specific entry is marked "G.S.W. Left side Head."

27. National Archives, MSR for Francis W. Hoffman; Andrus, *The Brooke, Fauquier, Loudoun and Alexandria Artillery*, 85.

28. Stribling, "From Markham to Appomattox with the Fauquier Artillery," 196.

29. Ibid., 196.

30. Taylor, *Ancestral Record of Francis William Hoffman and Anna Barbara Esser*, Chapter IV.

31. www.fold3.com, MSR for Henry Wentz.
32. Koleszar, *Ashland, Bedford and Taylor Virginia Light Artillery*, 25.
33. www.fold3.com, MSR for Henry Wentz.
34. Koleszar, *Ashland, Bedford and Taylor Virginia Light Artillery*, 29, 40.
35. Ibid., 40.
36. www.fold3.com, MSR for Henry Wentz.
37. Stribling, "From Markham to Appomattox with the Fauquier Artillery," 197.

Fourteen: Reconstruction

1. www.encyclopediavirginia.org, "Martinsburg during the Civil War."
2. Willis F. Evans, *History of Berkeley County, West Virginia* (Westminster, Md.: Heritage Books, 2001, originally published 1928), 119.
3. 1870 U.S. Federal Census, Martinsburg, Berkeley, West Virginia.
4. Advertisement in *Spirit of Jefferson*, March 17, 1868, www.wvgeohistory.org.
5. 1870 U.S. Census, Martinsburg, Berkeley, West Virginia.
6. *Spirit of Jefferson*, March 17, 1868.
7. Evergreen Cemetery, Wentz family plot tombstones; Adams County Deed Book BB, 281–83.
8. "Martinsburg Gas Company," Constitution and Schedule Adopted in Convention at Charleston, April 9, 1972, https://books.google.com/books?id=V_JOAQAAIAAJ&pg=PA848&lpg=PA848&dq=henry+wentz+martinsburg&source=bl&ots=fXg7wO2gHd&sig=muOpSolyTo44k5CfpPUpy9t-ixo&hl=en&sa=X&ved=0ahUKEwiNtoKSqObOAhVC7yYKHVYdCM04ChDoAQhSMA8#v=onepage&q=henry%20wentz%20martinsburg&f=false, 847–48.

9. Public Documents, Vol. 3, State of West Virginia: Biennial Report of the Board of Health, 1904–1905, 19 (for address of Everett House); J Steven Wilkins, *All Things for Good: The Steadfast Fidelity of Stonewall Jackson*, 196.

10. *Martinsburg Statesman*, "Sudden Death," December 14, 1875.

11. Site visit to Green Hill Cemetery in Martinsburg; Clouse, *Battlefield Dispatch*, Vol. 17. No. 10, October 1998, 6–10.

12. Henry Wentz Will, Berkeley County Courthouse.

13. Ibid.

14. Taylor, *Ancestral Record of Francis William Hoffman and Anna Barbara Esser*, Chapter IV.

15. "Reports of Cases Decided in the Supreme Court of Appeals of Virginia," Vol. XXXI, 442–455.

16. Taylor, *Ancestral Record of Francis William Hoffman and Anna Barbara Esser*, Chapter V.

17. U.S. Federal Census, Marshall District, Fauquier County, Virginia. Wesley is listed as "Westley H. Hoffman."

18. *Shenandoah Herald*, Vol. 69, No. 42, November 22, 1889.

19. *Gettysburg Compiler*, November 19, 1889.

20. Site visit to Prospect Hill Cemetery in Front Royal.

21. Taylor, *Ancestral Record of Francis William Hoffman and Anna Barbara Esser*, Chapter IV, Third Generation; 1870 U.S. Federal Census, First Revenue District, Fauquier County, Virginia.

22. Site visit to Linden Church Hill Cemetery in Linden.

23. Taylor, *Ancestral Record of Francis William Hoffman and Anna Barbara Esser*, Chapter VII.

24. Ibid.

25. www.fold3.com, City Directories for Dallas, Texas, 1878–1897.

26. U.S. Federal Census, Justice Precinct 1, Armstrong, Texas; www.ancestry.com, Texas Land Title Abstracts, 1700–2008, Robert N.

Hoffman; "Alabama, Texas and Virginia Confederate Pensions, 1884–1958, for Robert N. Hoffman (Robert's application)."

27. Taylor, *Ancestral Record of Francis William Hoffman and Anna Barbara Esser*, Third Generation; http://cemeterycensus.com/tx/armstr/cem001h.htm, "Claude Cemetery" (cemetery records list a "J. N. Hoffman," as opposed to "R. N. Hoffman," but that is likely a typographical error).

28. www.ancestry.com, "Alabama, Texas and Virginia Confederate Pensions, 1884–1958, for Robert N. Hoffman (Ellen's application)."

29. Ibid.

30. Taylor, *Ancestral Record of Francis William Hoffman and Anna Barbara Esser*, Third Generation,

31. Ibid., Chapter IV.

32. Official Register of the United States, Officers and Employees, Civil, Military and Naval Service, "The Post-Office Department," 1889 and 1895; 1920 U.S. Federal Census, Washington, District of Columbia; *Washington Times*, "Pennsylvania Man Who Fought for Confederacy Dead; Francis Hoffman Lived at Crooked Run, Va. After War," October 17, 1920.

33. *Culpeper Exponent*, "Frank W. Hoffman Dead," October 14, 1920.

34. *Washington Times*, "Pa. Man Who Fought for Confederacy Dead: Francis Hoffman Lived at Crooked Run, Va. After War," October 17, 1920.

35. Taylor, *Ancestral Record of Francis William Hoffman and Anna Barbara Esser*, Third Generation. All three brothers had children who lived into the 1970s. Wesley's daughter, Martha, died on November 3, 1970. Robert's daughter, Pauline, died on May 20, 1972.

Epilogue

1. 1870 U.S. Federal Census, Gettysburg, Adams, Pennsylvania.
2. Bradsby, Sheely, and Leeson, *History of Adams County, Pennsylvania*, 84–87, 202–3.
3. www.hgaconline.org/id6.html, "Historic Gettysburg Adams County, Inc.: GAR Building," 1–5.
4. Bradsby, Sheely, and Leeson, *History of Adams County, Pennsylvania*, 202.
5. "William David Holtzworth" photo and caption on display at Evergreen Cemetery office, Gettysburg.
6. 1880 U.S. Federal Census, Chambersburg, Franklin, Pennsylvania; National Archives, Pension Records for William E. Culp; Culp obituary, *Valley Spirit* (Chambersburg), October 18, 1882, 3.
7. Author's visit to Culp family plot at Evergreen Cemetery, Gettysburg.
8. *Gettysburg Times*, "Park Service Will Remove Wentz House," April 29, 1960; ACHS, *Survey Report for Restoration and Rehabilitation of Historic Structures, Gettysburg National Military Park: Wentz Buildings*, "Conclusions and Recommendations, 12, 14.
9. ACHS, *Survey Report for Restoration and Rehabilitation of Historic Structures: Wentz Buildings*, "Location of Wentz Farm Buildings," 6 (monuments to the Sixty-Third and Sixty-Eighth Pennsylvania, Third Michigan and Third Maine, which are visible in the Tipton photos, were erected in 1888 and 1889); "Statements of War-Period and Early Post-War Residents of the Wentz Property and Vicinity," 7–9.
10. Ibid., 7. Others interviewed were W. C. Storrick, who wrote a book about the battle that is referenced elsewhere in the text; Mrs. Isaac Hereter, a daughter of Joseph Sherfy, who owned a nearby farm; and Miss Ella Spangler.

11. Ibid., "Conclusions and Recommendations," 11.

12. Ibid., "References of Conveyances of the Wentz Farm," 9–10; "Statements of War-Period and Early Post-War Residents of the Wentz Property and Vicinity," 8.

13. Ibid., "Conclusions and Recommendations," 11.

14. *Gettysburg Times*, "Park Service Will Remove Wentz House," April 29, 1960.

15. ACHS, *Survey Report for Restoration and Rehabilitation of Historic Structures: Wentz Buildings*, "Conclusions and Recommendations," 11.

16. Vanessa Pellechio, *Hanover Evening Sun*, "The Culp Brothers Gettysburg Memorial Revealed, July 6, 2013 (reprinted by Baltimore Civil War Roundtable); www.journal-news.net, "Local soldier to be honored with statue at Gettysburg," July 6, 2013; for more information on the Culp Brothers' Memorial, see also http://www.gettysburgscv.org/culpmemorial.html.

17. Text of wayside marker at Culp Brothers Memorial, Steinwehr Ave., Gettysburg, "A Tale of Two Brothers."

18. Sign posted at 117–19 Chambersburg Street, Gettysburg.

19. "The Confederate Veteran: Address of Gen. E. Porter Alexander, Delivered on Alumni Day, West Point Military Academy Centennial, June 9, 1902," 1–6.

20. www.georgiaencyclopedia.org, "Edward Porter Alexander (1835–1910).

21. "The Confederate Veteran: Address of Gen. E. Porter Alexander," 10–11.

22. Ibid., 11–12.

23. http://housedivided.dickinson.edu/sites/civilwar/files/2012/07/PDF-Race-and-Reunion.pdf; Frederick Douglass, "The Unknown Loyal Dead," Arlington National Cemetery, Virginia, on

Decoration Day 1871; Andy Hall, *The Atlantic*, "The Other Decoration Day Speech," January 19, 2011.

24. "The Confederate Veteran: Address of Gen. E. Porter Alexander, 3–4, 9, 14–15.

25. Ibid., 15; Edwin Anderson Alderman, *Classics Old and New, A Fifth Reader*, 7, 249. The poem is attributed to Frank L. Stanton.

Index